MY FARE CITY

My Fare City

A TAXI-DRIVER'S GUIDE
TO THE CAPITAL

B O B M C C U L L O C H

SERENDIPITY

Copyright © Bob McCulloch, 2004

First published in 2003 by
Serendipity
Suite 530
37 Store Street
Bloomsbury
London

British Library Cataloguing-in-Publication data
A catalogue record for this book is available from the British Library

ISBN 1-84394-075-2

Printed and bound in Europe by the Alden Group, Oxford

To Bill McKelvie, who loved the city and whose knowledge and enthusiasm was a great inspiration

Acknowledgements to Ron Leask,
Master M. V. Gardyloo

Foreword

Edinburgh is a beautiful, dynamic, prosperous European city with a unique architectural heritage and a magnificent natural setting. It is host to many thousands of visitors who come here throughout the year to enjoy numerous cultural events such as Edinburgh's Hogmanay and the world renowned Edinburgh International Festival and to visit attractions such as Edinburgh Castle and the Royal Yacht Britannia.

Edinburgh is the UK's second financial centre. It is the home of government, the law, the churches and banking in Scotland and enjoys an international reputation for academic excellence and for offering a superb quality of life to those who live and work here. As the home of Scotland's first parliament in three hundred years, Edinburgh is now a more complete capital city than ever before.

Whatever your business in Edinburgh, I hope you have a successful and enjoyable visit.

Councillor Eric Milligan
The City of Edinburgh Council

Introduction to Edinburgh

Edinburgh began as a fortified garrison on the castle rock, a hard volcanic mass of basalt rock which had withstood the movement of the ice during the Ice Age. The ice moving west to east split against this rock and gouged out the valley of the Grassmarket to the south and what is now Princes Street Gardens to the north, leaving the long ridge sloping down to flat ground. The first fortress would probably have been a wooden palisade to protect soldiers who chose this locality as the most easily defended place from which to control the tracks and trade routes of the area. Gradually the huts of the merchants whose business it was to supply the garrison were built in the lee of the fort so that they could quickly take shelter should danger threaten. Inevitably these huts began to extend down the ridge of the High Street, so we had a castle of a kind and one long street stretching down the ridge with many closes and wynds between the houses.

After King David I built Holyrood Abbey in the 12th century a separate burgh of the Canongate was formed, continuing from the High Street but administered by the Canons of Holyrood. This was known as the Canons Gait or walk.

During the fifteenth century King James II built a defensive wall round the town, but this wall did not include the Canongate. Thus Edinburgh extended from the Castle as far as St Mary's Street where a wall crossed the ridge with a gate called the Netherbow Port, while on the north side they created the Nor Loch, where Princes Street Gardens is now, by damming a stream.

The population continued to grow but owing to the wall they could not expand outwards so they built upwards, adding storeys to their houses until they had skyscrapers of up to seventeen floors, each floor being a separate dwelling house served by a single turnpike stair. All classes lived in these 'lands', lords and ladies, nobles and bishops, in the same stair as artisans, tradesmen, and beggars. They all got on well together and knew each other by Christian names. As there was no sanitation in the old town any waste was thrown onto the street.

The need for defence was no longer necessary after the Union of Scotland and England and so in 1763 it was decided that because of the cramped and unsanitary conditions a new town should be built to the north. The first North Bridge was constructed and the first new town was designed by James Craig and built to such a standard that it is still one of the finest deliberately planned towns in Europe.

The plan was for a formal layout of wide streets and elegant houses, and basically it consisted of a wide main street – George Street, with a grand square at either end, Charlotte Square and St Andrews Square. Parallel to George Street were Princes Street and Queen Street. These three streets were to be crossed by Hanover, Frederick, and Castle Streets and by a stroke of clear thinking they decided that no houses were to be built on the south side of Princes Street, so giving a clear view of the Castle from Princes Street. The 'Mound' was constructed using material from the excavations and became known as 'Geordie Boyd's mud brig'.

Later further new towns (or extensions to the first one) were constructed, all with the grace and elegance in the effective Grecian style which makes our city so interesting. We have both an old town of great historical interest and a new town of beauty combined into one.

There are imposing buildings in Edinburgh which reflect practically every major aspect of Scottish history. The Castle, the High Kirk of St Giles, the Palace of Holyrood House, Parliament Hall, the Tron Kirk, Moray House, Huntly House, Canongate Tolbooth, the Universities and many more.

Edinburgh has been the home of the famous and the illustrious, Robert the Bruce, all the Stewart kings, Mary, Queen of Scots, John Knox, Sir Walter Scott, Robert Louis Stevenson, Bonnie Prince Charlie and many more historical figures.

Being built on seven hills Edinburgh has marvellous views from exceptional vantage points.

Edinburgh is the centre of the legal profession, the Scottish Church, the Royal College of Surgeons, the Royal College of Physicians,

Banking, Insurance, the Army Scottish Command and, since 1999, the home of the new Scottish Parliament. Each year hosts the International Festival of the Arts. The ceremonial dignity of the City is enhanced by the presence of the Royal Company of Archers and the court of the Lord Lyon King of Arms with heralds and pursuivants. A popular nickname for Edinburgh was 'Auld Reekie' due to the smoke from coal fires that hung over the city, on some days it was so bad the city could not be seen from the Pentland Hills. In the 1960s the council passed legislation enforcing the use of smokeless fuels which greatly improved the situation.

It is indeed the capital of Scotland.

Water Supply and Sewage, 1440-1675

The Ancient Royalty of Edinburgh grew up as a huddle of houses on the long eastern slope of the Castle Rock, on which some sort of fortification must have existed from the earliest times. Walls were built at different dates to enclose and guard the town.

The North (Nor) Loch, now the site of Princes Street Gardens, was created to the north of the Castle Rock by the damming of the Craig Burn in 1440, this being a part of the defensive barrier.

Between the Netherbow and Holyrood Abbey, to the east of Edinburgh arose a separate town, the Burgh of the Canongate. Both Edinburgh and Canongate, being situated on a ridge, could easily shed water to the north and south. In other words drainage from the ridge passed either to the Nor Loch or the Cowgate.

At this time the amount of water used for domestic purposes was very small, more especially as all of it had to be carried into the town from draw-wells or springs. One such spring was in Holyrood Park, thought to date from the tenth century and now known as St Margaret's Well. The stonework surrounding the well was only erected in 1859, having been removed from the site of the original St Margaret's Well in Restalrig, due to the building of St Margaret's railway depot, now the site of local government offices.

In 1583 and 1598 there were proposals to supply water from the Burgh (south) loch, now the site of the Meadows. The proposal of 1598 resulted in a resolution being passed and this water was used to supplement that from the Wells.

In the year 1560, the population of Edinburgh was 10,000 and over the next two centuries this figure increased to 30,000. The population largely remained within the limits of the Ancient Royalty,

4

138 acres. The expanding population had nowhere to go but up, and 'Lands' of up to ten or twelve storeys high became a characteristic feature of the City, accommodating a great variety of classes living, as it were, in a vertical street, with the most distinguished near the top where the air was fresher.

Such chronic overcrowding, coupled with the meagre supplies of water and lack of drainage, not surprisingly resulted in a high mortality rate. Frequent outbreaks of pestilence or plague are recorded. On 4 October 1514 following an outbreak of the pest a Burgh statute was passed restricting entry to the town ports or gates.

There were severe visitations of the plague in 1568–9, 1574, 1585–6 and 1587. Penalties for concealing plague victims were severe. An offender who put a plague-stricken woman out of his house while concealing the fact that she had the plague was sentenced to be burnt on the cheek.

On 2 August 1530, one David Duly, tailor, was convicted of having concealed the fact that his wife had contracted pestilence. He was sentenced to be hanged on a gibbet before his own door, but the rope broke while the hanging was taking place, this was regarded as a sign that God willed that he should live. He was simply banished from the town for life.

The High Street was first paved or causewayed in 1532, under the supervision of a Frenchman named Marlin, it can still be seen under the Tron Church known as Marlins Wynd. In 1562 the Town Council took measures to mend the causeways and paved streets. Regular measures were taken for cleaning the town especially during and after visitations of the 'Pest'.

Accumulations of filth in the streets were quite normal and sometimes the Council ordered individuals to remove filth from before their houses. In Acts of the Council of 1553–5 mounds of household garbage were ordered to be removed and swine to be prevented from being pests in the street; each household had a dunghill in the street and swine were allowed to roam the streets and act the part of scavengers.

In October 1556 the Council decreed that all butchers of the Burgh should have their 'feilth' carried to the Nor Loch. The frequency of legislation for removing filth suggests that it was not wholly effective.

The condition of the Nor Loch at this time can well be imagined and the Town Council were apparently aware of this, for an order of 22 May 1562 made special arrangements for the ducking of 'fornicators' in the Nor Loch, severe punishment indeed. Women accused of witchcraft had their hands tied behind their backs and were thrown in, if they survived they were taken to Castle Hill and burned at the stake. Between the 15th and 18th centuries over 300 women met this fate.

Drains of a sort existed as early as 1527, open sewers draining into streams which ran to the north and south of the town, in an easterly direction. It is perhaps significant that the date of the first drains more or less coincides with the paving of the High Street.

Throughout the fourteenth and early fifteenth centuries outbreaks of the plague continued, culminating in 1645 in one of the most serious, and also the last recorded outbreak of bubonic plague in Edinburgh.

The High School was closed in April and remained closed for eleven months. The University moved to Linlithgow and Parliament fled to Stirling. Prisoners in the Tolbooth and the castle were set free because of the fear of uprising among them. The death toll was enormous, in Leith less than half the population of 4,000 survived.

Punishment for those who concealed the plague in their homes was ruthless: parents who concealed that a child of theirs had the plague were searched out by a special official with a white St Andrews cross on the front and the back of his gown: a guilty father could be hanged at his own door and a guilty mother taken to be drowned in one of the quarry holes on the Burgh Muir.

The First Piped Water Supply, 1675

An Act of the Scottish Parliament of 1621 gave powers to bring a supply of piped water into the town. However, it was not until 1674 that the Town Council agreed to pay a German engineer called Peter Bruschi the sum of £2950 for the laying of a three inch lead pipe to bring water from Comiston, about four miles from the city, to supply a reservoir to be made on Castlehill.

From the reservoir it was conveyed by pipes to five public wellheads or cisterns, these proved insufficient in number and a further nine were later added. At least six of these are still in existence, four on the Royal Mile, one at the foot of the West Bow and one in Old Tolbooth Wynd.

The reservoir on Castlehill had a capacity of 75,000 gallons and the supply was declared as working satisfactorily on 28 April 1675. The original reservoir was replaced by a new one with a capacity of 1.7 million gallons.

The water at Comiston was collected from springs, these were later directed into a small tank, enclosed in a stone building (collecting house), this is still standing and is now in a green patch in the heart of Oxgangs housing scheme. Initially, only one spring was tapped (Fox Spring No. 1), further springs were added until eventually nine were used, all named after animals, e.g. swan, hare, peewee. Lead models of the animals were sited on the pipes delivering the spring water to the collecting house. The surviving models are now in Huntly House Museum in the Canongate.

Gardez l'eau, 1675–1763

As already indicated the population of Edinburgh was rapidly increasing, while still being confined within the limits of the Ancient Royalty. By the year 1763 the population had reached 30,000. With no proper drainage, conditions on the streets became even worse. Several notable people wrote of their experiences when visiting Edinburgh during this period. A recent book on the Life and Times of Rob Roy MacGregor contains the following description of the Edinburgh he would find on his first visit in 1688–89:

'Like all other visitors they would time arrival to avoid the horrors of the night drum. When Edinburgh's clock struck ten, the people were allowed by beat of drum to throw their slops and excrement out of windows on to the streets. Since there were 30,000 people living within a square mile, all on the flank of the long ridge that sloped down from the Castle to Holyrood Palace, this avalanche from ten storeys high was too grim a penalty to be paid for late arrival, however much it might save on the morrow. Rob on his first visit may well have felt appalled by the vision summoned up. The pleasant surprise of the morning's arrival would seem all the greater, when they climbed up to the High Street Rob would find no trace of the expected sludge.

Scavengers daily swept all clean when the bell of St Giles tolled seven. First they had a struggle getting up the narrow stairs, which in the mornings were always congested with male and female carriers bearing water-casks to the houses from the public wells in the main street. The bedrooms and kitchen, which opened off the common room, each had a close-stool, or chamber pot set in a wooden box, and the scents from that source were augmented from windows opened to 'air the rooms', for the close was freely used by passers-by, including the tenants, to relieve themselves at all times of day .... . Since there was no street lighting each hired a cadie, one of the numerous lads who hung around coffee houses and all other public places to serve as guides or run errands. On the ten o'clock drumbeat the town resounded to the cries of 'Gardyloo'(a corruption of the French *Gardez l'eau*) as folk emptied pots and buckets. Then from the streets came the stench called the 'Flowers of Edinburgh' pouring in at the windows. Conversation stopped indoors while counter measures were taken. Men tried to fumigate the rooms by scattering bits of lit paper across floors and tables .... . A cadie bearing a paper lantern would go ahead to cry 'haud yur haunde' in answer to any cries of 'Gardyloo' from above'.

Daniel Defoe in the third volume of his *Tour Thro the Whole Island of Great Britain, Divided into Circuits of Journeys,* published in 1726 described the conditions he found in early eighteenth century Edinburgh. He noted the 'Stench and Nastiness' of the streets, 'as if the people were not as willing to live as sweet and clean as other Nations'. People live in a 'rocky and mountainous situation, thronged buildings from seven to ten or twelve storey high, a scarcity of water, and that little they have difficult to be had, and to the uppermost lodgings far to fetch'. He observed that 'I believe that in no city in the world so many people live in so little room as at Edinburgh'.

Early in the eighteenth century people were prohibited from staying on at taverns after the town drum had beaten its nightly tattoo in the High Street at ten o'clock and though the regulation remained throughout much of the century, it came to be ignored by determined drinkers (including the city's magistrates) at club meetings in taverns.

But they had to be careful going home at night, for at any moment the cry of 'Gardyloo' could be heard from an upper window as a warning that a chamber pot was about to be emptied onto the heads of any unfortunate passing below unless he was quick witted enough to shout out 'haud yur haund' and briskly step out of the way. 'How long can it be suffered,' wrote John Wesley in his Journal in 1762 'that all manner of filth should be flung into the streets? How long shall the capital city of Scotland and the chief street of it stink worse than a common sewer'.

Water, or the lack of it, also remained a problem throughout this period and between 1704 and 1720.

The original three inch lead pipe from Comiston was replaced by one of five inches. Once again a German engineer named Corvie was employed to carry out the work. At the opening ceremony in 1720, when the supply was turned on, water failed to come through to the reservoir on Castlehill, Corvie duly sped off on horseback to the collecting house at Comiston but could not locate the problem, panicking he fled and was never seen again, he had not yet been paid. One of his workmen being a little more practical found an air lock in the pipe and giving the pipe a few healthy blows with a hammer restored the supply.

An Act of 1756 gave power to take water from Swanston, seven-inch wooden pipes made from hollowed out elm trees were used to convey the water to Comiston from where it was conveyed in a parallel pipe to the reservoir on Castlehill. This supply was not actually brought into use until the 1780s. On the north side of Cannan Lane and the East Side of Whitehouse Loan the numerals 5 and 7 are set in the wall following the route of the pipe.

Demand for the water available from the wellheads was so great that considerable congestion was caused in the High Street, also the supply frequently ran out, especially during dry summers. For this reason, it became customary for it to be turned on only between midnight and three o'clock in the morning. This gave rise to the ritual of 'waiting at the well'. Places were bookable in advance by leaving vessels at the wellheads, and an array of miscellaneous containers could often be found stretching back from each of the wells. The most popular vessel was the one made especially for the purpose, called the water-stoup, these were usually carried in pairs.

Citizens who had no wish to queue halfway through the night for water and had no servant to fetch it for them employed the services of a water cadie, (a corruption of the French word cadet and now called cadie as in golf). These were sometimes old soldiers, or even their wives or daughters. Each cadie generally had his or her own customers, though they seldom had to be called they knew the habits and wants of each family and the capacity of each cistern, which was replenished at the cadie's own discretion. Because they supplied a vital need of the community, they assumed an air of great self-importance, and became a somewhat unruly class.

In an attempt to abate this nuisance the Town Council instituted the Society of Water Cadies, but this only lasted from 1718 to 1727.

The Draining of the North Loch – the first sewer, 1763

The North Loch continued to receive the drainage from much of the Town, and in addition a flesh market and slaughterhouse were situated on its banks, as was a tannery.

In 1721 the Town Council consulted the College of Physicians as to the measures to be taken to clean up the loch.

They recommended the draining of the North Loch, then a pestilent swamp, and the formation of a 'canal' in the valley to carry off impurities; the effective cleaning of the streets, closes and courts; the erection of conveniences at various sites and the provision of dust carts to which servants might bring the 'fulzie' of houses, in place of the universal 'gardyloo.'

The draining of the North Loch began in 1759 and marked the first move to provide a proper and adequate system of drainage. It was completed in 1763.

A Time of Expansion: The New Town, 1763–1864

The narrow limits of the Ancient Royalty led to the publishing in 1752 of a pamphlet entitled 'Proposals for carrying out certain Public Works in the City of Edinburgh', written by Sir Gilbert Elliot but heavily influenced by six times Lord Provost, George Drummond, whose vision it was. These proposals suggested an extension of the city. A bill was presented to the House of Commons on the 31 January 1767 entitled

'An Act for Extending the Royalty of the City of Edinburgh over certain adjoining Lands; and for giving powers to the Magistrates of Edinburgh, for the benefit of the said City; and to enable His Majesty to grant Letters Patent for establishing a theatre in the City of Edinburgh, or Suburbs thereof.'

It passed on 16 April and received the Royal Assent on 20 May. A new town to the north then became an immediate possibility.

In 1766, anticipating the passing of the Act the Town Council published an advertisement announcing a competition for a plan to fill the site to the north of the Nor Loch. On 17 April 1767 it was announced that James Craig was 'Entitled to the primum for the best plan of a New Town in terms of the advertisement in the newspapers for that purpose'.

The site of the New Town was determined partly by the physical features of the area and partly by existing boundaries of property. It extended from east to west for about three quarters of a mile along the top of a low, broad ridge just north of the Nor Loch. The North Bridge, linking the Old Town with this ridge and spanning the valley of the Nor Loch was completed in 1772.

A so-called second New Town was laid out at the beginning of the nineteenth century and by the year 1831 the Georgian development of Edinburgh was completed.

The building of the New Town brought about a shift in population. One after another the nobles and gentry and substantial burghers deserted their old quarters in the High Street and Canongate and moved into the elegant New Town.

In the Old Town their mansions were subdivided, their gardens built over and occupied by the humbler trading classes; the houses of these classes were in turn occupied by lower grades of inhabitants.

Water Supply for the New Town

The New Town houses were gradually equipped with piped supplies of water, although when it failed the servants were sent out with stoups to the nearest well.

Further supplies of water were required and under an Act of 1775, two reservoirs, fed by springs were constructed at Bonaly. These were the first impounding reservoirs to be built and the water was conveyed to Swanston and from there to the reservoir on Castlehill. The reservoir on Castlehill became surplus to requirements and was drained in 1992 and it is now the only Tartan Weaving mill in the Old Town.

Following a great water shortage in 1810, Thomas Telford and James Jardine were commissioned to prepare a report in 1813. The Town Council failed to act but in 1819 a public meeting was held at which it was decided to make application to Parliament for powers to set up a water company.

The Act of 2 July 1819 created the Edinburgh Joint Stock Water Company. The Act also incorporated powers to abstract water from Crawley Springs and to build Glencorse reservoir.

This was completed in 1822 to provide compensation water to the mill owners on the River North Esk.

Between 1842 and 1863, several hundred springs were tapped along the North Pentlands. This water was conveyed into the town via the North Pentland Aqueduct.

As with the River North Esk, the mill owners on the Bavelaw Burn and Water of Leith were provided with compensation water reservoirs, at Thriepmuir and Harlaw (1847–8). A further reservoir was built at the head of the Water of Leith at Harperrig in 1859 its purpose being both compensation and supply.

Drainage

Reference has already been made to the draining of the Nor Loch, the sewer from here passed via the North Back of the Canongate (Calton Road). By the beginning of the nineteenth century, a further two sewers had been constructed, one serving the Cowgate and the other originating in the George Square district.

These three sewers, all draining the old town, delivered their contents into a wide open ditch near Clockmill, the stream being known as the Foul Burn and flowing in open channel to the sea.

By the year 1841 this stream was led into a network of irrigation-type ditches for simple land treatment over a large area known as the Craigentinny Meadows, the run off being led to the Forth estuary. This land treatment lasted until 1922 when the sewage was carried directly to the estuary.

Exactly how much sewage was actually piped to these early sewers is open to speculation but reference was made in the 'Contract for the Building of the City Chambers 1753' to drains 4½ft high being fed by pipes passing through of the walls of the building to the kitchens and water closets. Coincidentally the Cowgate sewer was 4½ ft high.

This early reference to water closets was no doubt an isolated instance as they were only introduced into the better parts of the city when a greater supply of water became available from Crawley Springs.

Even in the New Town disposal methods were a matter for the individual household until the middle of the nineteenth century. Carts still came round in the early morning for 'night soil' and Edinburgh was described as being second only to Madrid for filthiness amongst European Cities. It therefore seems likely that most of the drainage reaching the three sewers serving the Old Town was conveyed there by open channels laid at the sides of streets and closes. Drainage of the New Town was evidently considered at the planning stage in 1767 and it was minuted that 'no-one here is capable of giving instructions about sewers' and James Craig was said to be willing to go to London. A year later the committee agreed to consult architects John and William Adam on the subject and the following year, 14 September 1768, a ten-guinea prize was offered for the best plan of the sewers. Drainage from the New Town found its way to the Water of Leith and, as the nineteenth century progressed concern about the polluted condition of the river increased.

Acts were passed in 1822, 1832 and 1848 but these were merely permissive. An Act of 1854 sought to improve matters but this proved ineffective and it was not until the passing of a further Act in 1864 that real action was taken. This resulted in the construction of a new sewer which intercepted numerous drains and minor sewers up to Roseburn and discharged its contents into the estuary of the Forth.

Edinburgh grew in population and in area during the nineteenth century. Its population, i.e. the population of the area now included in the city boundaries, was 90,768 in 1801, 150,674 in 1821, 179,897 in 1841, 222,015 in 1861, 320,549 in 1881 and 413,008 in 1901. The most rapid increase was in the first two decades of the century and between 1860 and 1880.

Increase in population brought its own problems, even though it was associated with an increase in area (unlike earlier centuries when the increasing numbers were confined to the boundaries of the Ancient Royalty). The city's notorious carelessness in the matter of sanitation was at last tackled in the Victorian period. By the mid 1860s the task of laying sewers on the lines of all the streets was completed.

The Public Health Act of 1867

The collapse of a tenement in the High Street called Paisley Close (Heave Awa Close) killing 35 people prompted the passing of this Act.

The Public Health Act gave important powers to local authorities in dealing with matters relevant to public health and required the appointment of Medical Officers of Health. Edinburgh was fortunate in its first MOH, Dr H. D. Littlejohn, who in 1865 published his 'Report on the Sanitary Conditions of the City of Edinburgh'.

Dr Littlejohn was the first MOH to be appointed in Scotland, he was specially charged with duties connected with epidemic diseases and sanitary reforms. A cholera epidemic in 1832 claimed 600 lives in six months and there were further epidemics in 1848 and 1849. In his report Dr Littlejohn stated that these epidemics were instrumental in stimulating the provision of sewers, in Edinburgh and elsewhere.

He also reported on the three sewers serving the Old Town stating that they were 'of the best construction and carried off rainfall and drainage of certain elevated districts', but as far as the closes were concerned, for any sewage they conveyed from such poor localities, they might never have existed at all.

The introduction of water closets was made compulsory in 1864. Dr Littlejohn reported that this had only been applied in a few closes and added that, in any case, no sooner were they put in than they went out of order and pools of sewage appeared in common stairs and passages. He concluded that the poor of the city were not prepared to make proper use of the conveniences and that they required preliminary education before they could be trusted.

The report also referred to the irrigated meadows. 250 acres were irrigated by the Foul Burn at Craigentinny, and the Jordan Burn was put to similar use, about 11 acres being irrigated. The Lochrin Burn irrigated 90 acres in the Dalry area and the Broughton Burn 5 acres.

There was also an attempt at irrigation at Claremont Crescent and an extensive tract at Corstorphine.

This system increased the value of estates by tenfold. The proprietors established, by certain decisions of the court, a right to the sewage of the City, and they interdicted such concerns as the Gas Company from contaminating the sewage so as to interfere with its profitable use.

Dr Littlejohn's opinion was that the 'emanations' from these irrigated meadows affected the health of the City. His report concluded with four recommendations, two of these were;

The satisfactory paving and draining of closes.

The improvement of the housing accommodation of the poor by insisting on the introduction of water and gas and the cleaning of common stairs.

On 5 December 1865 Lord Provost Chambers made a statement to the Council on the subject of sanitary improvements. He stated that two things required to be done: -

To obtain, by a provisional order, new powers in respect of drainage and general sanitary improvements.

Extensive structural alterations throughout the Old Town to open up the closes to give facilities for thorough cleansing.

At this time, fever was on the increase and Dr Littlejohn had ordered the closes to be flushed with water and purified with chloride of lime.

The Growth of the Present Water Supply System, 1867–1982

The Public Health Act of 1867 has already been referred to; this stands out as a real effort to ensure, not only the introduction of sanitary conveniences, adequate drainage and sewerage facilities, but also an ample and pure water supply.

An earlier Act of 1862 gave local authorities the power to require landlords to introduce water into houses, at this time houses in slums were still totally devoid of water. As water was introduced, the Water Company complained of an enormous waste of water reporting that tenants had to be educated in its use.

It was also reported that staff of the Water Company were occupied in the disciplining of offenders.

In 1870 the Edinburgh and District Water Trust took over from the former Water Company and the supply of water remained in the hands of the trust until 1920 when it was transferred to the Edinburgh Corporation.

In the 1870s supplies from the North and South Pentlands were inadequate and Edinburgh had to look further afield for its water. These further supplies were obtained from the Moorfoot Hills, following the passing of an Act in July 1874. Gladhouse and Portmore reservoirs were built with a pipeline to Alnwickhill Filter Station; this was officially opened in June 1879. This was the first real water treatment works, utilising four slow sand filters. The works are still in use, although they have since been extended and treatment now consists of lime addition followed by sand filtration and chlorination.

At the time two compensation reservoirs were also built at Rosebery and Edgelaw.

By the 1890s the Moorfoot supplies became insufficient and a further source of supply was sought.

Talla reservoir was constructed on the upper reaches of the River Tweed. This was completed in 1905 and an aqueduct 35 miles long was laid to a new treatment works at Fairmilehead. As at Alnwickhill, slow sand filters were used. The 35 mile long aqueduct consisted of 12 miles of built aqueduct (underground), 9 miles in tunnel and the remainder in cast iron pipes.

In 1914 a 3ft pipeline was laid from the Talla aqueduct to Glencorse reservoir and this acts as a balancing reservoir.

In 1949, the County of Midlothian and the Burghs of Musselburgh, Dalkeith, Bonnyrigg and Lasswade, Loanhead and Penicuik were added to the area of supply. A new filtration plant was also constructed at Rosebery.

In 1969 the Fruid reservoir was constructed and this completed the works at the head of the Tweed.

Responsibility for the supply of water remained in the hands of Edinburgh Corporation from 1920 until 1968 when the South East of Scotland Water Board was created. This survived until 15 May 1975 when Lothian Regional Council was created.

The Meggat Scheme

The Meggat Scheme was first considered in 1963. In 1968 the South

East of Scotland Water Board promoted a scheme and legal authorisation was finally granted with the passing of the South East of Scotland Water Board (Meggat Reservoir) Water Order 1974. The reservoir yields 22.5 million gallons of water and was estimated to provide adequate supplies until the late 1990s. Four miles of tunnel take water to the head of the Manor Valley from where it is piped to the Talla Aqueduct, a branch was provided to the works at Rosebery, Glencorse and Gladhouse reservoirs acting as balancing reservoirs.

A further 22.5 million gallons can be obtained by pumping water from St Mary's Loch into the Meggat reservoir, this second phase will provide adequate supplies up to 2020–30.

The scheme cost over £43 million.

The Growth of the Present Main Drainage System, 1864–1967

By the year 1864, all that existed of the present main drainage system was the 1864 Water of Leith sewer and the three sewers draining the Old Town via the Foul Burn to Craigentinny Meadows.

Considerable development was taking place to the south of the city in the Newington, Grange and Morningside areas, areas in which the natural drainage gravitates to the Braid Burn.

In 1889 a new sewer was completed from Seafield, traversing Craigentinny and Duddingston and then following the valley of the Braid Burn, Powburn and Jordan Burn as far as Morningside Road. An extension was later laid up Comiston Road and this served to take the foul discharges from a very considerable area. The sewer was constructed in brick and varied in dimension from 5ft x 3½ft at Seafield to 3ft x 2ft at Morningside.

Pollution of the Water of Leith continued and while the 1864 sewer constituted a very considerable step forward it was neither sufficient for the increasing loads it was called upon to receive nor did it deal with the stretches of the river above Roseburn. The sewer had been constructed of brick and it varied in diameter from 3½ft at its outlet to the sea to 2ft at Roseburn.

In 1889 the Water of Leith Commissioners were appointed to make proper provision for a really effective purification system for the whole river, and the construction of a second sewer commenced. The outfall was close to that of the earlier sewer, the diameter being 5ft at the outfall and 10 inches at the summit. The sewer received drainage from trunk sewers at Haymarket, Lochrin, Merchiston and Gorgie. An extension was laid along the Stank Burn from Roseburn to Broomhouse Road. A further sewer, the Greenside Burn sewer, was laid to serve the area between Leith Walk and Easter Road, a connection being made to the 1864 Water of Leith sewer at Great Junction Street.

Thus at the end of the nineteenth century, the system to the Craigentinny and the Water of Leith sewers served most of the area within the boundaries existing at that time with the exception of such coastal areas as Granton, Newhaven, Leith and Portobello which were served by local sewers discharging directly to the sea, usually at low water mark but, in some cases, on the foreshore at high water mark.

This drainage sufficed until after the First World War when, in 1920, the boundaries of the city were extended to include Cramond, Davidsons Mains, Corstorphine, Colinton, Liberton and Gilmerton. This enlargement tripled the area from 10,877 acres to 32,664 acres. These areas were already partially sewered; Corstorphine and Colinton by the Water of Leith sewer, Davidsons Mains by a sewer from Granton, Liberton and Gilmerton by the county sewer with a sea outfall at Eastfield.

This extension of the boundaries and the extensive development of the post World War I era was accompanied or followed by the construction of many new sewers, including the Craigentinny and new Powburn sewers in 1922, the Pipe Street sewer in 1924, the Gogar Burn sewer in 1929–32, the Blackhall sewer in 1930 and the Davidsons Mains in 1931.

The first of these is of particular interest as it extended from Seafield through the Craigentinny Meadows and up the Foul Burn to take in the contents of the three original Old Town sewers. It was therefore 1922 before the original drains from the Old Town were piped through to the sea outfall.

The first complaints about the nuisance caused by pollution of the Forth were raised about this time and, as a result, screening and disintegration plants were installed on the Trinity, Granton and Seafield outfalls in 1930, 1936 and 1939 respectively. At the same time intercepting sewers were constructed to group together some of the main sewers and bring their points of discharge to new outfalls. Sewers serving Granton, Wardie, Trinity and Newhaven were brought to a point of discharge between Granton and Newhaven with a new outfall extending well beyond low water mark.

The Granton outfall served the Granton/Corstorphine sewer, the old Davidsons Mains sewer and part of West Granton. The third and largest installation to give screening and disintegration dealt with the flow in the Salamander Street, Craigentinny, Powburn and Pipe Street sewers. Two of these, on account of their depth required pumping and a new 7ft diameter outfall was constructed extending into the estuary, 455 yards below low water mark.

The boom in development after the Second World War required extensive sewerage work to relieve overloaded existing sewers and to provide sewerage in hitherto undeveloped areas, and the programme carried out included the Burdiehouse/Seafield sewer in1947/52, the Corstorphine/Sighthill sewer in 1947, the Sighthill/Balerno sewer in 1951 on behalf of Midlothian County Council, the North Junction Street sewer serving Northeast Leith, the Glasgow Road/Drumbrae Road sewer in 1952, the Cramond/Davidsons Mains sewer in 1953, the Western Boundary sewer in 1955 from Cramond Village to Sighthill and the Lochrin relief sewer from Tollcross to Princes Street Gardens in 1960. Also to meet further expression of concern at pollution of the Forth, comminutors were installed on the Joppa, Eastfield and Cramond outfalls in the period 1953–54.

In the period 1960–67 no major sewerage schemes were carried out.

From Drainage to Water Pollution Control, 1967–82

The Rivers (Prevention of Pollution) Act of 1951 allowed the River Purification Boards control over new discharges to designated tidal waters, and called for an assessment of the extent of pollution by existing discharges. A Tidal Waters Order of 1960 and a further Act in 1965 meant that by November 1966, application to the Lothian River Purification Board was necessary for consent to continue the existing discharges to the Firth of Forth.

At this time there were nine discharge points to the estuary dispersed over a nine mile length of the city's coastline, the only treatment being screening and disintegration or comminution on some of the outfalls.

In August 1967, a 'Report on a Scheme for the Treatment of the City's sewage to Reduce Pollution of the River Forth' was published by the City Engineer. This was approved in principle in February 1968 by the Edinburgh Corporation and by the Scottish Development Department, from whom borrowing consent was required.

The report, in its introduction, stated that 'The application of recent legislation has added compulsion by statute to the need for a reduction in pollution of the River Forth by the City's sewage'. At long last, some 200 years after the construction of the first sewer, the need for more than just drainage had been officially recognised. The report also referred to the need to make charges on the traders for the reception and treatment of trade effluents and a charging scheme was subsequently approved by the Lothian Regional Council in 1975.

The scheme for collection and treatment of the city's sewage involved construction of interceptor sewers and pumping stations to convey the sewage to a new treatment works to be built on reclaimed land in Seafield Bay. The sewage works was officially opened on 18 April 1978 and provides for primary treatment prior to discharge via an outfall of overall length of 1.75 miles.

By the early 1980s 92% of the city's sewage was intercepted for treatment and the overall cost to that date was £52 million. Sludge removed during sedimentation was disposed of at sea by the specially built sludge disposal vessel most appropriately named M. V. *Gardyloo*.

M. V. *Gardyloo* was built by Ferguson Brothers at Port Glasgow and launched on 4 February 1976, the approximate cost was £1.8 million and she had an expected service life of 25 years, capable of carrying 2515 tons of sludge in two tanks situated on the port and starboard sides.

Berthed in Edinburgh Dock alongside sludge holding tanks, the sludge was pumped aboard, the operation taking about an hour to complete.

Two areas in the North Sea were licensed by the Dept. Agriculture and Fisheries for controlled dumping, one at St Abbs Head, 38 miles from Leith and the other in the Bell Rock Area, 44 miles from Leith. The round trip to the dumping grounds took about nine hours.

With a crew of 5 officers and 6 crewmen and able to cater for a maximum of 12 passengers it was possible to book a trip as a day out. The M. V. *Gardyloo* was decommissioned in December 1998 when dumping at sea was made illegal. The last Master of M. V. *Gardyloo* was Captain Ron Leask whom I would like to thank for supplying me with this information and the notes of G. P. Tetlaw, Senior Trade Effluent Officer, Department of Drainage. Thanks also for answering endless questions while I was on board.

Characters of Edinburgh

Few cities anywhere can equal the contribution to the advancement of civilisation made by the citizens of Edinburgh.

Edinburgh has been the home, either through birth or choice, of many people who have reached the top of their chosen profession and who have made an impact on the lives of people all over the world.

In the period between 1775 and 1850 known as the 'Age of Enlightenment' an Englishman reported that standing at the Mercat Cross of Edinburgh he could within a few minutes shake by the hand 50 men of genius.

It was the home of famous people from communications e.g. Telephone, Alexander Graham Bell who was trying to help deaf people; Television, Swinton who had the theory but not the mechanical skills; also from Medical science, Joseph Bell, who is the model on which the character of Sherlock Holmes is based; Syme, who was known as the Napoleon of surgery; Joseph Lister, and Sir James Y. Simpson who discovered the anaesthetic properties of chloroform and Dr Elsie Inglis who was regarded as a saint in the Balkans.

The literary world would be a poorer place without the writings of Sir Walter Scott, Robert Louis Stevenson and Robert Burns, also Ian Rankin, Muriel Spark, Conan Doyle, Irving Welsh, Dorothy Dunnet and J. K. Rowling, who through the adventures of her character Harry Potter made school children switch off television and read books.

Generations of schoolchildren struggling to master logarithm tables would hesitate to thank John Napier for inventing them and those playing with their Kaleidoscope would not know that David Brewster thought that it would be a great help in the design of carpets.

There were philosophers like David Hume who could write a convoluted sentence in Latin with his right hand while simultaneously writing the same with his left in Greek, and that at the age of ten.

Adam Smith, whose book *The Wealth of Nations* has been the foundation of many a fiscal policy; James Hutton, the father of modern Geology who studied the rocks of Arthur's Seat and Salisbury Crags and came to the conclusion that the Earth was older than previously thought and denied the biblical theory of creation and instead suggested it was created by fire and ice.

Architects Robert Adam and William Playfair left a legacy of beautiful buildings which have enabled Edinburgh to achieve World Heritage status.

James Braidwood organised the first co-ordinated fire service in the city before moving to London.

The imposing building, Heriots School, on Lauriston Place owes its existence to George Heriot, goldsmith to King James IV who had the nickname of 'Jinglin Geordie' and who left his fortune to found the school.

Daniel Defoe acted as a spy for the English Government whilst editor of the *Courant*.

In sport Ken Buchanan won the world lightweight boxing title and in a poll of American sports writers came top, beating Muhammad Ali and Joe Frazier into second and third place. Eric Liddle, the runner and missionary, inspired the film 'Chariots of Fire', Dougal Haston was the first Briton to conquer the North Face of the Eiger in 1966 and was tragically killed in an avalanche while skiing in the Alps in 1977. Allan Wells the sprinter won gold in the Moscow Olympics, Ronnie Shade was the most successful amateur golfer and Tommy Armour, 'The Silver Scot', was a grand slam winner and learned the game of golf on the Braid Hills.

In rugby the Hastings brothers, Scott and Gavin captained the British Lions on their tour to Australia. In swimming W. E. (Ned) Barnie who swam the English Channel in 1950 and in 1951 became the first man to swim it in both directions; David Wilkie who won the Gold Medal in the 1976 Moscow Olympics, and Peter Heatly the high diver who won gold at three successive Empire Games in 1950–54–58.

In bowling one name stands out, Richard Corsie, triple world singles indoor champion, twice winner of indoor pairs with another great Edinburgh bowler Alex 'Tattie' Marshall, Gold, Silver and Bronze medallist at the Commonwealth Games and undisputed world champion, he now runs his own bowling complex on Milton Road.

In entertainment, Sir Harry Lauder born in Bridge Street, Portobello went on to become the first person to sell 1 million records and to be the highest paid entertainer earning £1,000 a week in the early part of the century and was knighted in 1919. Ronnie Corbet from Dalry; The Bay City Rollers, the Tartan clad pop group who took the world by storm in the 1970s. The Corries folk singing duo of Ronnie Browne and Roy Williamson who wrote the song 'Flower of Scotland' now our National Anthem and Sir Sean Connery the milkman from Fountainbridge who played James Bond, a spaceman and a Russian submariner all with a Scottish accent.

During the Golden Age of Steam one man became the outright leader in Steam Engine design, Sir Nigel Gresley, born in Dublin Street, he went on to design the L.N.E.R. Pacific class locomotive.

On 3rd July 1938 the A4 Pacific *Mallard* set the world steam speed record at 126 m.p.h., this record has never been broken.

Deacon Brodie was the model for Robert Louis Stevenson's *Dr Jeykll and Mr Hyde*. Burke and Hare murdered 16 people and sold their bodies to the Medical School, James Steele the forger from Dalry, whose coins fooled the Royal Mint on three separate occasions and Dora Noyce who ran Edinburgh's most famous brothel, but preferred it to be called the Y.M.C.A with extras.

In all a rich tapestry of the great and the good mixed with a sprinkling of rogues.

Burke and Hare

William Burke (1792–1829) was not a body snatcher at any time, so he said. As he was confessing to sixteen murders at the time his words merit some respect.

Burke grew up an Irish speaking labourer in West Tyrone and joined the Donegal Militia. He reverted to his trade as a tramping artisan when he was thrown out of the British Army after the Battle of Waterloo. He came to Scotland in 1818 to work on the Union Canal. Although he had a wife and family in Ireland he fell in love with a Scots girl called Helen MacDougal. He was a charming and garrulous man who made friends easily.

The Society of High Constables

The founding date is unknown but is generally accepted as 1611, when the Magistrates decided to elect Constables, half from the Merchants and half from the Tradesmen. They were an early form of police force and their powers were many and far-reaching.

There are twenty-three wards of twelve members in the Society, giving a total membership of two hundred and seventy-six. You cannot apply to join but must be invited, and today their function is confined to having dinners and to act as ushers on ceremonial occasions, but these were not their original duties.

The twelve Officers and twenty-six Constables who were appointed had a great variety of duties.

They were expected to apprehend and imprison suspects, such as vagabonds and night walkers, they were to challenge anyone in possession of a pistol or dagger, and present them to the Lord Provost or Bailies for punishment. They were to intervene at times of public disorder, such as riots or street fighting, and were given the power to break down doors to investigate noise and nuisance.

They were duty bound to search for Jesuits, Seminarians, priests or trafficking papists and deal with beggars and gypsies as well as idle persons. They were empowered to deal with murders, theft, or other capital crimes and also to clear the streets of filth, middens and swine.

They were to see that those liable for King's service had adequate armour, and to apprehend swearers and blasphemers in the streets, markets or at the wells.

With such superhuman tasks before them, it is little wonder that the Constables were unsuccessful in cleansing the streets where refuse lay 'like mountains' and roads had to be cut through it to reach the closes and booths.

The Constables seemed to be used for everything, they oversaw the sending of beggars and vagrants to the workhouse and the Correction House in the Calton district.

They were used as tax gatherers, as officers of the local census, for billeting soldiers and for street patrol at Hogmanay to prevent 'The throwing of dead cats' and other riotous behaviour.

They were also ordered to quell snowball fights, Chartist

demonstrations and to assist at fires in the High Street or in public buildings elsewhere in the City.

Lord Provost's Badge and Chain

William de Dederyk is generally accepted as Edinburgh's first Provost in 1296. Over the years the position has not been without its dangers.

In 1561 Mary Queen of Scots dismissed the Provost and Bailies on religious grounds.

Provost Sir Alexander Lauder was killed at the Battle of Flodden in 1513, and Adam Otterburne was assassinated in office. Provost Archibald Stewart was seen by the Government as too closely tied to the Jacobite cause and was tried for treason.

Provost Andrew Ramsey has served the longest, a total of fourteen years, and was the first to be called Lord Provost. Sir James Millar of the building firm is the only man to have held both positions of Lord Provost of Edinburgh and Lord Mayor of London, albeit at different times. The only Englishman to hold the position has been Sir James Falshaw in 1874, the only women Eleanor McLaughlin in 1988–92, and Lesley Hynds in 2003.

It was the custom for the Provosts to be knighted but the practice ceased when Jack Kane refused the honour in 1972.

Sir George Drummond was elected six times during which time he pushed through his vision for a 'New Town'.

The Lord Provost's present badge and chain was first worn by Lord Provost Sir Mitchell Thomson in 1899, on the occasion of the freedom of the city to HRH the Prince of Wales, afterwards King Edward VII. Designed by W. S. Black, it was made by Messrs. Brook and Son, George Street.

The chain is 18 carat gold, 46 inches in length, 1½ inches broad and weighs between 40 and 50 ounces. The centre square link has the letters 'E' facing each other and joined by a heart of laurel, symbolical of the 'Heart of Midlothian'. It also has in the centre of the two 'E's, a replica of the old Scottish Crown.

The other plaques on the chain show the other offices or titles held by the Lord Provost – Triton of the Sea; the mermaid and the ship and anchor associated with the title, Lord High Admiral of the Firth of Forth; the figure of justice and scales as chief magistrate; the crown sentenced him to two years in jail, his sight in his remaining eye became worse and he was released before he completed his sentence. He died in Edinburgh in 1968.

During an interview after his arrest he solved a mystery which had baffled Royal Mint officials since 1917. On his release from the army it had been his intention to make sovereigns and he had started production when, to his disgust, sovereigns ceased to be made so in a fit of pique rather than destroy the dies he sent them anonymously to the mint were they remained a mystery for 50 years.

Robert Louis Stevenson, 1850–94

Born at No. 8 Howard Place into a family of lighthouse engineers, the young Robert was a sickly child.

The family moved to Inverleith Terrace, but the house was subject to damp and so when he was seven years old they moved again, this time to 17 Heriot Row, which was to be his final home in Edinburgh.

He was christened Robert Lewis Balfour Stevenson in favour of his maternal grandfather, but when he grew up he dropped the Balfour and changed the spelling to the French, Louis, as he thought this more avant garde.

Whilst living in Howard Place R. L. S. attended Canonmills School (opposite the Canonmills service station) where a plaque on the wall commemorates the fact.

As a child he was often in bed ill and his nurse, Alison Cunningham, (Cummy to the family) would read him stories about the Covenanters and from the Bible. During this time he would watch for 'Leerie' the Lamplighter coming along the street and was always pleased when he gave him a wave. He later immortalised him in the poem, which is inscribed on a brass plaque on the railings of No. 17.

From his bedroom window he could see the ornamental pond in Queen Street Gardens East from which he conceived the idea of *Treasure Island*.

While visiting his grandfather, Robert Stevenson, who was the greatest Lighthouse Engineer and lived at Baxter's Place now called Stevenson House, he purchased cardboard from an adjacent shop (now an Italian Restaurant) which he used to make a small theatre He used this for his poem 'Penny Plain Twopence Coloured'.

His maternal grandfather was minister at Colinton Church and as a young boy he would spend the summers with him at Swanston Cottage in Swanston Village. He loved to roam the Pentland Hills and would listen avidly to the stories told to him by Jock Todd the Swanston shepherd. In later life he would always yearn for what he called 'The Hills of Home'.

In 1867 he studied Engineering at Edinburgh University but had to give up through ill health, as some days he could not even wear a jacket as it caused his lungs to haemorrhage. He wanted to become a writer but his father was not keen on the idea so, as a compromise, he agreed to study Law so that he would have a profession to fall back on. In 1875 he was called to the Scottish Bar, but his heart was not in it and he only had one client.

To recover from another bout of illness he went to France where he met an American woman named Fanny Van Degrift Osbourne and they struck up a friendship. She returned to America and R.L.S. returned to Scotland but he followed her to California in 1879, almost dying on the journey. When he had recovered she divorced her husband and they were married in 1880. For the sake of his health they decided to live in a warmer climate and after wandering round the Pacific they finally settled in Samoa.

He wrote *Treasure Island* in 1882, *Dr Jeykll and Mr Hyde* in 1886 (which was based on the character of Deacon Brodie) and the following year *Kidnapped*.

He was a prolific writer and as well as novels and poems he also wrote travelogues for tour companies and he based many of his stories around the Edinburgh area.

When he died on 3 December 1894 the natives of Samoa, who revered him and called him 'Tusitala'(the teller of tales) hacked a path through the undergrowth to the top of Mount Vaea where he was buried.

At the time of his death he was working on the novel *The Weir of Hermiston*.

His childhood nurse Alison Cunningham (Cummy) is buried in Morningside cemetery.

Streets in the Clermiston area are named after places and characters in his novels.

was convened there by Alexander II in 1215. His son, Alexander III, made it a repository for the Kingdom's records and regalia. On his death the succession to the throne was disputed and the English King, Edward I, called in as umpire, settled this by burning the town and seizing the castle in 1296 after a three day seige. The Scots virtually razed the castle to the ground in 1313 to prevent further domination by their foes from this stronghold. Only St Margaret's Chapel was left standing.

In 1313 while the castle was in English hands, Randolph, Earl of Moray scaled the castle rock with 20 men, surprised the garrison of 200 and captured the castle for his uncle, Robert the Bruce. Randolph had under his command a soldier called William Francis, who had in earlier times been a soldier in the castle garrison and who had discovered a secret route out and had used the route to visit his girlfriend in the Grassmarket. This was the way Randolph used to take the castle.

The castle began to take on more of its present form in the late fourteenth century. King David II returned from captivity in England in 1356 and built a 60ft high tower on the site of the present Half Moon Battery to protect the castle's east side. This defence, known as David's Tower, was so strong it withstood a major attack by Henry IV and only succumbed to the massive bombardment of English cannon in 1573.

The next monarchs strengthened David's fortifications along the east, extending them to end in Constable's Tower. In the 1430s James I moved the royal accommodation out of David's tower stronghold to the site of the present palace block.

This move did not prove as fatal for James I as his choice of Perth as a centre for his court and parliament. His assassination there in 1437 increased the importance of Edinburgh as its castle was considered the safest in the land.

Perhaps it was safe for the nation's rulers but not for others with any claim to the throne. In 1440 when the boy King James II lived there, his regents Crichton and Livingstone lured two rivals, the young Douglas brothers, to a feast in the castle's hall. When the food was brought to the table, the main course was a black bull's head, a symbol of death. The boys were taken from this meal, since known as the Black Dinner, to a mock trial, after which they were both beheaded.

James III was so suspicious of his own brothers claiming his crown that he kept them imprisoned, holding the Duke of Albany in David's Tower in 1479 while he lived in the adjacent royal apartments.

Albany escaped after luring his guards into his chambers to drink wine before a blazing fire, killing them when they became drowsy and roasting them in full armour on the fire. Ironically before James III was imprisoned for two months in David's Tower, to be released by the intervention of his former captive brother Albany. Under James III, Edinburgh was finally declared the chief town in the kingdom and the permanent seat for the Scottish Parliament.

After James IV was crowned in 1489 he held tournaments that were famed throughout Europe and embarked on a massive building programme that included the splendid Great Hall that still stands.

This era of success ended on Flodden Field in 1513 when James IV and his army of 10,000 suffered at the hands of the English, the worst military disaster in Scottish history.

By the time Mary Queen of Scots began her reign, the castle was the nation's main armoury, making and storing gunpowder and artillery. In 1566 the armaments included at least 25 cast bronze guns, many of which were used in sieges around the country.

Although Holyrood Palace was preferred as a residence Mary chose to give birth to the future King of Scotland and England, James VI (and I), in the castle so long a symbol of the Scottish crown.

The castle was the last place to uphold Mary's cause in the most destructive siege in its history.

Sir William Kirkcaldy of Grange held the castle against incredible odds for three years for the exiled Queen Mary. The attackers sent for help to Queen Elizabeth I. These reinforcements included 30 cannon sent by sea and by May 1573 five batteries were set up surrounding the castle. David's Tower eventually collapsed, blocking the castle's main well, and within weeks there was no water, food or provisions. The castle surrendered but contrary to the agreement made Kirkcaldy and other leaders were hanged, beheaded and their heads displayed.

The castle was put into Regent Morton's hands and he rebuilt the eastern defences in their present form. Records show the massive Half and sword as Lord Lieutenant of the county of the City of Edinburgh, the Queen's representative and first citizen in the capital city of Scotland. Spaced throughout is the figure of St Andrew with the cross.

Suspended from the chain is the jewel, which has the owl loop, the bird of Minerva, symbolising wisdom and referring to the old connection between the town and university. There are 470 brilliants and 22 rose diamonds, in all 492, and they weigh between 23 and 24 carats. The jewel weighs 4½ ounces and has in blue and white enamel the city crest of arms and the motto; *Nisi Dominus Frustra*, the intepretation being 'except the Lord in vain'. The full meaning is: 'Except the Lord build the house, they labour in vain that build it, except the Lord keep the city, the watcher waketh but in vain,' taken from the 127th psalm.

Edinburgh Castle

The impenetrable fortress of Edinburgh Castle has been besieged and attacked numerous times in its 1300-year history but it has rarely been overwhelmed. It stands today as a memorial to the turbulent history of a nation.

The castle dominates the city below. This is no accident but a deliberate strategy of its many military designers and part of the secret of its success as a fortress. For nearly 500 years the stone edifice topping the Castle Rock was regularly under siege and, though famine and maybe even betrayal led their garrisons to surrender, the castle was never once successfully stormed.

Today the castle is the biggest tourist attraction in Scotland, the HQ of the army in Scotland and the army's School of Piping. Each August the castle provides the setting for the Military Tattoo on the Esplanade. The Crown Room houses the Honours of Scotland, The Crown, The Sceptre, and The Sword of Scotland, and also The Stone of Destiny.

Malcolm Canmore, son of Shakespeare's Duncan and successor to McBeth, had his capital in Dunfermline but his Saxon Queen, Margaret, thought civilisation lay further south. The crude fortress on the hill was converted into a royal residence and the name Castle Rock originates from this period. She was living there when news of her husband's and eldest son's deaths in England reached her in 1093 and she died on the rock the same year.

Her death was followed by events to be repeated frequently in the nation's history- a disputed succession and siege of the castle. Both attempts failed and her youngest son was crowned Scotland's next king in 1124. David I built the summit's only surviving 12th century structure, a chapel dedicated to her memory. He also shaped the first real settlement around the castle. David I was the first to use the castle for the assembly of earls, barons and churchmen, which later became the Scottish Parliament.

The pattern of alternating occupation of the fortress by Scots and English started in the late 12th century.

It was held by an English garrison between 1174 and 1186 but was safely back in Scottish hands when their first official parliament of the Esplanade as the nursery rhyme about the 'Grand Old Duke of York' says, at 'the top of the hill.'

As Commander of the British Army against the French in Flanders during the campaign of 1793 he began well and was acclaimed King of France but a series of tactical blunders led to his recall in 1794.

In 1799 he was again Commander of the British Army in Holland when 10,000 Russians who advanced too eagerly, causing an unexpected engagement on unfamiliar ground, joined them, the result was a humiliating negotiation and withdrawal. Such events produced derision as in the familiar nursery rhyme and even Wellington (then a young soldier) confessed many years later, 'I learnt what one ought not to do, and that is always something.' Off the field of battle the Duke was an able administrator, building up the British Army into a force that would enable Wellington to defeat Napoleon.

Sasine of Nova Scotia

The rank of Baronet had originally been introduced by James I and VI as a way of raising money and colonising the provinces of Ulster. Charles I revived the custom in order to persuade settlers to emigrate to Nova Scotia, a territory which had been granted to Sir William Alexander of Menstrie, Earl of Stirling.

The number of baronetcies was to be limited to 150, each baronet paying £3,000 for the privilege. To overcome the difficulty of giving rights of possession to a land overseas, the earth and stones of the castle hill were converted by Royal Mandate into that of Nova Scotia and the new baronets were given the right of castle, pit and gallows in a ceremony supervised by the Lord Lyon and his Heralds.

The first baronet was created on 26 May 1625, between that date and 1649 some 64 baronets took Sasine (possession) of their Nova Scotia territory.

Mons Meg

'Mons Meg' is a huge siege gun which was forged in Flanders in 1449, one of a pair given to James II by his uncle in marriage, the Duke of Burgundy, in 1457. It consists of wrought iron bars welded into a cylinder over a wooden core and bound with iron hoops. It was probably used as a muzzle loader and could fire a 500lb cannonball

(4½ cwt or 227 Kilos) nearly two miles. It was moved to sieges around the country, its wheels greased with Orkney butter. It took 100 men, 5 carpenters and a large number of oxen to move the 5-ton Meg. The gun was named after its maker's wife and town of origin. It was in use until 1862 when it burst firing a salute in honour of the Duke of York – later James VII. It was taken to London in 1754 to be repaired and was only restored to Edinburgh in 1829, largely by the efforts of Sir Walter Scott. Records show that two men and a cart were employed to retrieve the cannonballs.

Stone of Destiny

Called the Stone of Scone it was alleged to be Jacobs's pillow, and was kept at Scone Palace where Scottish Kings were crowned, including McBeth. The last Scottish King to be crowned on it was Edward Balliol in 1292.

It was stolen by Edward I and kept in England for 700 years under the Coronation Throne in Westminster Abbey.

On Christmas Eve 1950, Ian Hamilton, a law student at Glasgow University, assisted by three others, stole the Stone. Despite a massive police search it was not recovered for a few weeks.

It was returned to Scotland by John Major, Prime Minister in 1996, in an attempt to win votes and is now kept in the Crown Room in the Castle.

John Knox House

The unique Town House known as John Knox House, is the only one of its type left in Edinburgh.

In the 15th and 16th centuries people prominent in Scottish society would all have lived in houses such as this.

The house, up to 1565, was owned by the Arres Family and possibly let to John Knox as his manse during the latter part of his life while he was minister at St Giles. Knox, however, had four different manses in the period after 1560 and all that can be said with certainty is that he lived in a house like this. Knox died in 1572 but the connection with him was strong enough to save the house from demolition when the city council wanted to widen the road.

This town house, typical of its time, is four storeys high with a

Moon Battery cost £743 6s 6d and the expense led Morton to devalue the Scots currency.

The castle came under serious siege three times within 50 years during the seventeenth century though no assault breached the walls. In 1649 and 1650 it was made even more impregnable when the citizens of Edinburgh were used as forced labour to demolish the spur in front of it. Though the castle, ammunition and provisions all seemed to be holding up against Cromwell's attack, in 1650 General Dundas surrendered to him. The castle's reputation was redeemed by the Duke of Gordon, holding it for the Old Pretender in 1689 against the forces of William and Mary. In three months the brave and steadfast Duke cost his attackers 500 lives before famine and disease forced him to give in.

The castle came under attack only twice more, both attempts made by Jacobite forces and neither coming near success. The first was in 1715 when a plan was formulated to scale the walls at night but a combination of betrayal and bad planning turned this assault into a fiasco. Bonnie Prince Charlie fared no better in 1745. He was welcomed into Edinburgh by the citizens but the castle troops fired on Holyrood Palace, then on nearby houses, giving one the name Cannonball House from a shot that embedded in its gable which can still be seen today. The Stuart colours finally reached the castle, displayed as spoils of war after the Young Pretender's defeat at Culloden.

A regular army, an innovation introduced in the mid seventeenth century, kept a permanent garrison there until 1923 when Redford Barracks south of the city was built.

During the Seven Years and the Napoleonic Wars with France the castle was used as a Military Prison. At the beginning of the nineteenth century as many as 1,000 prisoners of war were kept there. Most were lodged in the vaults under the great hall, since known as the French Prison. Their skill in carving can be seen in graffiti on the vault walls and handiwork made for sale, now on view in the Military Museum. But they also carved mutton bones to make watermarks on forged banknotes. So skilful were these forgeries that advertisements appeared in the press offering rewards for information on the prisoners' lucrative sideline.

The prisoners were kept in humane conditions but soldiers stationed at the castle did not enjoy a much higher standard of accommodation. Up to a 1,000 could be lodged in barracks there at one time and a 1791 census includes 159 women and 131 children. A mid nineteenth century report described the married quarters as the worst in Britain with no privacy and so insanitary that epidemics were rife.

The Esplanade

The Esplanade did not exist when the Castle was under siege. It was built as a parade ground in 1753, using earth from the foundations of the Royal Exchange building to level and widen the ridge formed by glacial action. The Esplanade, with its magnificent views of the city, is where the world famous Military Tattoo takes place each August, also there are a number of military statues.

Kings Own Scottish Borderers

A plaque commemorates the raising of the K. O. S. B. on 19 March 1689 by David Leslie, 3rd Earl of Leven, a thousand men enlisted in the space of two hours. The Edinburgh Regiment of Foot, as it was first called, was raised to defend the Lowlands against the Jacobite Highlanders fighting in the name of James II (then in France) in support of William of Orange who was now on the English Throne. At the Battle of Killiecrankie in 1689 Leven's regiment was one of only two who did not run away against the Highlanders. The Highlanders' leader was John Graham of Claverhouse, known as 'Bonnie Dundee', and while his regiment won the battle he himself was killed. After the battle the regiment took the song 'Bonnie Dundee' as its regimental march.

In order to honour its achievement the Magistrates of the City of Edinburgh conferred on Leslie's Regiment the unique right of recruiting by beat of drum in the city and of marching through the city at any time with drums beating, colours flying and bayonets fixed.

Duke of York and Albany

Fredrick, Duke of York and Albany, stands in the robes of a Knight of the Garter holding a Field Marshall's Baton as Commander of the British Army. The statue was erected in 1836 and placed at the top

66

the Arms of the twelfth Earl of Leven. The Lord Lyon King of Arms has been Secretary of the Order since 1926. Lord Home of Hirsel is the present Chancellor and the Sword Bearer is the Earl of Elgin and Kincardine.

All the materials used in the construction of the Chapel came from Scotland. The woodwork is of carved oak by the brothers W. & A. Clow of Edinburgh. The floor is granite from Ailsa Craig with small squares of Iona marble, and the stone is from Cullalo quarry near Aberdour.

The Sovereign's stall has the Royal Arms of the United Kingdom in the Scottish version on the front book board with the Coat of Arms of James VII on the south haffit and that of Queen Anne on the north. On the right hand side is the stall of the Queen Mother and the Duke of Edinburgh, and to the left is Prince Charles' showing the Arms of the Duke of Rothesay, his Scottish title. As there are eight stalls on the south side and six on the north side, the two stalls at either end of the West Side are for ordinary Knights.

The Sovereign's stall has elaborate stepped canopies with groups of three Angels holding scrolls. Carved and moulded supports also enhance the stall. The back is divided into three panels, with the stall plate the Royal Arms –Scottish version. The dexter panel of the canopy shows the Thistle and the sinister, the Rose. Above is a group representing St Margaret teaching some children, with on the left St Kentigren, and on the right St Columba. Above are the Sword, Royal Helmet, Mantling, and Crown. The finial is the Scottish Royal Crest – a Lion sejant affronte, holding a Sword in the dexter paw and a sceptre in the sinister.

The stalls for the Knights each have a richly carved canopy supported on slim twisted columns. On the elbows of the seats are carved beasts taken from Armorial bearings. The haffits have emblems such as the Evangelist and the Hound which is itself a Knightly animal.

The crests above the finials are changed when a new Knight is installed and each corresponds to that on the Heraldic plate of the Knight occupying the stall, although the old stall plates remain to record the earlier occupiers. Phoebe Traquair enamelled those dating from 1911, and Kirkwoods of Albany Street have manufactured the others to the present day.

In the east is housed the Holy Table and Cross. George V, who inaugurated the Chapel, replaced the original Chair of Investiture and put the Hanging here. South is the Dean's chair with faldstool, with opposite, the lectern with four buttresses terminating in the emblems of the Evangelists. On the cresting of the canopy around the apsidal end, angels support a shield with the descending Dove of Peace. Shields show the Cross of Queen Margaret of Scotland on dexter and the St Andrew's Cross on sinister. The shields on the ceiling vaulting are of the original Knights of the Order. The bosses at the apex, carved by Alexander Carrick, A.R.A. are the Royal Arms, St Cues, the Star of the Order, St Andrew, and 'The Pelican in all her Piety' showing loving self sacrifice, plucking feathers from her breast to feed blood to her young. The non-heraldic bosses are the Thistle, Rose, Acorn, Hawthorn, Horse Chestnut, and Vine.

The Heraldic windows are by Louis Davis of London, and with the carvings on the two blank windows, are the Arms of the Sovereign and Knight members during the building of the Chapel. In the tracery of the windows are the signs of the zodiac. The east window by Douglas Strachan of Edinburgh is St Andrew fishing by the Sea of Galilee. Overhead two Angels hold a Cross and a Crown, while below is the Lion Rampant within the wreath of the Order, with the motto 'Nemo Me Impune Lacessit'.

On the ceiling are various angels playing musical instruments to drive out evil spirits. One is playing bagpipes. While to the east of the door inside, fairly high up, is a delightful wooden carving of another angel, again playing bagpipes.

As there is no room inside the Chapel, the Knight's Banners are outside in the Preston Aisle, and are changed like the finial crests on appointment of a new Knight. The Preston Aisle is where the Sovereign and Knights sit during the normal church service.

The coronets on both stall plates and finials vary according to the rank of the wearer. Thus the Sovereign's Crown is an Imperial Crown with two crossing arches. That of Price Charles as immediate heir to the Throne is similar to the Queen's but with only one arch. Royal Dukes have coronets without arches, with crosses and fleur-de-lis alternating. Royal Crowns and coronets are on top of the helmets; coronets of those below Royal rank are below the helmets.

garret in the roof and a basement or laigh below street level. According to records, the first residents of the house were the Arres family. In 1525 Christina Arres inherited and in turn transferred it to her son. In 1566 the house became the home of Christina's granddaughter, Mariota Arres, who had married James Mossman, the goldsmith and moneylender. As a man of some standing Mossman had his family Armorial bearing recorded in the Court of the Lord Lyon now at New Register House. This can be seen on the west wall above the shop door, I. M for James Mossman and M. A. for Mariota Arres. It is I. M. and not J. M as there was no 'J' in the Scots alphabet at that time. On the corner facing up the High Street is a plaque denoting Moses receiving the Ten Commandments and on the sun God is written in three languages, English, Latin and Hebrew. The Marriage Lintel reads 'Love God above all and your neighbours as yourself'.

James Mossman became Master of the Mint and Assayer to Mary Queen of Scots and in taking up his appointment moved into the Castle, thereby giving up his home and later his life since he was executed for supporting Mary Queen of Scots and Roman Catholicism.

John Mossman, James' father, was a skilled Goldsmith in his own right. He was the jeweller who re-designed and fashioned the Scottish Crown, which can be seen in the Crown Room of Edinburgh Castle.

The building has always had shops on the ground and basement floors, of varying trades: Wigmaker, Spirit Shop, Painter, Fishmonger, Bookseller and Kiltmaker.

Moubray House (next door) was built some years earlier in 1488 and on the second floor you can see the original gable end which was discovered in 1982 during restorations.

Residents of note were George Jameson, painter, and Daniel Defoe when he was editor of the *Courant* and a spy for the English Government; his mission was to assess the mood of the people to the union of the Parliaments.

The Thistle Chapel

The Most Ancient and Most Noble Order of the Thistle is the highest Order of Chivalry in Scotland, as is the Order of the Garter in England. There are only sixteen Knights of the Thistle in addition to any Royal Knights the Sovereign may appoint. The Order is a personal appointment by the Sovereign without any ministerial advice or recommendation. The robes are olive green with the large Silver Star of the Order on the left breast. The hat is black velvet with an ostrich feather. The foundation of the Order is accredited to James VII in 1687, revived by Queen Anne in 1703 but there is evidence that the Collar of the Thistles and the Badge of St Andrew was in use in James III's time. It is possible that an Order of Scotland, or of St Andrew, or of the Unicorn, was in being which later gave rise to the present Order of Knighthood of the Thistle.

In 1687 James VII took over the Nave of the Abbey of Holyrood as the Chapel of the Order, but the mob destroyed it in 1688 on his abdication. Investitures of the Knights of the Order continued to be held in Holyrood Palace, the Privy Council Chambers in Edinburgh, and even abroad, but there was no Chapel until the eleventh Earl of Leven and Melville left £40,000 to rebuild Holyrood Chapel Royal.

This was not possible, so the twelfth Earl and his brothers used the bequest to commission Robert Lorimer, who was knighted for this work, to build the present chapel as an extension to St Giles, and Lorimer's genius effectively made it a part of the church, not just an addition. Therefore it is quite small in area being only 35ft by 18ft but the height of 42ft gives it a dignity and it contains a wealth of detail.

The Chapel was inaugurated in 1911 when George V performed the first installation of the Knights here, but the practice continued of investing at different places, and the next ceremony here was not until 1937 when George VI installed his Queen, Elizabeth, as the First Lady of the Order, before their coronation in May, along with two other Knights, although on the Sunday following St Andrew's day each year, there has usually been a short service in the Chapel, conducted by the Dean of the Thistle attended by the Knights before the normal morning service. On these occasions, and at installations, the Lord Lyon's court of Heralds and Pursuivants attend to precede the Knights into and out of the Chapel.

The Ante Chapel contains the names of members from 1687 until 1911, since when the names are on stall plates inside the Chapel. The ceiling of the Ante Chapel has bosses of the Royal Arms of Scotland and also of St Andrew. On the right of the door into the Chapel are

Rationalisation of rail requirements and the 'Beeching' plan resulted in closure of the Waverley route and all passenger branch lines except the North Berwick/Drem which plies from the east end of the station and that part was not used to capacity.

The car-parking problem was solved by drastically shortening platforms 8 and 9, filling in and surfacing the area, which now is a car park for 110 cars. Platforms 2, 3, 4 and 5 were shortened and half of the reclaimed area was acquired by the Post Office who erected a mail-bag sorting compound with hook and chain conveyer linked directly to the General Post Office. The remaining space was used as a parcel handling area, with platforms 3,4,5 and 6 being used exclusively for parcel trains and vehicles. The shortened platforms 8 and 9 served as a Motorola Terminal and a daily service to London was operated with a less frequent service to Bristol.

Up to 400 hundred trains enter or leave the station daily and empty carriage trains go to Craigentinny Carriage Sidings for maintenance and cleaning. Very few parcel trains now use the station, but at one time there were trains conveying parcels, mails, newspapers, fruit and flowers. Few freight trains pass through the station, the majority using the suburban lines. The former parcel office on Waverley Bridge is now a public house. Passenger trains arrive and depart from and to the following points: Aberdeen, Dundee, Ladybank, Kirkcaldy, Cardenden, Cowdenbeath, Dunfermline Perth, Inverness, Stirling, Dunblane, Glasgow Queen Street, Glasgow Central, Hamilton, Motherwell, Shotts, Kingsknowe, (this station was reopened on 1 February 1971) Plymouth, Bristol, Birmingham, Manchester, Liverpool, Carlisle, London Kings Cross, Leeds, York, Newcastle, North Berwick, Dunbar, Livingston.

The Edinburgh/Glasgow route introduced rail travel to the population of Edinburgh and now has a 15 minute service with a journey time of approx. 40 minutes. An unusual feature was introduced during the 1960s in that 6 coaches were hauled by one loco. When the loco was at the rear of the train the driver operated from a small cab in the leading coach, these became known as 'Push and Pulls'. Locos were serviced at Haymarket Motive Power Depot.

Between 1936 and 1937, two signal boxes, Waverley East and Waverley West, were built to replace in modern form, four old manual signal boxes. The two are not now in use having been replaced by a Signalling Centre built on the site of the former goods yard in New Street, but the former Waverley West signal box (one of the largest manual signal boxes ever constructed with 230 levers in a continuous frame) remains and is situated in Princes Street Gardens West.

Considerable modernisation of the station buildings has been carried out in recent years and the programme continues. The Booking Hall has been converted into a modern travel centre without destroying many of the grand design features of the original building. The ceiling has been preserved intact, and the raised numerals '1897' are recorded no less than 36 times.

Edinburgh Signalling Centre was opened in October 1976, the area of control was initially in the vicinity of Waverley, but the final stage was completed in 1981. The Centre now controls the movement of trains on the following routes:

1. East Coast Main Line to Berwick.
2. West Coast Main Line to Carstairs.
3. Glasgow Central Line to Fauldhouse.
4. Glasgow Queen Street Line to Linlithgow.
5. The North lines over the Forth Bridge.
6. The majority of Fife Lines almost to Cupar and the branch line Ladybank to Perth is controlled to Hilton Junction.
7. Local Edinburgh Freight Lines.

While traffic over these routes had originally been controlled by over 100 signal boxes various rationalisation schemes saw this number reduce to 60 and they too have now been closed. In addition to signalling, the centre operates the train information displays at Waverley and certain other stations, and the broadcast announcements to passengers at Waverley.

The Area Manager's sphere of control embraces the East Coast Line to Berwick, all Edinburgh Stations and yards, the lines to the Forth Bridge, Fauldhouse and Linlithgow.

Edinburgh, Leith & Granton Railway

The Edinburgh Leith & Newhaven Railway was incorporated on the 13 August 1836.

A Duke's coronet has eight strawberry leaves.

A Marquis has four pearls between four strawberry leaves.

An Earl has eight pearls impaled and eight strawberry leaves,

A Viscount has sixteen pearls,

A Baron has six large pearls.

The style and position of the helmet is also a mark of distinction displayed like the coronet on both stall plate and finial. A Royal helmet is gold facing front with bars. That of a Peer is silver in profile, generally facing dexter, with gold bars. A Baronet or Knight's helmet is steel with open visor facing front, an Esquire's or Gentleman's is steel, in profile, with visor closed.

Helmets on finials all face front. So because the crest is correctly a fixture on the helmet, a Peer's crest will face dexter on the stall plate, but will face front on the finial unless perhaps in some cases of bad Heraldry when the crest is only two-dimensional and cannot be turned along with the helmet on the finial.

Dexter is the shield bearer's right, the viewer's left.

Sinister is the shield bearer's left, the viewer's right.

Waverley Station

The station is built on a site formerly occupied by the Edinburgh Physic Garden between 1675–1763 before being relocated to a site in Leith Walk with a final move to Inverleith in 1820, becoming the Royal Botanical Gardens. The garden is commemorated by a plaque opposite platform 10 and beside the War Memorial listing the names of railway employees who gave their lives during two World Wars.

The station opened with the name North Bridge on 21 February 1842, as the Edinburgh terminus of the Edinburgh and Glasgow railway. This day also marked the inception of Edinburgh Leith and Granton railway, which plied from North Bridge through Scotland Street Tunnel. The two services were not connected, the platforms being at right angles.

Railway development boomed during this period and four years later the line was built and services commenced between Edinburgh and Berwick. The river Tweed acted as a barrier between Scotland and England for some time, but the erection of the Border Bridge in

1850 enabled trains to run from Edinburgh to London. Lines were being laid down in Fife and from Dundee to Aberdeen and beyond.

The rivers Forth and Tay were major obstacles, but the latter was bridged in 1878, although it had a brief life. On 28 December 1879 the bridge collapsed and a passenger train fell into the river. All the passengers and crew perished. A new Tay bridge was built in 1887 and in 1890 the magnificent Forth Bridge was opened, connecting Edinburgh directly to Aberdeen.

A branch line to Hawick was opened in 1849 but through running of trains over the line to London was not established until 1876. This became known as the 'Waverley' route.

The development of new lines and increased services resulted in chaotic conditions in Waverley, as the station was too small to cope with the increased services and the double line connections to the East and West were also inadequate. The Act of 5 July 1891 allowed the North British Railway to encroach further upon Princes Street Gardens, (despite violent opposition from the City Fathers) allowing an additional line in each direction to be laid down westwards to Saughton Junction and eastwards through Calton tunnel to Abbeyhill.

The station was rebuilt as an 'Island' with footbridge links northwards to Princes Street and Leith Street and southwards to Market Street. Road traffic access is by way of two carriageways from Waverley Bridge, with two beams and girder supporting fairly steeply inclined roadways.

The station design is a double back to back terminus with through platform lines on either flank i. e platforms 1 and 19, 10 and 11 and 20 and 21 which are on what is known as the 'Sub' or suburban line. The area comprises 23 acres and Waverley became the largest station in the British Isles. There were 19 platforms with an aggregate length of 13,980ft, which at the time could accommodate 358 carriages. Through platforms 20 and 21 were completed shortly afterwards and are sited to the south of the main station area. Work commenced in 1892 and was completed in 1900. Extensive office accommodation was built in 1897, part of which housed the General Manager and staff of the North British Railway. The original Booking Hall has a magnificent ceiling, including roof lights extensively embellished with decorative wrought iron work.

5. MacFie of Dreghorn.

This was intended to represent John MacFie who was senior Bailie at the landing of George IV in 1822. This spelling of MacFie is also on the metal plaque on the side of the wharf showing where the landing took place.

6. The Burgh of Leith.

Argent in the sea proper, an ancient galley with two masts, sails furled sable, flagged gules, seated therein the Virgin Mary with the infant saviour in her arms and a cloud azure resting over their heads proper.

This is the matriculated version of 1889. The earlier version showed the Madonna and Child seated below a church canopy as can be seen on the Mercat Cross of Edinburgh and many other sites. But in 1887 Leith Town Council had been asked to supply a banner of their arms for the Paris exhibition of 1889. On realising that the arms had never been matriculated the town clerk of Leith approached the Lord Lyon to effect the registration. He produced a copy of the seal of Leith and Lyon changed the charge to show a cloud instead of a church canopy. This is of course, correct.

The Duke of Buccleuch was outraged by this decision and attempted (unsuccessfully) to have it changed, as it would appear that the Madonna and Child are under a cloud.

7. Sir William Millar of Manderston Bart.

Sometime merchant in St Petersburg (1853), son of James Millar, merchant in Leith. This is correct. The arms were granted in November 1853.

8. Lamont of that Ilk.

The arms were intended for Oliver Cromwell the Lord Protector, whose arms are similar.

9. Lord Bellenden of Broughton.

This coat is correct for the Abbot of Holyrood who built St Ninian's church and the now demolished bridge over the water of Leith at Coalhill.

10. Leith of Restalrig.

This is a reference to this family who in the reign of Alexander III owned Restalrig and many extensive possessions in Midlothian. An heiress married into the Logans. The Leiths were burgesses in Edinburgh and gave their name to Leith Wynd. This is correct heraldry.

It was also decided to put the name of the Provost Thomas Aitken on the ceiling.

The Royal Arms in the centre panels were intended to be:

11. Queen Margaret of Denmark, spouse of James III. While some have suggested that this may be mistaken for Anne of Denmark, Queen of James VI, the intention of the Town Council was clearly Margaret and James III. This is correct.

12. Queen Mary (Mary Queen of Scots).

The arms, however, are quartered with England and Ireland in the English marshalling used after 1603 by James VI, Charles I, Charles II and James VII, and are exactly as used by Mary II, joint Sovereign with William of Orange in 1689. Mary Queen of Scots should have the arms of Scotland alone. The letters 'M' and 'R' on the panel would mean 'Maria Regina'.

13. King George IV.

14. Queen Victoria.

These are both correct.

On the ceiling there are four dates:

1563, this was the date when Queen Mary authorised Leith to have its own Tolbooth and is the date on many representations of the earlier arms of Leith.

1833 was the date Leith became a parliamentary borough.

1877 was when the Town Council of Leith and the police commissioners amalgamated into one legislative body.

The first section to open, on 31 August 1842 was from Canonmills to Trinity.

The company's name was changed to Edinburgh Leith & Granton Railway in 1844. The line was extended on 19 February 1846 from Trinity to Granton, the branch line from Bonnington junction to Leith opened on 10 May 1846.

Scotland Street tunnel and Canal Street Station opened on 17 May 1847. Trains were worked from Scotland Street to Canal Street by a stationary engine at Canal Street.

The Edinburgh Leith & Granton Railway was amalgamated with the Edinburgh Northern Railway to form the Edinburgh Perth & Dundee Railway in 1847 and this was incorporated in the North British Railway on 1 August 1862.

On 2 March 1868 in connection with the opening of the line from Abbeyhill junction to Easter Road the tunnel and Canal Street were closed.

Between 1868 and 1867 the tunnel was used as a wagon store, during the Second World War as an air raid shelter and at various times since has been used as a mushroom farm and a car park. The entrance is still visible in Scotland Street adventure playground.

Today the station is operated by Scotrail, with G. N. E. R. operating the prestigious East Coast Main Line Service and Virgin the West Coast.

Leith Council Chamber

When Leith became a Parliamentary borough in 1833 the Town Council, consisting of a Provost, four Bailies, Treasurer and ten councillors met in the Tollbooth until it moved to Charlotte Street in 1848. (Altered to Queen Charlotte Street on 1 February 1968.) Until they merged in 1877, there were two separate and distinct bodies dealing with the administration of Leith, occupying the same building, built as the Police and Sheriff's Office in 1827. Leith was absorbed into Edinburgh in 1920 when Leith Town Council ceased to exist. The public can visit Leith Town Council chambers on limited occasions courtesy of Leith division of Lothian and Borders Police.

There is a booklet giving an interpretation of the heraldry on the ceiling. These coats of arms have been correctly identified by the Lyon court, but, unfortunately, they are not always representative of the individuals whom the council of 1892 wished to commemorate.

James Simpson started alterations to the building in July 1891 and the cost of painting the restored council meeting room was estimated at £98. The Leith Council minutes of 2 February 1892 (now in the archives of Edinburgh City Chambers) clearly state the intention of Leith Council to honour certain individuals, but it was not noticed that the painter's and the council's knowledge of heraldry was faulty. The coats of arms as shown in the booklet are not at all correct for the intended persons. It would appear that this was never noticed until Bill McKelvie pointed it out. None of the well-known books on Leith have references to any of these errors.

The Leith Town Council minutes were consulted to determine what these distinguished gentlemen had done for Leith to be so honoured. This required research as, unlike the Edinburgh Council minutes, those of Leith are not indexed and for 1892 there are three thick volumes to be studied. Thus we have:

1. The arms of the Earl of Home, chief of the family of Home.

This was intended to represent the Revd. John Home, author of the controversial play 'Douglas' who was born in Leith, buried in South Leith churchyard and was the son of a Leith Town clerk.

2. George Wishart, Bishop of Edinburgh.

He was Bishop in 1622. However the intention was to show the martyr, George Wishart, who was burned at the stake in St Andrews on the orders of David, Cardinal Beaton in 1546. He had occasionally preached at South Leith Church.

3. Gladstone of Fasque Bt. Father of the Prime Minister William Ewart Gladstone.

Sir John Gladstone was born in Leith and founded St Thomas church, this is correct.

4. Lindsay, Earl of Crawford, Chief of the family of Lindsay.

This was intended to represent the Rev. David Lindsay, minister of South Leith Church who sailed to Norway to conduct the marriage of James VI and Anne of Denmark.

The Tay Bridge took seven years to build and had been opened only 19 months when on 28 December 1879, Bouch at the zenith of his powers was at home in Edinburgh when he received the following telegram:
'Terrible accident on bridge, one or more of high girders blown down. Am not sure of the safety of last Edinburgh train'. Daylight revealed that the bridge had collapsed into the Tay estuary taking with it the Edinburgh train and an estimated 75 passengers to their deaths.

An Act of Parliament stopped work on the Forth Bridge; public confidence in Bouch was shattered and although trains still operated on over 300 miles of railway he had constructed that counted for nothing.

The Tay Bridge had fallen. Due to the disaster there entered into the language a saying 'To make a Bouch of it', meaning to make a mess of things.

Bouch retreated to his house in Moffat where he hid for four months after the report on the disaster, which destroyed him, was published. He died on 1 November 1890 and is buried in the Dean cemetery.

It would take more than a disaster to stop the growth of the railways, and before 1880 was out the railway companies were looking at other designs. Almost three years to the day since the Tay Bridge disaster the contract to build the Forth Bridge was awarded to Tancred, Arrol and Company. The designers were Fowler and Baker. The statistics are 5000 men laboured day and night for seven years. The work cost £3 million, it has a length of 1½ miles, has two spans of 1710ft and two spans of 690ft. The highest point above sea level at high tide is 361ft. The height of the rails above sea level at high tide is 158ft. The depth below sea level is 91ft.

During construction the following quantities were used:
Concrete 64,300 cubic yards.
Steel 54,160 tons.
Cement 21,000 tons.
Granite 740,000 cubic ft
Ordinary stone 48,400 cubic yards.
Rivets 6,500,000 which equals 4,200 tons.
Paint oils 35,527 gallons.

Paint 250 tons.

The grim cost of the bridge was 57 lives.

In the 1990s it was estimated that the cost to British Rail of maintaining the bridge was £750,000 per annum.

On a hot day the bridge is one metre longer than in winter due to heat expansion.

To gain a perspective of the work involved, stand on Waverley Bridge and look towards the castle and imagine trying to span the distance with a structure weighing 150,000 tons with no central supports, the rail level would be as high as the Esplanade, and the highest point would be the same height as the Scott Monument.

The Marquess of Tweedale drove the first train across the completed bridge, on 21 January, 1890.

Two trains were taken onto the bridge, their gross weight of 1,800 tons was made up of 100 coal wagons and 6 locos weighing 73 tons apiece; board of trade inspectors took readings along the bridge and were satisfied that the structure was rigid and safe.

On Tuesday 4 March 1890 the bridge was opened by the Prince of Wales who drove home the last of the rivets.

During construction firms were invited to tender as suppliers of paint and the contract was won by Craig and Rose of Leith which has supplied the paint ever since. The painting area is estimated to be 145 acres and 7,000 gallons of paint are required to paint the bridge from end to end. Contrary to popular belief the bridge is not painted from end to end but done over a four to six year cycle. There are 16 men employed as painters and the 'climbing season' is from April to September.

The tradition of throwing a coin over the bridge 'for luck' has faded now but in years gone by it provided a source of income for the maintenance squads.

Royal College of Surgeons

Surgeons Hall is probably known to most people as a bus stop and not as a college and museum of the Fellows of the Royal College of Surgeons.

This building, designed by William Playfair, (1790–1857) was formally opened on 7 July 1832 on a site previously occupied by the

1892 was the year the ceiling was painted.

Now that the real intentions of the Leith town council have been discovered, the Lord Lyon has requested that the officials who conduct visitors round the historic chambers are made aware of the correct persons intended to be honoured, but that the coats should not be altered as they are of interest both artistically and because of the errors.

Mr Charles Burnett, Ross Herald, passed the comment:

'This is the largest decorative scheme employing heraldry in Leith. We are fortunate that the Town Council of 1892 decided to record some of the history of this ancient port by an armorial presentation. It is also an excellent example of late Victorian internal decoration. One can speculate that the inspiration for this display was the 1891 heraldry exhibition held to celebrate the opening of the National Portrait Gallery'.

One o'clock Gun

At 1pm in Edinburgh four things happen, the gun fires, pigeons take flight, tourist take fright and locals check their watches.

The one o'clock gun was first fired in 1861 as a signal for shipping in the Forth.

John Hewat, an Edinburgh Banker, put forward the suggestion in 1846 after seeing a time gun operate in Paris. In response to this a visual time ball was established on the Nelson Monument on Calton Hill in 1851 which moved at a set time each day. Prior to this mariners in the Forth had to bring their chronometers in a wheelbarrow to the City Observatory to have them checked, they did this using what was known as a 'Politicians' clock' i.e. one with two faces, one facing into the Observatory and the other facing out.

Professor Charles Piazza Smyth, the Astronomer Royal for Scotland, worked out the details for a linked time gun system, the Royal Artillery supplied an early version of the existing cannon with an 18lb. gun placed on the Half Moon Battery of the castle and operated by gunners of the Royal Artillery.

The first gun was replaced in the early part of the century by a breechloader in the 1920s and this was replaced by the type of field gun used by the British Army during the First World War. A 25lb. field gun was introduced after World War Two. The gun in use today is another 25lb. and was used during the battle of El Alamein.

Tom McKay, also known as 'Tam the Gun', who has fired the gun on a daily basis for over two decades is the longest serving gunner since the gun was established in 1861. His only days off are Sundays, Christmas Day and Good Friday. Today he relies on the speaking clock for a time check but it was not always so. In the early days, by a fantastic feat of nineteenth century electrical engineering by the Royal Engineers a clock beside the time gun was connected to the time ball on the Nelson Monument by a 4,000ft overhead wire (the longest in Europe) which in turn was connected to the City Observatory's mean time clock, a chain connected to the Castle clock was attached to the gun's fuse and at 1p.m. a weight dropped and the gun was fired automatically.

In 1896 when the Royal Observatory was opened on Blackford Hill the wire was laid underground.

Because of the speed of sound the people in Leith hear the gun at ten seconds past one.

An exhibition of the time gun opened on 21 February 2000, the 100th anniversary of the death of Charles Piazza Smyth.

Anecdotes surrounding the gun say that when it was first decided to have a time signal copied from the French who fired their signal 12 times at noon the canny Scots decided to wait an hour and save 11 shots.

Tourists are told to watch the time ball on Nelson Monument and if the gunner's aim is accurate he will knock the ball down.

Forth Rail Bridge

With the expansion of the railways and the competition between the rival companies to open up the routes to Dundee and Aberdeen the need for a crossing over the Forth and Tay rivers became imperative. The North British Railway Company recruited an engineer called Thomas Bouch and he convinced the directors that the two rivers could be bridged.

The foundation stone of the Tay Bridge was laid in July 1871 and on the Forth Bridge in 1873.

the time the chapel was dedicated. The other three windows display the Lion Rampant and the bottom two commemorate Mitchell MacQuhane and Janet Rynd. These windows are part of the Scottish National Treasures and during World War Two were removed for safekeeping and then restored when hostilities were ended.

In 1560 the Chapel became the focal point of the reformation, and one writer described it as the 'workshop of the reformation'. This is certainly an apt description for, although John Knox made St Giles the preaching centre, it was in the Magdalen Chapel that much of the work was completed on the essential documents required for maintaining the Reformation. John Knox and his fellow reformers, all of whom had the Christian name of John, discussed and drew up such documents as the Scots Confession of Faith, one of the most important documents to come out of the Reformation.

They also prepared the First Book of Discipline, which catered for every aspect of Scotland's national life; not only religious, but also social, cultural and educational aspects were handled in it. If this document had been accepted and implemented the whole of Scotland would have been better even than it became through the Reformation.

It was also in this little Chapel that the first General Assembly of the Reformed Church in Scotland took place. Those present numbered 6 ministers and 36 elders and John Knox presided over that first Assembly. Various other leaders also met in this Chapel. Andrew Melville presided over another Assembly in 1578, which was another historic occasion. John Craig, one of Knox's colleagues, preached in the Chapel on a regular basis.

One item, which has recently come to light, is that chaplains of Cromwell used the Chapel while the Lord Protector was in Edinburgh. In 1765 Robert Carmichael and seven others rented the Chapel for the establishing of a Baptist cause in the city and so the Scots Baptist cause was constituted as a direct result and they worshipped in the Chapel for nine years.

In the last century the complex of both hospital and Chapel was taken over by the Edinburgh Medical Missionary Society who carried on dispensary work for the district in the training of those who were to become Medical Missionaries. This work closed when Edinburgh University took over the dispensary and made it their family doctor service clinic, this part of the building is now administered by the Lothian Health Board.

The Chapel was leased to Heriot Watt University for use as its Chaplaincy centre until the university transferred to Riccarton Campus and its main function was for the use of the music society. Many well known musicians played there, taking advantage of the excellent acoustic qualities of the building.

Golf in the city

Today St Andrews is regarded as the home of golf and the Royal and Ancient Club as golf's rule giving authority. This was not always the case, and Edinburgh's claim has the most historical validity.

Golf was played at Leith Links during the reign of the Stewarts, and Mary Queen of Scots is said to have played there.

The world's oldest golf club is the Honourable Company of Edinburgh Golfers which played for its first trophy, a silver club, on the Links at Leith on 7 March 1744. They also devised a set of rules for the competition. The paper on which the original 13 rules of golf were drafted is in the archives of the Honourable Company and a copy is on show at their clubhouse at Muirfield.

The Royal and Ancient Club simply adopted the Leith club's rules and it was not until 1754 that St Andrews played for a silver club. It was in 1834 that the St Andrews club successfully petitioned King William IV to designate it Royal and Ancient.

The original course at Leith was of five holes, Thorntree 414 yards, Braehead 461 yards, Sawmill 426 yards, North-mid 495 yards, South-mid 435 yards. Bearing in mind the equipment available the game was all about strength and if the five holes had been eighteen as today the course would measure over 8000 yards with an SSS of 79.

In the mid nineteenth century Leith Links was becoming overcrowded with grazing animals and women drying their washing so the Honourable Company moved to Musselburgh and in 1891 moved to their present home at Muirfield.

The second and third oldest clubs are the Edinburgh Burgess Golfing Society and the Bruntsfield Links Golf Club. The Burgess claims to have existed since 1735 but its records only go back to 1773,

Royal Academy of Exercises, (a riding school) in a 1763 building. In 1908 the architect Balfour Paul added an extension.

Inside is a reception room which is used as a meeting room and a waiting room for examination candidates, thousands of whom sit for numerous diplomas, coming to Edinburgh from all over the world. The library contains a modern medical library and instruments from through the ages and is heavily used by fellows and candidates world wide. In the Playfair Hall is housed the museum's 15,000 pathological specimens.

On the walls are some sixteen paintings by Sir Charles Bell, of war wounds as seen by him on the return of troops from the battles of Corunna and Waterloo.

In the Sir Jules Thorn Hall is the college's permanent exhibition of the history of medicine in Scotland, especially Edinburgh, over the last 500 years. There is also the remarkable Menzies Campbell collection of historical dental instruments.

Anyone can visit the museum by prior arrangement.

The Magdalen Chapel

The Magdalen Chapel is one of the few remaining pre-Reformation Church buildings in Edinburgh with the stained glass windows still intact. Recent reports indicate that the building stands as third in historic interest and value as a listed building in the city of Edinburgh.

The building itself dates from 1541 although not completed until 1547. Since its founding various additions have been made, especially after a fire ravaged the building in the 18th century. It was part of a small complex which included a small hospital. This plan was conceived by Mitchell MacQuhane and his wife Janet Rynd.

From the records it appears that the whole venture cost in the region of £2,700 Scottish currency. Janet Rynd was the person who after her husband's death saw the whole venture brought to completion. She is buried in the chapel and her tomb is in the south east corner of the chapel. The original charter is to be found in the north west corner and makes interesting reading.

Externally the tower was added in 1628 and a clock and bell were installed. The clock was removed in recent times by the department of Mechanical Engineering of Heriot Watt University who have since restored it to full working order and reinstalled it after the renovation programme was completed.

Other items of interest are the inscriptions around the north and east walls. These begin at the top left and work round to the end of the east wall then return to the north wall. These permanent receipts are called 'Brods' and make interesting reading as the names, descriptions and trades are examined. The various forms of currency are also very interesting.

The balustrade around the platform is a later innovation to indicate some of the trades, which were found in the incorporation of hammermen. This Trade Guild who used the chapel as their Guildhall were patrons of the chapel and hospital from its earliest days. Their symbols are seen in different parts of the chapel in the hammer surmounted by a crown. This association was continued until the last century, when they asked the then Protestant Institute of Scotland, (now incorporated into the Scottish Reformation Society) to assume ownership of the chapel. Happily this association of the hammermen has been resumed and they celebrated their 500th anniversary in the chapel in 1983.

The large chair on the platform also belongs to the hammermen and was the deacon's chair. It is something which is now priceless although it only cost £33 Scots currency to make which in 1916 was calculated to be the equivalent of £2.65p sterling.

The old table, which stands on the platform, was used as a mortuary table as this was one of the uses the chapel had in its chequered history. This was because the chapel was close to the place of public execution in the Grassmarket. During the 'Killing Times' of the Covenanters, when over a hundred were executed in the Grassmarket, their remains were brought to the chapel and dressed for burial.

This service was rendered by a team of ladies under Helen Alexander, who regarded it as part of their Christian duties to honour their fellow Covenanters in this way before their bodies were buried in the common grave at Greyfriars Churchyard.

The chapel has witnessed many varied situations in the pageant of Scottish history. Prior to 1560 the chapel was a Roman Catholic Chapel. This is seen in the stained glass windows, where the top right window is the coat of arms of Mary of Lorraine, the Queen Regent at sentenced him to two years in jail, his sight in his remaining eye became worse and he was released before he completed his sentence. He died in Edinburgh in 1968.

During an interview after his arrest he solved a mystery which had baffled Royal Mint officials since 1917. On his release from the army it had been his intention to make sovereigns and he had started production when, to his disgust, sovereigns ceased to be made so in a fit of pique rather than destroy the dies he sent them anonymously to the mint were they remained a mystery for 50 years.

Robert Louis Stevenson, 1850–94

Born at No. 8 Howard Place into a family of lighthouse engineers, the young Robert was a sickly child.

The family moved to Inverleith Terrace, but the house was subject to damp and so when he was seven years old they moved again, this time to 17 Heriot Row, which was to be his final home in Edinburgh.

He was christened Robert Lewis Balfour Stevenson in favour of his maternal grandfather, but when he grew up he dropped the Balfour and changed the spelling to the French, Louis, as he thought this more avant garde.

Whilst living in Howard Place R. L. S. attended Canonmills School (opposite the Canonmills service station) where a plaque on the wall commemorates the fact.

As a child he was often in bed ill and his nurse, Alison Cunningham, (Cummy to the family) would read him stories about the Covenanters and from the Bible. During this time he would watch for 'Leerie' the Lamplighter coming along the street and was always pleased when he gave him a wave. He later immortalised him in the poem, which is inscribed on a brass plaque on the railings of No. 17.

From his bedroom window he could see the ornamental pond in Queen Street Gardens East from which he conceived the idea of *Treasure Island*.

While visiting his grandfather, Robert Stevenson, who was the greatest Lighthouse Engineer and lived at Baxter's Place now called Stevenson House, he purchased cardboard from an adjacent shop (now an Italian Restaurant) which he used to make a small theatre He used this for his poem 'Penny Plain Twopence Coloured'.

His maternal grandfather was minister at Colinton Church and as a young boy he would spend the summers with him at Swanston Cottage in Swanston Village. He loved to roam the Pentland Hills and would listen avidly to the stories told to him by Jock Todd the Swanston shepherd. In later life he would always yearn for what he called 'The Hills of Home'.

In 1867 he studied Engineering at Edinburgh University but had to give up through ill health, as some days he could not even wear a jacket as it caused his lungs to haemorrhage. He wanted to become a writer but his father was not keen on the idea so, as a compromise, he agreed to study Law so that he would have a profession to fall back on. In 1875 he was called to the Scottish Bar, but his heart was not in it and he only had one client.

To recover from another bout of illness he went to France where he met an American woman named Fanny Van Degrift Osbourne and they struck up a friendship. She returned to America and R.L.S. returned to Scotland but he followed her to California in 1879, almost dying on the journey. When he had recovered she divorced her husband and they were married in 1880. For the sake of his health they decided to live in a warmer climate and after wandering round the Pacific they finally settled in Samoa.

He wrote *Treasure Island* in 1882, *Dr Jeykll and Mr Hyde* in 1886 (which was based on the character of Deacon Brodie) and the following year *Kidnapped*.

He was a prolific writer and as well as novels and poems he also wrote travelogues for tour companies and he based many of his stories around the Edinburgh area.

When he died on 3 December 1894 the natives of Samoa, who revered him and called him 'Tusitala'(the teller of tales) hacked a path through the undergrowth to the top of Mount Vaea where he was buried.

At the time of his death he was working on the novel *The Weir of Hermiston*.

His childhood nurse Alison Cunningham (Cummy) is buried in Morningside cemetery.

Streets in the Clermiston area are named after places and characters in his novels.

The Society of High Constables

The founding date is unknown but is generally accepted as 1611, when the Magistrates decided to elect Constables, half from the Merchants and half from the Tradesmen. They were an early form of police force and their powers were many and far-reaching.

There are twenty-three wards of twelve members in the Society, giving a total membership of two hundred and seventy-six. You cannot apply to join but must be invited, and today their function is confined to having dinners and to act as ushers on ceremonial occasions, but these were not their original duties.

The twelve Officers and twenty-six Constables who were appointed had a great variety of duties.

They were expected to apprehend and imprison suspects, such as vagabonds and night walkers, they were to challenge anyone in possession of a pistol or dagger, and present them to the Lord Provost or Bailies for punishment. They were to intervene at times of public disorder, such as riots or street fighting, and were given the power to break down doors to investigate noise and nuisance.

They were duty bound to search for Jesuits, Seminarians, priests or trafficking papists and deal with beggars and gypsies as well as idle persons. They were empowered to deal with murders, theft, or other capital crimes and also to clear the streets of filth, middens and swine.

They were to see that those liable for King's service had adequate armour, and to apprehend swearers and blasphemers in the streets, markets or at the wells.

With such superhuman tasks before them, it is little wonder that the Constables were unsuccessful in cleansing the streets where refuse lay 'like mountains' and roads had to be cut through it to reach the closes and booths.

The Constables seemed to be used for everything, they oversaw the sending of beggars and vagrants to the workhouse and the Correction House in the Calton district.

They were used as tax gatherers, as officers of the local census, for billeting soldiers and for street patrol at Hogmanay to prevent 'The throwing of dead cats' and other riotous behaviour.

They were also ordered to quell snowball fights, Chartist

demonstrations and to assist at fires in the High Street or in public buildings elsewhere in the City.

Lord Provost's Badge and Chain

William de Dederyk is generally accepted as Edinburgh's first Provost in 1296. Over the years the position has not been without its dangers.

In 1561 Mary Queen of Scots dismissed the Provost and Bailies on religious grounds.

Provost Sir Alexander Lauder was killed at the Battle of Flodden in 1513, and Adam Otterburne was assassinated in office. Provost Archibald Stewart was seen by the Government as too closely tied to the Jacobite cause and was tried for treason.

Provost Andrew Ramsey has served the longest, a total of fourteen years, and was the first to be called Lord Provost. Sir James Millar of the building firm is the only man to have held both positions of Lord Provost of Edinburgh and Lord Mayor of London, albeit at different times. The only Englishman to hold the position has been Sir James Falshaw in 1874, the only women Eleanor McLaughlin in 1988–92, and Lesley Hynds in 2003.

It was the custom for the Provosts to be knighted but the practice ceased when Jack Kane refused the honour in 1972.

Sir George Drummond was elected six times during which time he pushed through his vision for a 'New Town'.

The Lord Provost's present badge and chain was first worn by Lord Provost Sir Mitchell Thomson in 1899, on the occasion of the freedom of the city to HRH the Prince of Wales, afterwards King Edward VII. Designed by W. S. Black, it was made by Messrs. Brook and Son, George Street.

The chain is 18 carat gold, 46 inches in length, 1½ inches broad and weighs between 40 and 50 ounces. The centre square link has the letters 'E' facing each other and joined by a heart of laurel, symbolical of the 'Heart of Midlothian'. It also has in the centre of the two 'E's, a replica of the old Scottish Crown.

The other plaques on the chain show the other offices or titles held by the Lord Provost – Triton of the Sea; the mermaid and the ship and anchor associated with the title, Lord High Admiral of the Firth of Forth; the figure of justice and scales as chief magistrate; the crown and sword as Lord Lieutenant of the county of the City of Edinburgh, the Queen's representative and first citizen in the capital city of Scotland. Spaced throughout is the figure of St Andrew with the cross.

Suspended from the chain is the jewel, which has the owl loop, the bird of Minerva, symbolising wisdom and referring to the old connection between the town and university. There are 470 brilliants and 22 rose diamonds, in all 492, and they weigh between 23 and 24 carats. The jewel weighs 4½ ounces and has in blue and white enamel the city crest of arms and the motto; *Nisi Dominus Frustra*, the intepretation being 'except the Lord in vain'. The full meaning is: 'Except the Lord build the house, they labour in vain that build it, except the Lord keep the city, the watcher waketh but in vain,' taken from the 127th psalm.

Edinburgh Castle

The impenetrable fortress of Edinburgh Castle has been besieged and attacked numerous times in its 1300-year history but it has rarely been overwhelmed. It stands today as a memorial to the turbulent history of a nation.

The castle dominates the city below. This is no accident but a deliberate strategy of its many military designers and part of the secret of its success as a fortress. For nearly 500 years the stone edifice topping the Castle Rock was regularly under siege and, though famine and maybe even betrayal led their garrisons to surrender, the castle was never once successfully stormed.

Today the castle is the biggest tourist attraction in Scotland, the HQ of the army in Scotland and the army's School of Piping. Each August the castle provides the setting for the Military Tattoo on the Esplanade. The Crown Room houses the Honours of Scotland, The Crown, The Sceptre, and The Sword of Scotland, and also The Stone of Destiny.

Malcolm Canmore, son of Shakespeare's Duncan and successor to McBeth, had his capital in Dunfermline but his Saxon Queen, Margaret, thought civilisation lay further south. The crude fortress on the hill was converted into a royal residence and the name Castle Rock originates from this period. She was living there when news of her husband's and eldest son's deaths in England reached her in 1093 and she died on the rock the same year.

Her death was followed by events to be repeated frequently in the nation's history- a disputed succession and siege of the castle. Both attempts failed and her youngest son was crowned Scotland's next king in 1124. David I built the summit's only surviving 12th century structure, a chapel dedicated to her memory. He also shaped the first real settlement around the castle. David I was the first to use the castle for the assembly of earls, barons and churchmen, which later became the Scottish Parliament.

The pattern of alternating occupation of the fortress by Scots and English started in the late 12th century.

It was held by an English garrison between 1174 and 1186 but was safely back in Scottish hands when their first official parliament was convened there by Alexander II in 1215. His son, Alexander III, made it a repository for the Kingdom's records and regalia. On his death the succession to the throne was disputed and the English King, Edward I, called in as umpire, settled this by burning the town and seizing the castle in 1296 after a three day seige. The Scots virtually razed the castle to the ground in 1313 to prevent further domination by their foes from this stronghold. Only St Margaret's Chapel was left standing.

In 1313 while the castle was in English hands, Randolph, Earl of Moray scaled the castle rock with 20 men, surprised the garrison of 200 and captured the castle for his uncle, Robert the Bruce. Randolph had under his command a soldier called William Francis, who had in earlier times been a soldier in the castle garrison and who had discovered a secret route out and had used the route to visit his girlfriend in the Grassmarket. This was the way Randolph used to take the castle.

The castle began to take on more of its present form in the late fourteenth century. King David II returned from captivity in England in 1356 and built a 60ft high tower on the site of the present Half Moon Battery to protect the castle's east side. This defence, known as David's Tower, was so strong it withstood a major attack by Henry IV and only succumbed to the massive bombardment of English cannon in 1573.

The next monarchs strengthened David's fortifications along the east, extending them to end in Constable's Tower. In the 1430s James I moved the royal accommodation out of David's tower stronghold to the site of the present palace block.

This move did not prove as fatal for James I as his choice of Perth as a centre for his court and parliament. His assassination there in 1437 increased the importance of Edinburgh as its castle was considered the safest in the land.

Perhaps it was safe for the nation's rulers but not for others with any claim to the throne. In 1440 when the boy King James II lived there, his regents Crichton and Livingstone lured two rivals, the young Douglas brothers, to a feast in the castle's hall. When the food was brought to the table, the main course was a black bull's head, a symbol of death. The boys were taken from this meal, since known as the Black Dinner, to a mock trial, after which they were both beheaded.

James III was so suspicious of his own brothers claiming his crown that he kept them imprisoned, holding the Duke of Albany in David's Tower in 1479 while he lived in the adjacent royal apartments.

Albany escaped after luring his guards into his chambers to drink wine before a blazing fire, killing them when they became drowsy and roasting them in full armour on the fire. Ironically before James III was imprisoned for two months in David's Tower, to be released by the intervention of his former captive brother Albany. Under James III, Edinburgh was finally declared the chief town in the kingdom and the permanent seat for the Scottish Parliament.

After James IV was crowned in 1489 he held tournaments that were famed throughout Europe and embarked on a massive building programme that included the splendid Great Hall that still stands.

This era of success ended on Flodden Field in 1513 when James IV and his army of 10,000 suffered at the hands of the English, the worst military disaster in Scottish history.

By the time Mary Queen of Scots began her reign, the castle was the nation's main armoury, making and storing gunpowder and artillery. In 1566 the armaments included at least 25 cast bronze guns, many of which were used in sieges around the country.

Although Holyrood Palace was preferred as a residence Mary chose to give birth to the future King of Scotland and England, James VI (and I), in the castle so long a symbol of the Scottish crown.

The castle was the last place to uphold Mary's cause in the most destructive siege in its history.

Sir William Kirkcaldy of Grange held the castle against incredible odds for three years for the exiled Queen Mary. The attackers sent for help to Queen Elizabeth I. These reinforcements included 30 cannon sent by sea and by May 1573 five batteries were set up surrounding the castle. David's Tower eventually collapsed, blocking the castle's main well, and within weeks there was no water, food or provisions. The castle surrendered but contrary to the agreement made Kirkcaldy and other leaders were hanged, beheaded and their heads displayed.

The castle was put into Regent Morton's hands and he rebuilt the eastern defences in their present form. Records show the massive Half

Moon Battery cost £743 6s 6d and the expense led Morton to devalue the Scots currency.

The castle came under serious siege three times within 50 years during the seventeenth century though no assault breached the walls. In 1649 and 1650 it was made even more impregnable when the citizens of Edinburgh were used as forced labour to demolish the spur in front of it. Though the castle, ammunition and provisions all seemed to be holding up against Cromwell's attack, in 1650 General Dundas surrendered to him. The castle's reputation was redeemed by the Duke of Gordon, holding it for the Old Pretender in 1689 against the forces of William and Mary. In three months the brave and steadfast Duke cost his attackers 500 lives before famine and disease forced him to give in.

The castle came under attack only twice more, both attempts made by Jacobite forces and neither coming near success. The first was in 1715 when a plan was formulated to scale the walls at night but a combination of betrayal and bad planning turned this assault into a fiasco. Bonnie Prince Charlie fared no better in 1745. He was welcomed into Edinburgh by the citizens but the castle troops fired on Holyrood Palace, then on nearby houses, giving one the name Cannonball House from a shot that embedded in its gable which can still be seen today. The Stuart colours finally reached the castle, displayed as spoils of war after the Young Pretender's defeat at Culloden.

A regular army, an innovation introduced in the mid seventeenth century, kept a permanent garrison there until 1923 when Redford Barracks south of the city was built.

During the Seven Years and the Napoleonic Wars with France the castle was used as a Military Prison. At the beginning of the nineteenth century as many as 1,000 prisoners of war were kept there. Most were lodged in the vaults under the great hall, since known as the French Prison. Their skill in carving can be seen in graffiti on the vault walls and handiwork made for sale, now on view in the Military Museum. But they also carved mutton bones to make watermarks on forged banknotes. So skilful were these forgeries that advertisements appeared in the press offering rewards for information on the prisoners' lucrative sideline.

The prisoners were kept in humane conditions but soldiers stationed at the castle did not enjoy a much higher standard of accommodation. Up to a 1,000 could be lodged in barracks there at one time and a 1791 census includes 159 women and 131 children. A mid nineteenth century report described the married quarters as the worst in Britain with no privacy and so insanitary that epidemics were rife.

The Esplanade

The Esplanade did not exist when the Castle was under siege. It was built as a parade ground in 1753, using earth from the foundations of the Royal Exchange building to level and widen the ridge formed by glacial action. The Esplanade, with its magnificent views of the city, is where the world famous Military Tattoo takes place each August, also there are a number of military statues.

Kings Own Scottish Borderers

A plaque commemorates the raising of the K. O. S. B. on 19 March 1689 by David Leslie, 3rd Earl of Leven, a thousand men enlisted in the space of two hours. The Edinburgh Regiment of Foot, as it was first called, was raised to defend the Lowlands against the Jacobite Highlanders fighting in the name of James II (then in France) in support of William of Orange who was now on the English Throne. At the Battle of Killiecrankie in 1689 Leven's regiment was one of only two who did not run away against the Highlanders. The Highlanders' leader was John Graham of Claverhouse, known as 'Bonnie Dundee', and while his regiment won the battle he himself was killed. After the battle the regiment took the song 'Bonnie Dundee' as its regimental march.

In order to honour its achievement the Magistrates of the City of Edinburgh conferred on Leslie's Regiment the unique right of recruiting by beat of drum in the city and of marching through the city at any time with drums beating, colours flying and bayonets fixed.

Duke of York and Albany

Fredrick, Duke of York and Albany, stands in the robes of a Knight of the Garter holding a Field Marshall's Baton as Commander of the British Army. The statue was erected in 1836 and placed at the top

66

of the Esplanade as the nursery rhyme about the 'Grand Old Duke of York' says, at 'the top of the hill.'

As Commander of the British Army against the French in Flanders during the campaign of 1793 he began well and was acclaimed King of France but a series of tactical blunders led to his recall in 1794.

In 1799 he was again Commander of the British Army in Holland when 10,000 Russians who advanced too eagerly, causing an unexpected engagement on unfamiliar ground, joined them, the result was a humiliating negotiation and withdrawal. Such events produced derision as in the familiar nursery rhyme and even Wellington (then a young soldier) confessed many years later, 'I learnt what one ought not to do, and that is always something.' Off the field of battle the Duke was an able administrator, building up the British Army into a force that would enable Wellington to defeat Napoleon.

Sasine of Nova Scotia

The rank of Baronet had originally been introduced by James I and VI as a way of raising money and colonising the provinces of Ulster. Charles I revived the custom in order to persuade settlers to emigrate to Nova Scotia, a territory which had been granted to Sir William Alexander of Menstrie, Earl of Stirling.

The number of baronetcies was to be limited to 150, each baronet paying £3,000 for the privilege. To overcome the difficulty of giving rights of possession to a land overseas, the earth and stones of the castle hill were converted by Royal Mandate into that of Nova Scotia and the new baronets were given the right of castle, pit and gallows in a ceremony supervised by the Lord Lyon and his Heralds.

The first baronet was created on 26 May 1625, between that date and 1649 some 64 baronets took Sasine (possession) of their Nova Scotia territory.

Mons Meg

'Mons Meg' is a huge siege gun which was forged in Flanders in 1449, one of a pair given to James II by his uncle in marriage, the Duke of Burgundy, in 1457. It consists of wrought iron bars welded into a cylinder over a wooden core and bound with iron hoops. It was probably used as a muzzle loader and could fire a 500lb cannonball

(4½ cwt or 227 Kilos) nearly two miles. It was moved to sieges around the country, its wheels greased with Orkney butter. It took 100 men, 5 carpenters and a large number of oxen to move the 5-ton Meg. The gun was named after its maker's wife and town of origin. It was in use until 1862 when it burst firing a salute in honour of the Duke of York – later James VII. It was taken to London in 1754 to be repaired and was only restored to Edinburgh in 1829, largely by the efforts of Sir Walter Scott. Records show that two men and a cart were employed to retrieve the cannonballs.

Stone of Destiny

Called the Stone of Scone it was alleged to be Jacobs's pillow, and was kept at Scone Palace where Scottish Kings were crowned, including McBeth. The last Scottish King to be crowned on it was Edward Balliol in 1292.

It was stolen by Edward I and kept in England for 700 years under the Coronation Throne in Westminster Abbey.

On Christmas Eve 1950, Ian Hamilton, a law student at Glasgow University, assisted by three others, stole the Stone. Despite a massive police search it was not recovered for a few weeks.

It was returned to Scotland by John Major, Prime Minister in 1996, in an attempt to win votes and is now kept in the Crown Room in the Castle.

John Knox House

The unique Town House known as John Knox House, is the only one of its type left in Edinburgh.

In the 15th and 16th centuries people prominent in Scottish society would all have lived in houses such as this.

The house, up to 1565, was owned by the Arres Family and possibly let to John Knox as his manse during the latter part of his life while he was minister at St Giles. Knox, however, had four different manses in the period after 1560 and all that can be said with certainty is that he lived in a house like this. Knox died in 1572 but the connection with him was strong enough to save the house from demolition when the city council wanted to widen the road.

This town house, typical of its time, is four storeys high with a garret in the roof and a basement or laigh below street level. According to records, the first residents of the house were the Arres family. In 1525 Christina Arres inherited and in turn transferred it to her son. In 1566 the house became the home of Christina's granddaughter, Mariota Arres, who had married James Mossman, the goldsmith and moneylender. As a man of some standing Mossman had his family Armorial bearing recorded in the Court of the Lord Lyon now at New Register House. This can be seen on the west wall above the shop door, I. M for James Mossman and M. A. for Mariota Arres. It is I. M. and not J. M as there was no 'J' in the Scots alphabet at that time. On the corner facing up the High Street is a plaque denoting Moses receiving the Ten Commandments and on the sun God is written in three languages, English, Latin and Hebrew. The Marriage Lintel reads 'Love God above all and your neighbours as yourself'.

James Mossman became Master of the Mint and Assayer to Mary Queen of Scots and in taking up his appointment moved into the Castle, thereby giving up his home and later his life since he was executed for supporting Mary Queen of Scots and Roman Catholicism.

John Mossman, James' father, was a skilled Goldsmith in his own right. He was the jeweller who re-designed and fashioned the Scottish Crown, which can be seen in the Crown Room of Edinburgh Castle.

The building has always had shops on the ground and basement floors, of varying trades: Wigmaker, Spirit Shop, Painter, Fishmonger, Bookseller and Kiltmaker.

Moubray House (next door) was built some years earlier in 1488 and on the second floor you can see the original gable end which was discovered in 1982 during restorations.

Residents of note were George Jameson, painter, and Daniel Defoe when he was editor of the *Courant* and a spy for the English Government; his mission was to assess the mood of the people to the union of the Parliaments.

The Thistle Chapel

The Most Ancient and Most Noble Order of the Thistle is the highest Order of Chivalry in Scotland, as is the Order of the Garter in England. There are only sixteen Knights of the Thistle in addition to any Royal Knights the Sovereign may appoint. The Order is a personal appointment by the Sovereign without any ministerial advice or recommendation. The robes are olive green with the large Silver Star of the Order on the left breast. The hat is black velvet with an ostrich feather. The foundation of the Order is accredited to James VII in 1687, revived by Queen Anne in 1703 but there is evidence that the Collar of the Thistles and the Badge of St Andrew was in use in James III's time. It is possible that an Order of Scotland, or of St Andrew, or of the Unicorn, was in being which later gave rise to the present Order of Knighthood of the Thistle.

In 1687 James VII took over the Nave of the Abbey of Holyrood as the Chapel of the Order, but the mob destroyed it in 1688 on his abdication. Investitures of the Knights of the Order continued to be held in Holyrood Palace, the Privy Council Chambers in Edinburgh, and even abroad, but there was no Chapel until the eleventh Earl of Leven and Melville left £40,000 to rebuild Holyrood Chapel Royal.

This was not possible, so the twelfth Earl and his brothers used the bequest to commission Robert Lorimer, who was knighted for this work, to build the present chapel as an extension to St Giles, and Lorimer's genius effectively made it a part of the church, not just an addition. Therefore it is quite small in area being only 35ft by 18ft but the height of 42ft gives it a dignity and it contains a wealth of detail.

The Chapel was inaugurated in 1911 when George V performed the first installation of the Knights here, but the practice continued of investing at different places, and the next ceremony here was not until 1937 when George VI installed his Queen, Elizabeth, as the First Lady of the Order, before their coronation in May, along with two other Knights, although on the Sunday following St Andrew's day each year, there has usually been a short service in the Chapel, conducted by the Dean of the Thistle attended by the Knights before the normal morning service. On these occasions, and at installations, the Lord Lyon's court of Heralds and Pursuivants attend to precede the Knights into and out of the Chapel.

The Ante Chapel contains the names of members from 1687 until 1911, since when the names are on stall plates inside the Chapel. The ceiling of the Ante Chapel has bosses of the Royal Arms of Scotland and also of St Andrew. On the right of the door into the Chapel are the Arms of the twelfth Earl of Leven. The Lord Lyon King of Arms has been Secretary of the Order since 1926. Lord Home of Hirsel is the present Chancellor and the Sword Bearer is the Earl of Elgin and Kincardine.

All the materials used in the construction of the Chapel came from Scotland. The woodwork is of carved oak by the brothers W. & A. Clow of Edinburgh. The floor is granite from Ailsa Craig with small squares of Iona marble, and the stone is from Cullalo quarry near Aberdour.

The Sovereign's stall has the Royal Arms of the United Kingdom in the Scottish version on the front book board with the Coat of Arms of James VII on the south haffit and that of Queen Anne on the north. On the right hand side is the stall of the Queen Mother and the Duke of Edinburgh, and to the left is Prince Charles' showing the Arms of the Duke of Rothesay, his Scottish title. As there are eight stalls on the south side and six on the north side, the two stalls at either end of the West Side are for ordinary Knights.

The Sovereign's stall has elaborate stepped canopies with groups of three Angels holding scrolls. Carved and moulded supports also enhance the stall. The back is divided into three panels, with the stall plate the Royal Arms –Scottish version. The dexter panel of the canopy shows the Thistle and the sinister, the Rose. Above is a group representing St Margaret teaching some children, with on the left St Kentigren, and on the right St Columba. Above are the Sword, Royal Helmet, Mantling, and Crown. The finial is the Scottish Royal Crest – a Lion sejant affronte, holding a Sword in the dexter paw and a sceptre in the sinister.

The stalls for the Knights each have a richly carved canopy supported on slim twisted columns. On the elbows of the seats are carved beasts taken from Armorial bearings. The haffits have emblems such as the Evangelist and the Hound which is itself a Knightly animal.

The crests above the finials are changed when a new Knight is installed and each corresponds to that on the Heraldic plate of the Knight occupying the stall, although the old stall plates remain to record the earlier occupiers. Phoebe Traquair enamelled those dating from 1911, and Kirkwoods of Albany Street have manufactured the others to the present day.

In the east is housed the Holy Table and Cross. George V, who inaugurated the Chapel, replaced the original Chair of Investiture and put the Hanging here. South is the Dean's chair with faldstool, with opposite, the lectern with four buttresses terminating in the emblems of the Evangelists. On the cresting of the canopy around the apsidal end, angels support a shield with the descending Dove of Peace. Shields show the Cross of Queen Margaret of Scotland on dexter and the St Andrew's Cross on sinister. The shields on the ceiling vaulting are of the original Knights of the Order. The bosses at the apex, carved by Alexander Carrick, A.R.A. are the Royal Arms, St Cues, the Star of the Order, St Andrew, and 'The Pelican in all her Piety' showing loving self sacrifice, plucking feathers from her breast to feed blood to her young. The non-heraldic bosses are the Thistle, Rose, Acorn, Hawthorn, Horse Chestnut, and Vine.

The Heraldic windows are by Louis Davis of London, and with the carvings on the two blank windows, are the Arms of the Sovereign and Knight members during the building of the Chapel. In the tracery of the windows are the signs of the zodiac. The east window by Douglas Strachan of Edinburgh is St Andrew fishing by the Sea of Galilee. Overhead two Angels hold a Cross and a Crown, while below is the Lion Rampant within the wreath of the Order, with the motto 'Nemo Me Impune Lacessit'.

On the ceiling are various angels playing musical instruments to drive out evil spirits. One is playing bagpipes. While to the east of the door inside, fairly high up, is a delightful wooden carving of another angel, again playing bagpipes.

As there is no room inside the Chapel, the Knight's Banners are outside in the Preston Aisle, and are changed like the finial crests on appointment of a new Knight. The Preston Aisle is where the Sovereign and Knights sit during the normal church service.

The coronets on both stall plates and finials vary according to the rank of the wearer. Thus the Sovereign's Crown is an Imperial Crown with two crossing arches. That of Price Charles as immediate heir to the Throne is similar to the Queen's but with only one arch. Royal Dukes have coronets without arches, with crosses and fleur-de-lis alternating. Royal Crowns and coronets are on top of the helmets; coronets of those below Royal rank are below the helmets.

A Duke's coronet has eight strawberry leaves.

A Marquis has four pearls between four strawberry leaves.

An Earl has eight pearls impaled and eight strawberry leaves,

A Viscount has sixteen pearls,

A Baron has six large pearls.

The style and position of the helmet is also a mark of distinction displayed like the coronet on both stall plate and finial. A Royal helmet is gold facing front with bars. That of a Peer is silver in profile, generally facing dexter, with gold bars. A Baronet or Knight's helmet is steel with open visor facing front, an Esquire's or Gentleman's is steel, in profile, with visor closed.

Helmets on finials all face front. So because the crest is correctly a fixture on the helmet, a Peer's crest will face dexter on the stall plate, but will face front on the finial unless perhaps in some cases of bad Heraldry when the crest is only two-dimensional and cannot be turned along with the helmet on the finial.

Dexter is the shield bearer's right, the viewer's left.

Sinister is the shield bearer's left, the viewer's right.

Waverley Station

The station is built on a site formerly occupied by the Edinburgh Physic Garden between 1675–1763 before being relocated to a site in Leith Walk with a final move to Inverleith in 1820, becoming the Royal Botanical Gardens. The garden is commemorated by a plaque opposite platform 10 and beside the War Memorial listing the names of railway employees who gave their lives during two World Wars.

The station opened with the name North Bridge on 21 February 1842, as the Edinburgh terminus of the Edinburgh and Glasgow railway. This day also marked the inception of Edinburgh Leith and Granton railway, which plied from North Bridge through Scotland Street Tunnel. The two services were not connected, the platforms being at right angles.

Railway development boomed during this period and four years later the line was built and services commenced between Edinburgh and Berwick. The river Tweed acted as a barrier between Scotland and England for some time, but the erection of the Border Bridge in

1850 enabled trains to run from Edinburgh to London. Lines were being laid down in Fife and from Dundee to Aberdeen and beyond.

The rivers Forth and Tay were major obstacles, but the latter was bridged in 1878, although it had a brief life. On 28 December 1879 the bridge collapsed and a passenger train fell into the river. All the passengers and crew perished. A new Tay bridge was built in 1887 and in 1890 the magnificent Forth Bridge was opened, connecting Edinburgh directly to Aberdeen.

A branch line to Hawick was opened in 1849 but through running of trains over the line to London was not established until 1876. This became known as the 'Waverley' route.

The development of new lines and increased services resulted in chaotic conditions in Waverley, as the station was too small to cope with the increased services and the double line connections to the East and West were also inadequate. The Act of 5 July 1891 allowed the North British Railway to encroach further upon Princes Street Gardens, (despite violent opposition from the City Fathers) allowing an additional line in each direction to be laid down westwards to Saughton Junction and eastwards through Calton tunnel to Abbeyhill.

The station was rebuilt as an 'Island' with footbridge links northwards to Princes Street and Leith Street and southwards to Market Street. Road traffic access is by way of two carriageways from Waverley Bridge, with two beams and girder supporting fairly steeply inclined roadways.

The station design is a double back to back terminus with through platform lines on either flank i. e platforms 1 and 19, 10 and 11 and 20 and 21 which are on what is known as the 'Sub' or suburban line. The area comprises 23 acres and Waverley became the largest station in the British Isles. There were 19 platforms with an aggregate length of 13,980ft, which at the time could accommodate 358 carriages. Through platforms 20 and 21 were completed shortly afterwards and are sited to the south of the main station area. Work commenced in 1892 and was completed in 1900. Extensive office accommodation was built in 1897, part of which housed the General Manager and staff of the North British Railway. The original Booking Hall has a magnificent ceiling, including roof lights extensively embellished with decorative wrought iron work.

Rationalisation of rail requirements and the 'Beeching' plan resulted in closure of the Waverley route and all passenger branch lines except the North Berwick/Drem which plies from the east end of the station and that part was not used to capacity.

The car-parking problem was solved by drastically shortening platforms 8 and 9, filling in and surfacing the area, which now is a car park for 110 cars. Platforms 2, 3, 4 and 5 were shortened and half of the reclaimed area was acquired by the Post Office who erected a mail-bag sorting compound with hook and chain conveyer linked directly to the General Post Office. The remaining space was used as a parcel handling area, with platforms 3,4,5 and 6 being used exclusively for parcel trains and vehicles. The shortened platforms 8 and 9 served as a Motorola Terminal and a daily service to London was operated with a less frequent service to Bristol.

Up to 400 hundred trains enter or leave the station daily and empty carriage trains go to Craigentinny Carriage Sidings for maintenance and cleaning. Very few parcel trains now use the station, but at one time there were trains conveying parcels, mails, newspapers, fruit and flowers. Few freight trains pass through the station, the majority using the suburban lines. The former parcel office on Waverley Bridge is now a public house. Passenger trains arrive and depart from and to the following points: Aberdeen, Dundee, Ladybank, Kirkcaldy, Cardenden, Cowdenbeath, Dunfermline Perth, Inverness, Stirling, Dunblane, Glasgow Queen Street, Glasgow Central, Hamilton, Motherwell, Shotts, Kingsknowe, (this station was reopened on 1 February 1971) Plymouth, Bristol, Birmingham, Manchester, Liverpool, Carlisle, London Kings Cross, Leeds, York, Newcastle, North Berwick, Dunbar, Livingston.

The Edinburgh/Glasgow route introduced rail travel to the population of Edinburgh and now has a 15 minute service with a journey time of approx. 40 minutes. An unusual feature was introduced during the 1960s in that 6 coaches were hauled by one loco. When the loco was at the rear of the train the driver operated from a small cab in the leading coach, these became known as 'Push and Pulls'. Locos were serviced at Haymarket Motive Power Depot.

Between 1936 and 1937, two signal boxes, Waverley East and Waverley West, were built to replace in modern form, four old manual signal boxes. The two are not now in use having been replaced by a Signalling Centre built on the site of the former goods yard in New Street, but the former Waverley West signal box (one of the largest manual signal boxes ever constructed with 230 levers in a continuous frame) remains and is situated in Princes Street Gardens West.

Considerable modernisation of the station buildings has been carried out in recent years and the programme continues. The Booking Hall has been converted into a modern travel centre without destroying many of the grand design features of the original building. The ceiling has been preserved intact, and the raised numerals '1897' are recorded no less than 36 times.

Edinburgh Signalling Centre was opened in October 1976, the area of control was initially in the vicinity of Waverley, but the final stage was completed in 1981. The Centre now controls the movement of trains on the following routes:

1. East Coast Main Line to Berwick.
2. West Coast Main Line to Carstairs.
3. Glasgow Central Line to Fauldhouse.
4. Glasgow Queen Street Line to Linlithgow.
5. The North lines over the Forth Bridge.
6. The majority of Fife Lines almost to Cupar and the branch line Ladybank to Perth is controlled to Hilton Junction.
7. Local Edinburgh Freight Lines.

While traffic over these routes had originally been controlled by over 100 signal boxes various rationalisation schemes saw this number reduce to 60 and they too have now been closed. In addition to signalling, the centre operates the train information displays at Waverley and certain other stations, and the broadcast announcements to passengers at Waverley.

The Area Manager's sphere of control embraces the East Coast Line to Berwick, all Edinburgh Stations and yards, the lines to the Forth Bridge, Fauldhouse and Linlithgow.

Edinburgh, Leith & Granton Railway

The Edinburgh Leith & Newhaven Railway was incorporated on the 13 August 1836.

The first section to open, on 31 August 1842 was from Canonmills to Trinity.

The company's name was changed to Edinburgh Leith & Granton Railway in 1844. The line was extended on 19 February 1846 from Trinity to Granton, the branch line from Bonnington junction to Leith opened on 10 May 1846.

Scotland Street tunnel and Canal Street Station opened on 17 May 1847. Trains were worked from Scotland Street to Canal Street by a stationary engine at Canal Street.

The Edinburgh Leith & Granton Railway was amalgamated with the Edinburgh Northern Railway to form the Edinburgh Perth & Dundee Railway in 1847 and this was incorporated in the North British Railway on 1 August 1862.

On 2 March 1868 in connection with the opening of the line from Abbeyhill junction to Easter Road the tunnel and Canal Street were closed.

Between 1868 and 1867 the tunnel was used as a wagon store, during the Second World War as an air raid shelter and at various times since has been used as a mushroom farm and a car park. The entrance is still visible in Scotland Street adventure playground.

Today the station is operated by Scotrail, with G. N. E. R. operating the prestigious East Coast Main Line Service and Virgin the West Coast.

Leith Council Chamber

When Leith became a Parliamentary borough in 1833 the Town Council, consisting of a Provost, four Bailies, Treasurer and ten councillors met in the Tollbooth until it moved to Charlotte Street in 1848. (Altered to Queen Charlotte Street on 1 February 1968.) Until they merged in 1877, there were two separate and distinct bodies dealing with the administration of Leith, occupying the same building, built as the Police and Sheriff's Office in 1827. Leith was absorbed into Edinburgh in 1920 when Leith Town Council ceased to exist. The public can visit Leith Town Council chambers on limited occasions courtesy of Leith division of Lothian and Borders Police.

There is a booklet giving an interpretation of the heraldry on the ceiling. These coats of arms have been correctly identified by the Lyon court, but, unfortunately, they are not always representative of the individuals whom the council of 1892 wished to commemorate.

James Simpson started alterations to the building in July 1891 and the cost of painting the restored council meeting room was estimated at £98. The Leith Council minutes of 2 February 1892 (now in the archives of Edinburgh City Chambers) clearly state the intention of Leith Council to honour certain individuals, but it was not noticed that the painter's and the council's knowledge of heraldry was faulty. The coats of arms as shown in the booklet are not at all correct for the intended persons. It would appear that this was never noticed until Bill McKelvie pointed it out. None of the well-known books on Leith have references to any of these errors.

The Leith Town Council minutes were consulted to determine what these distinguished gentlemen had done for Leith to be so honoured. This required research as, unlike the Edinburgh Council minutes, those of Leith are not indexed and for 1892 there are three thick volumes to be studied. Thus we have:

1. The arms of the Earl of Home, chief of the family of Home.

This was intended to represent the Revd. John Home, author of the controversial play 'Douglas' who was born in Leith, buried in South Leith churchyard and was the son of a Leith Town clerk.

2. George Wishart, Bishop of Edinburgh.

He was Bishop in 1622. However the intention was to show the martyr, George Wishart, who was burned at the stake in St Andrews on the orders of David, Cardinal Beaton in 1546. He had occasionally preached at South Leith Church.

3. Gladstone of Fasque Bt. Father of the Prime Minister William Ewart Gladstone.

Sir John Gladstone was born in Leith and founded St Thomas church, this is correct.

4. Lindsay, Earl of Crawford, Chief of the family of Lindsay.

This was intended to represent the Rev. David Lindsay, minister of South Leith Church who sailed to Norway to conduct the marriage of James VI and Anne of Denmark.

5. MacFie of Dreghorn.

This was intended to represent John MacFie who was senior Bailie at the landing of George IV in 1822. This spelling of MacFie is also on the metal plaque on the side of the wharf showing where the landing took place.

6. The Burgh of Leith.

Argent in the sea proper, an ancient galley with two masts, sails furled sable, flagged gules, seated therein the Virgin Mary with the infant saviour in her arms and a cloud azure resting over their heads proper.

This is the matriculated version of 1889. The earlier version showed the Madonna and Child seated below a church canopy as can be seen on the Mercat Cross of Edinburgh and many other sites. But in 1887 Leith Town Council had been asked to supply a banner of their arms for the Paris exhibition of 1889. On realising that the arms had never been matriculated the town clerk of Leith approached the Lord Lyon to effect the registration. He produced a copy of the seal of Leith and Lyon changed the charge to show a cloud instead of a church canopy. This is of course, correct.

The Duke of Buccleuch was outraged by this decision and attempted (unsuccessfully) to have it changed, as it would appear that the Madonna and Child are under a cloud.

7. Sir William Millar of Manderston Bart.

Sometime merchant in St Petersburg (1853), son of James Millar, merchant in Leith. This is correct. The arms were granted in November 1853.

8. Lamont of that Ilk.

The arms were intended for Oliver Cromwell the Lord Protector, whose arms are similar.

9. Lord Bellenden of Broughton.

This coat is correct for the Abbot of Holyrood who built St Ninian's church and the now demolished bridge over the water of Leith at Coalhill.

10. Leith of Restalrig.

This is a reference to this family who in the reign of Alexander III owned Restalrig and many extensive possessions in Midlothian. An heiress married into the Logans. The Leiths were burgesses in Edinburgh and gave their name to Leith Wynd. This is correct heraldry.

It was also decided to put the name of the Provost Thomas Aitken on the ceiling.

The Royal Arms in the centre panels were intended to be:

11. Queen Margaret of Denmark, spouse of James III. While some have suggested that this may be mistaken for Anne of Denmark, Queen of James VI, the intention of the Town Council was clearly Margaret and James III. This is correct.

12. Queen Mary (Mary Queen of Scots).

The arms, however, are quartered with England and Ireland in the English marshalling used after 1603 by James VI, Charles I, Charles II and James VII, and are exactly as used by Mary II, joint Sovereign with William of Orange in 1689. Mary Queen of Scots should have the arms of Scotland alone. The letters 'M' and 'R' on the panel would mean 'Maria Regina'.

13. King George IV.

14. Queen Victoria.

These are both correct.

On the ceiling there are four dates:

1563, this was the date when Queen Mary authorised Leith to have its own Tolbooth and is the date on many representations of the earlier arms of Leith.

1833 was the date Leith became a parliamentary borough.

1877 was when the Town Council of Leith and the police commissioners amalgamated into one legislative body.

1892 was the year the ceiling was painted.

Now that the real intentions of the Leith town council have been discovered, the Lord Lyon has requested that the officials who conduct visitors round the historic chambers are made aware of the correct persons intended to be honoured, but that the coats should not be altered as they are of interest both artistically and because of the errors.

Mr Charles Burnett, Ross Herald, passed the comment:

'This is the largest decorative scheme employing heraldry in Leith. We are fortunate that the Town Council of 1892 decided to record some of the history of this ancient port by an armorial presentation. It is also an excellent example of late Victorian internal decoration. One can speculate that the inspiration for this display was the 1891 heraldry exhibition held to celebrate the opening of the National Portrait Gallery'.

One o'clock Gun

At 1pm in Edinburgh four things happen, the gun fires, pigeons take flight, tourist take fright and locals check their watches.

The one o'clock gun was first fired in 1861 as a signal for shipping in the Forth.

John Hewat, an Edinburgh Banker, put forward the suggestion in 1846 after seeing a time gun operate in Paris. In response to this a visual time ball was established on the Nelson Monument on Calton Hill in 1851 which moved at a set time each day. Prior to this mariners in the Forth had to bring their chronometers in a wheelbarrow to the City Observatory to have them checked, they did this using what was known as a 'Politicians' clock' i.e. one with two faces, one facing into the Observatory and the other facing out.

Professor Charles Piazza Smyth, the Astronomer Royal for Scotland, worked out the details for a linked time gun system, the Royal Artillery supplied an early version of the existing cannon with an 18lb. gun placed on the Half Moon Battery of the castle and operated by gunners of the Royal Artillery.

The first gun was replaced in the early part of the century by a breechloader in the 1920s and this was replaced by the type of field

gun used by the British Army during the First World War. A 25lb.
field gun was introduced after World War Two. The gun in use today
is another 25lb. and was used during the battle of El Alamein.

Tom McKay, also known as 'Tam the Gun', who has fired the gun
on a daily basis for over two decades is the longest serving gunner
since the gun was established in 1861. His only days off are Sundays,
Christmas Day and Good Friday. Today he relies on the speaking clock
for a time check but it was not always so. In the early days, by a
fantastic feat of nineteenth century electrical engineering by the Royal
Engineers a clock beside the time gun was connected to the time ball
on the Nelson Monument by a 4,000ft overhead wire (the longest in
Europe) which in turn was connected to the City Observatory's mean
time clock, a chain connected to the Castle clock was attached to the
gun's fuse and at 1p.m. a weight dropped and the gun was fired
automatically.

In 1896 when the Royal Observatory was opened on Blackford Hill
the wire was laid underground.

Because of the speed of sound the people in Leith hear the gun at
ten seconds past one.

An exhibition of the time gun opened on 21 February 2000, the
100th anniversary of the death of Charles Piazza Smyth.

Anecdotes surrounding the gun say that when it was first decided
to have a time signal copied from the French who fired their signal
12 times at noon the canny Scots decided to wait an hour and save
11 shots.

Tourists are told to watch the time ball on Nelson Monument and
if the gunner's aim is accurate he will knock the ball down.

Forth Rail Bridge

With the expansion of the railways and the competition between the
rival companies to open up the routes to Dundee and Aberdeen the
need for a crossing over the Forth and Tay rivers became imperative.
The North British Railway Company recruited an engineer called
Thomas Bouch and he convinced the directors that the two rivers
could be bridged.

The foundation stone of the Tay Bridge was laid in July 1871 and
on the Forth Bridge in 1873.

The Tay Bridge took seven years to build and had been opened only 19 months when on 28 December 1879, Bouch at the zenith of his powers was at home in Edinburgh when he received the following telegram:

'Terrible accident on bridge, one or more of high girders blown down. Am not sure of the safety of last Edinburgh train'. Daylight revealed that the bridge had collapsed into the Tay estuary taking with it the Edinburgh train and an estimated 75 passengers to their deaths.

An Act of Parliament stopped work on the Forth Bridge; public confidence in Bouch was shattered and although trains still operated on over 300 miles of railway he had constructed that counted for nothing.

The Tay Bridge had fallen. Due to the disaster there entered into the language a saying 'To make a Bouch of it', meaning to make a mess of things.

Bouch retreated to his house in Moffat where he hid for four months after the report on the disaster, which destroyed him, was published. He died on 1 November 1890 and is buried in the Dean cemetery.

It would take more than a disaster to stop the growth of the railways, and before 1880 was out the railway companies were looking at other designs. Almost three years to the day since the Tay Bridge disaster the contract to build the Forth Bridge was awarded to Tancred, Arrol and Company. The designers were Fowler and Baker. The statistics are 5000 men laboured day and night for seven years. The work cost £3 million, it has a length of 1½ miles, has two spans of 1710ft and two spans of 690ft. The highest point above sea level at high tide is 361ft. The height of the rails above sea level at high tide is 158ft. The depth below sea level is 91ft.

During construction the following quantities were used:
Concrete 64,300 cubic yards.
Steel 54,160 tons.
Cement 21,000 tons.
Granite 740,000 cubic ft
Ordinary stone 48,400 cubic yards.
Rivets 6,500,000 which equals 4,200 tons.
Paint oils 35,527 gallons.

Paint 250 tons.

The grim cost of the bridge was 57 lives.

In the 1990s it was estimated that the cost to British Rail of maintaining the bridge was £750,000 per annum.

On a hot day the bridge is one metre longer than in winter due to heat expansion.

To gain a perspective of the work involved, stand on Waverley Bridge and look towards the castle and imagine trying to span the distance with a structure weighing 150,000 tons with no central supports, the rail level would be as high as the Esplanade, and the highest point would be the same height as the Scott Monument.

The Marquess of Tweedale drove the first train across the completed bridge, on 21 January, 1890.

Two trains were taken onto the bridge, their gross weight of 1,800 tons was made up of 100 coal wagons and 6 locos weighing 73 tons apiece; board of trade inspectors took readings along the bridge and were satisfied that the structure was rigid and safe.

On Tuesday 4 March 1890 the bridge was opened by the Prince of Wales who drove home the last of the rivets.

During construction firms were invited to tender as suppliers of paint and the contract was won by Craig and Rose of Leith which has supplied the paint ever since. The painting area is estimated to be 145 acres and 7,000 gallons of paint are required to paint the bridge from end to end. Contrary to popular belief the bridge is not painted from end to end but done over a four to six year cycle. There are 16 men employed as painters and the 'climbing season' is from April to September.

The tradition of throwing a coin over the bridge 'for luck' has faded now but in years gone by it provided a source of income for the maintenance squads.

Royal College of Surgeons

Surgeons Hall is probably known to most people as a bus stop and not as a college and museum of the Fellows of the Royal College of Surgeons.

This building, designed by William Playfair, (1790–1857) was formally opened on 7 July 1832 on a site previously occupied by the

Royal Academy of Exercises, (a riding school) in a 1763 building. In 1908 the architect Balfour Paul added an extension.

Inside is a reception room which is used as a meeting room and a waiting room for examination candidates, thousands of whom sit for numerous diplomas, coming to Edinburgh from all over the world. The library contains a modern medical library and instruments from through the ages and is heavily used by fellows and candidates world wide. In the Playfair Hall is housed the museum's 15,000 pathological specimens.

On the walls are some sixteen paintings by Sir Charles Bell, of war wounds as seen by him on the return of troops from the battles of Corunna and Waterloo.

In the Sir Jules Thorn Hall is the college's permanent exhibition of the history of medicine in Scotland, especially Edinburgh, over the last 500 years. There is also the remarkable Menzies Campbell collection of historical dental instruments.

Anyone can visit the museum by prior arrangement.

The Magdalen Chapel

The Magdalen Chapel is one of the few remaining pre-Reformation Church buildings in Edinburgh with the stained glass windows still intact. Recent reports indicate that the building stands as third in historic interest and value as a listed building in the city of Edinburgh.

The building itself dates from 1541 although not completed until 1547. Since its founding various additions have been made, especially after a fire ravaged the building in the 18th century. It was part of a small complex which included a small hospital. This plan was conceived by Mitchell MacQuhane and his wife Janet Rynd.

From the records it appears that the whole venture cost in the region of £2,700 Scottish currency. Janet Rynd was the person who after her husband's death saw the whole venture brought to completion. She is buried in the chapel and her tomb is in the south east corner of the chapel. The original charter is to be found in the north west corner and makes interesting reading.

Externally the tower was added in 1628 and a clock and bell were installed. The clock was removed in recent times by the department of Mechanical Engineering of Heriot Watt University who have since restored it to full working order and reinstalled it after the renovation programme was completed.

Other items of interest are the inscriptions around the north and east walls. These begin at the top left and work round to the end of the east wall then return to the north wall. These permanent receipts are called 'Brods' and make interesting reading as the names, descriptions and trades are examined. The various forms of currency are also very interesting.

The balustrade around the platform is a later innovation to indicate some of the trades, which were found in the incorporation of hammermen. This Trade Guild who used the chapel as their Guildhall were patrons of the chapel and hospital from its earliest days. Their symbols are seen in different parts of the chapel in the hammer surmounted by a crown. This association was continued until the last century, when they asked the then Protestant Institute of Scotland, (now incorporated into the Scottish Reformation Society) to assume ownership of the chapel. Happily this association of the hammermen has been resumed and they celebrated their 500th anniversary in the chapel in 1983.

The large chair on the platform also belongs to the hammermen and was the deacon's chair. It is something which is now priceless although it only cost £33 Scots currency to make which in 1916 was calculated to be the equivalent of £2.65p sterling.

The old table, which stands on the platform, was used as a mortuary table as this was one of the uses the chapel had in its chequered history. This was because the chapel was close to the place of public execution in the Grassmarket. During the 'Killing Times' of the Covenanters, when over a hundred were executed in the Grassmarket, their remains were brought to the chapel and dressed for burial.

This service was rendered by a team of ladies under Helen Alexander, who regarded it as part of their Christian duties to honour their fellow Covenanters in this way before their bodies were buried in the common grave at Greyfriars Churchyard.

The chapel has witnessed many varied situations in the pageant of Scottish history. Prior to 1560 the chapel was a Roman Catholic Chapel. This is seen in the stained glass windows, where the top right window is the coat of arms of Mary of Lorraine, the Queen Regent at the time the chapel was dedicated. The other three windows display the Lion Rampant and the bottom two commemorate Mitchell MacQuhane and Janet Rynd. These windows are part of the Scottish National Treasures and during World War Two were removed for safekeeping and then restored when hostilities were ended.

In 1560 the Chapel became the focal point of the reformation, and one writer described it as the 'workshop of the reformation'. This is certainly an apt description for, although John Knox made St Giles the preaching centre, it was in the Magdalen Chapel that much of the work was completed on the essential documents required for maintaining the Reformation. John Knox and his fellow reformers, all of whom had the Christian name of John, discussed and drew up such documents as the Scots Confession of Faith, one of the most important documents to come out of the Reformation.

They also prepared the First Book of Discipline, which catered for every aspect of Scotland's national life; not only religious, but also social, cultural and educational aspects were handled in it. If this document had been accepted and implemented the whole of Scotland would have been better even than it became through the Reformation.

It was also in this little Chapel that the first General Assembly of the Reformed Church in Scotland took place. Those present numbered 6 ministers and 36 elders and John Knox presided over that first Assembly. Various other leaders also met in this Chapel. Andrew Melville presided over another Assembly in 1578, which was another historic occasion. John Craig, one of Knox's colleagues, preached in the Chapel on a regular basis.

One item, which has recently come to light, is that chaplains of Cromwell used the Chapel while the Lord Protector was in Edinburgh. In 1765 Robert Carmichael and seven others rented the Chapel for the establishing of a Baptist cause in the city and so the Scots Baptist cause was constituted as a direct result and they worshipped in the Chapel for nine years.

In the last century the complex of both hospital and Chapel was taken over by the Edinburgh Medical Missionary Society who carried on dispensary work for the district in the training of those who were to become Medical Missionaries. This work closed when Edinburgh University took over the dispensary and made it their family doctor service clinic, this part of the building is now administered by the Lothian Health Board.

The Chapel was leased to Heriot Watt University for use as its Chaplaincy centre until the university transferred to Riccarton Campus and its main function was for the use of the music society. Many well known musicians played there, taking advantage of the excellent acoustic qualities of the building.

Golf in the city

Today St Andrews is regarded as the home of golf and the Royal and Ancient Club as golf's rule giving authority. This was not always the case, and Edinburgh's claim has the most historical validity.

Golf was played at Leith Links during the reign of the Stewarts, and Mary Queen of Scots is said to have played there.

The world's oldest golf club is the Honourable Company of Edinburgh Golfers which played for its first trophy, a silver club, on the Links at Leith on 7 March 1744. They also devised a set of rules for the competition. The paper on which the original 13 rules of golf were drafted is in the archives of the Honourable Company and a copy is on show at their clubhouse at Muirfield.

The Royal and Ancient Club simply adopted the Leith club's rules and it was not until 1754 that St Andrews played for a silver club. It was in 1834 that the St Andrews club successfully petitioned King William IV to designate it Royal and Ancient.

The original course at Leith was of five holes, Thorntree 414 yards, Braehead 461 yards, Sawmill 426 yards, North-mid 495 yards, South-mid 435 yards. Bearing in mind the equipment available the game was all about strength and if the five holes had been eighteen as today the course would measure over 8000 yards with an SSS of 79.

In the mid nineteenth century Leith Links was becoming overcrowded with grazing animals and women drying their washing so the Honourable Company moved to Musselburgh and in 1891 moved to their present home at Muirfield.

The second and third oldest clubs are the Edinburgh Burgess Golfing Society and the Bruntsfield Links Golf Club. The Burgess claims to have existed since 1735 but its records only go back to 1773,

Bruntsfield dates back to 1761 as a society and 1787 as a club, both started at Bruntsfield Links on a six hole course with the Golf Tavern as their clubhouse. But again with overcrowding and the decline of the links they moved to Musselburgh before moving to their present homes at Barnton and Davidsons Mains. A pitch and putt course is still at Bruntsfield and is part of the original links so it has a claim to be the oldest course on which golf is still played.

There are 25 courses in the city boundaries, six of which are municipally owned, with a number of driving ranges.

Fearing a war with England and the lack of practice at archery, in 1457 James II laid down a statute 'futeball and golfe to be utterly cryed doon and not to be used' but it appears to have had little effect and in 1503 James IV played golf. Indeed when Captain Topham visited Edinburgh he wrote 'the diversion which is peculiar to Scotland, and in which all ages find great pleasure, is golf. They play at it with a small leathern ball and a piece of wood, flat on one side, in the shape of a small bat, which is fastened at the end of a stick three or four feet long, at right angles to it. The art consists of striking the ball with this instrument into a hole in the ground in a smaller number of strokes than your adversary. The game has the superiority of cricket and tennis in being less violent and dangerous, but in point of dexterity and amusement by no means to be compared with them.'

Tradition says that Golfers' Land in the Canongate was built by John Patterson, a shoemaker, with the winnings of a wager.

Two English nobles challenged the Duke of York, later James VII, (II), to a game of golf and he chose Patterson as his partner. When they won the Duke let Patterson keep the prize money which he used to build his house which was demolished in the 1950s but a plaque commemorating the feat is on the wall of the 'Jenny Ha's' pub along with the family crest.

In 1798 a bet was made that no two members of the Burgess society could be found capable of driving a ball over the spire of St Giles. A Mr Smellie, a printer, and a Mr Sceales of Leith were selected to perform this formidable task. They were allowed to use six balls each, it was reported that 'the balls passed considerably higher than the weathercock and were found nearly opposite in Advocates Close'.

The bet was decided early in the morning in case of accidents, the parties taking their stations at the south east corner of Parliament Square. The required elevation was obtained by a barrel stave, suitably fixed, and the height of the steeple, which is 161ft, together with the distance from the base of the church were found to be much less than a 'good stroke of the club'.

In 1815 a Mr Scott bet a guinea with a Mr McDowal that he would drive a ball from the golf house at Bruntsfield Links over Arthur's Seat in 45 strokes. Mr Scott, we learn, had reason to regret his hardihood, but better luck attended a Mr Brown who risked a gallon of whisky in a bet with a Mr Spalding that he would drive a ball over Arthur's Seat on the same terms. With his last shot Mr Brown won the whisky, having cleared the lion's crest in 44 strokes.

The Merchants Club has a record that will never be broken in that it had two members who each won a Victoria Cross in the First and Second World Wars.

Baberton, founded in 1893, has a clubhouse dating back to 1622 and Liberton (1920) has eighteenth century Kingston Grange as its clubhouse and Ratho Parks clubhouse dates from 1824.

James Braid who was born in Elie in Fife and won the Open five times between 1901 and 1910 designed ten courses in the city.

Two of the most famous golfers the city has produced are Tommy Armour and Ronnie Shade. Tommy Armour was brought up in Bruce Street and learned to play golf on the Braid Hills. He fought as a tank commander in the First World War in the course of which he leapt from his tank and strangled one of the enemy with his bare hands. He was gassed and wounded in the head and lost an eye. After the war he emigrated to America and became a professional golfer known as the 'Silver Scot'. He won the U S. open in 1927 and the USPGA. in 1930. When the Open was first held at Carnoustie in 1931 Armour was the winner.

Ronnie Shade whose initials were R D B M. and were said to mean 'right down the bloody middle' was Scotland's greatest amateur golfer. Playing out of Duddingston where his father was professional, he won the Scottish Amateur Championship five times in a row from 1963–67 after being the beaten finalist in 1962. He was a Walker Cup regular from 1961–1967. He won everything as an amateur and was awarded the MBE for services to amateur golf and turned professional in 1968.

He won the Scottish professional championship as well as European tour events but he did not enjoy professional golf and he gave it up. He was reinstated as an amateur shortly before he died aged 47 in 1989.

When the European team won the Ryder Cup at Oak Hills Rochester USA in 1995 the PGA were presented with 100 acorns which were grown into oak trees. To mark the PGA Centenary they were planted at 100 golf courses through out Britain and Ireland, one of which was planted at the Braid Hills on 18 December 2001 by Brian Donkin, captain of Braids United golf club, and Peter Lloyd, Scottish secretary of the PGA.

In March 2003 the Leith Rules Golf Society was inaugurated, their aim to revive a unique piece of golfing history that belongs to Leith.

This follows on from 2002 when they opened up Leith Links during the Open week in July when the Open was held at Muirfield, present home of the direct descendants of the authors and first players of Leith Rules which the Royal and Ancient adopted and are now recognised throughout the world.

Each year they intend to hold a Hickory Open whereby competitors will play using Hickory shafted clubs and play to the original thirteen rules on a replica of the original five hole course.

Banking

There have been many small, medium and large banking ventures in Scotland's long history.

Amalgamations by the dozen, collapses, buyouts and mergers have reduced the number to the current heavyweight players, Halifax Bank of Scotland, The Royal Bank of Scotland, Clydesdale Bank and Lloyds TSB.

Among the four Scottish clearing banks, Bank of Scotland has the distinction of being first born. In 1695, one year after the Bank of England was founded by Scotsman William Paterson, the Bank of Scotland was formed by Parliamentary decree and granted a 21 year monopoly to run banking services in Scotland.

One of the earliest acts of BoS was the introduction of paper money. At the time of its formation, Scots coinage was in short supply, and of uncertain value. This was seen as a blight on trade by Scottish merchants, so BoS introduced paper currency. Once it became clear that BoS was in a position to honour its 'promise to pay' the idea took off. Paper currency use soon spread beyond the merchant community and Scotland became one of the first countries in the world to use paper currency as a preferred means of exchange.

The Founding Act allowed the banks directors to raise a nominal capital of 1,200,000 Scots pounds, the equivalent at that time of £100,000 sterling. An interesting addendum to the Act was its final clause (only repealed in 1920) which stipulated that 'all forraigners who shall join as partners of this bank, shall thereby be and become Naturalised Scotsmen, to all intents and purposes whatsoever'.

The Royal Bank of Scotland came into being shortly after that monopoly lapsed. Founded as a corporation by Royal Charter in Edinburgh in 1727, it immediately set about introducing a series of innovations into banking practice. It pioneered the concept of the 'overdraft' in 1728 and introduced coloured banknotes in 1777. Double-sided bank notes were another Royal Bank innovation, introduced in 1826. As well as being commercial rivals, the two Edinburgh banks represented different political parties, with the Royal Bank championing the Duke of Argyll's interests. The next 15 years or so, from the Royal Bank's inception, were spent by the two banks trying to put each other out of business.

Although both banks were allowed to operate throughout Scotland, their activities were largely focused on Edinburgh. Glasgow merchants had to be well known in the capital to raise money from either bank. In the absence of any law in Scotland prohibiting the formation of banks, a number of private banks were founded to fill the gap in Scotland's provincial towns and in Glasgow. Waking up to the threat, the Edinburgh banks came to a secret arrangement to stop feuding with each other and to join forces to see off 'start ups' such as new Glasgow banks. The pact included the two colluding in legal action against the newcomers, organising hostile runs on their reserves and letting it be known that anyone dealing with them would be cut off by the Edinburgh Banks. Although the Glasgow banks proved resilient to their tactics, the Edinburgh banks did succeed in killing off a small Aberdeen bank.

By this stage, however, the honour of founding the first successful branch network in Scotland had slipped through their fingers, even though BoS had tried, without much joy, on two earlier occasions.

The British Linen Company, formed in 1746 to promote the Scottish Linen industry, had offices in towns all over Scotland and began providing banking services through its offices, in effect creating a branch network. It was on BoS' third attempt, in 1774, that the founding of its branch network was successful. The Royal Bank meanwhile, limited itself at the time to a prestigious branch in Glasgow.

In 1810 there were 21 banking companies operating in Scotland outside Edinburgh and Glasgow.

Eventually, the British Linen Bank amalgamated with the Bank of Scotland in 1971, and re-emerged as the bank's merchant banking subsidiary.

By the 1760s monetary instability loomed, as all the banks, including the tiny ones, had been launching their own notes. In 1765, Statutory Regulation limited the volume of notes that could be printed and a note exchange was opened.

But the history of Scotland's banknotes has not been without its moments of drama. In 1826 the English Parliament attempted to ban all notes less than five pounds. This went down very badly in Scotland, where the majority of the public relied on one pound notes. Sir Walter Scott weighed in on the side of the lowly note with a series of letters to the *Edinburgh Weekly Journal*. The government bowed to Scottish sentiment and the one pound note was saved. Scott's portrait still graces Bank of Scotland notes today.

More serious crises in the Scottish banking system involved the collapse of banks such as the Ayr Bank in 1772 and the even more disastrous failure of the City of Glasgow Bank in 1878. At the time, the City of Glasgow Bank had 133 branches, but reckless trading policies, which saw its directors approving nearly £5.4 million in loans to just three companies involved in highly speculative ventures, caused a catastrophic failure.

Individual shareholders however were not protected by limited liability and only 254 out of a total of 1,819 shareholders remained solvent at the end of proceedings. This failure had a sobering effect on the whole Scottish banking community, which moved to a system of more standardised, audited balance sheets. It also led to the 1879 Companies Act, which introduced a form of limited liability for the banks.

In 1838, Clydesdale Bank was founded in Glasgow by a local businessman James Lumsden. It grew rapidly, absorbing the Greenock Union Bank in 1844 and the Bank of Glasgow in 1845. By the mid 1840s, Scotland had a mature banking system comprising large-scale organisations with extensive and growing branch networks.

By 1810 another trend had emerged. The banks discussed so far were commercial banks. The rise of the Trustee Savings Banks, the first branch of which was established in Dumfriesshire in 1810 by Henry Duncan, aimed to provide working families with deposit facilities to encourage savings. This laid the foundation for today's retail banking. The Trustee Savings Bank movement, where trustees were elected by the depositors and ran the bank purely for the depositors, was designed to encourage thrift among poorer people and belongs to the same nineteenth century movement that saw the growth of building societies and friendly societies. In 1976, the number of individual trustee savings banks was reduced from 70 to 4. TSB Scotland was acquired by Lloyds Bank in 1995. By the 1860s the Scottish banks had begun to make inroads into the English banking arena and in 1874, Clydesdale Bank opened up three offices in the north of England – provoking the government to set up a committee of enquiry. The result was a tacit agreement between the English and Scottish banks, whereby it was decided that neither would open branches in the other's country.

By 1915 this century-long agreement began to fray. English banks began acquiring Scottish 'affiliates', which retained their Scottish identities.

An easing of government controls in the 1960s led to more aggressive competition between all the banks, north and south of the border. Services mushroomed, with the banks moving into the credit card and cheque guarantee card business. Banking began to be much more customer centric and automation and cost cutting began to receive a great deal of attention. Clydesdale Bank had become a wholly owned subsidiary of the joint City and Midland (later the Midland Bank) in 1920 merging with the North of Scotland Bank in 1950. In

1987 the Clydesdale was acquired by National Australia Bank (NAB) which now also owns the Yorkshire Bank. NAB requested parliamentary approval to merge Clydesdale with the Yorkshire Bank in 2000.

Bank of Scotland is reckoned to be the first U. K. bank in 1959 to install a computer to process its accounts. Technology continues, of course, to be a major theme in the development of banking with all the major banks initiating 'anytime anywhere' banking via telephone or the Internet.

In 1995, some three years before the Australians found their way to the Clydesdale, Bank of Scotland acquired the Bank of Western Australia, This followed the opening of international offices in Russia and Houston as a direct response to the bank's involvement with the oil industry. It merged with the Halifax Group in 2001 to form HBOS.

The Royal Bank was responsible for pioneering telephone banking, with the launch of Direct Banking in1994 and it launched the UK's first fully fledged on-line banking service in 1997. In March 2000 it acquired National Westminster Bank, making it the third largest bank in the UK.

Brewing

Brewing started in the 12th century when the Augustinian monks, brought in to build Holyrood Abbey, complained to King David that the water supply was not fit to drink, and he granted permission to brew ale. Commercial brewing began in the fifteenth century and in an attempt to drain the burgh loch in 1575 it was decreed that all breweries must draw water from the Guse dub by way of a windmill situated at Buccleuch Street and West Cross Causeway.

In 1596 the society of brewers was granted a monopoly and the area of land around Bristo Port was known as society, and indeed the word Bristo is a corruption of the word brewer. The society disbanded in 1619.

Water was in short supply and the town wells had to be locked at night to prevent brewers from using them. In 1654 there was a bad fire and the brewers were blamed. In 1840 there were 40 commercial breweries, seven in the Craigmillar and Duddingston area alone, employing 18,000 people.

The late eighteenth century saw the city levy an impost on ale over and above the government tax and many of the brewers moved to Holyrood (which was outside the city) to escape the levy.

William Younger opened his brewery in Leith in 1750 and moved to Edinburgh in 1778, this was to become the biggest of them all.

William McEwan started in 1856 and the two merged in 1931 but were kept separate until a full merger took place in 1959 to form Scottish Brewers.

They merged with a Newcastle brewery to become Scottish and Newcastle. They tended to rest on their laurels and were ripe for a take-over and in the 1980s the Australian brewer, Swan, backed by the Royal Bank of Scotland made a hostile bid. Such was the level of public outcry that the bank pulled out and the bid failed but it served to show the board how vulnerable they had become so they launched bids for English breweries and in the 1990s took over Courage and they are set to become the biggest in Britain.

In 1973 they opened a new brewery in Fountainbridge and stopped brewing in the Canongate in 1986. They kept offices in Holyrood Road and Horse Wynd until the 1990s when they sold the land for the site of the Scottish Parliament building.

At the start of the twentieth century there were 26 breweries producing 2.2 million barrels a year, after the First World War this figure fell to 800,000.

By the start of the second war Edinburgh was the second biggest brewing centre in Britain with 23 working breweries, but some stopped beer production and turned to making armaments for the duration of the war. When the war finished bad management, lack of investment in new technology, and a shortage of hops saw this number fall and a number of small operators were going cap in hand to the bigger ones asking to be taken over.

Up until 1958, when multiple licences were granted, the licensing trade was known as a free house, with licensees being the owners and the breweries were wholesale not retail.

At that time a Mr Eddie Taylor (of Carling Black Label) came over from Canada and bought over Aitchisons, Fowlers, Calders and Murrays to get his hands on their outlets for his beer.

In 1969 there were 7 breweries, in 1980 there were 4, and at the start of a new century only two.

The legacy of the brewing industry is that it has been responsible for two of the finest buildings in the city, the McEwan Hall at Teviot Place. used for graduation ceremonies by Edinburgh University, and the Usher Hall, built with a £100,000 donation from Andrew Usher. The 2,900-seat auditorium was opened in 1914.

Lothian & Borders Police Force

The Lothian & Borders Police Force is the second biggest force in Scotland. Highly mechanised and covering south east Scotland it is a far cry from the early days of policing when the Town Guard (known as 'The Toon Rats', protected the town. They were a collection of ex soldiers mainly Highlanders.

The Town Guard was disbanded in 1817

By 1850 the Police establishment consisted of one Superintendent, four Lieutenants, one Sergeant Major, thirty-one Sergeants, eight Criminal Officers, two senior reserve Sergeants and 262 Constables. The expenditure for the financial year 1848–49 amounted to £15,053.

The City Police Military Band, which consisted mainly of ex military bandsmen, was formed in 1822 but was discontinued eight years later. It reformed and celebrated its centenary in 1991.

Police telephone boxes were introduced in 1904 and were designed by the City Architect Ebeneezer Macrae. They are different from the rest of the country in that they have a classical design to fit in with the New Town, unlike the 'Doctor Who Tardis' design used elsewhere and have been likened to miniature Greek Temples. A radio controlled network of 141 boxes was established in 1933, radio communication with police cars was introduced the following year.

Police administration as we know it today came into operation in 1975, when the City, Lothian and Peebles and Border forces merged with new Headquarters in Fettes Avenue.

For administration purposes the City is split into four divisions, A. B. C. D. with A. being based at Fettes, B. at St Leonards, C. at Wester Hailes and D. at Queen Charlotte Street. This probably the most famous through the use of the tongue twister 'The Leith Police dismisseth us', used to determine if a suspect was under the influence of alcohol.

Today the force numbers 2,500 including a mounted division and a dog section which are based at Fettes.

Arthur's Seat

An 823-foot high (251 metres) extinct volcano of red indigenous rock it was probably named in the fifteenth century with a revival in

Arthurian romance. James Hutton was the founder of modern geology, whose studies of the rocks of Salisbury Crags allowed him to define how the earth was formed.

The Radical Road, an early job creation scheme, was suggested by Sir Walter Scott to keep men employed after the Napoleonic War so that they would not be swayed by radical orators.

In June 1836 17 miniature coffins, 8 of which are in the national museum of Scotland, were found. The coffins and the figures inside are carved from wood and the reason is unknown but two theories are put forward, the first is that they are connected to witchcraft and represent victims to be harmed, or a custom practised by sea faring folk who buried their menfolk in effigy if lost at sea.

Princes Street Gardens

The Nor Loch was drained and by 1820 5 acres of land had been laid out as gardens with 77,000 trees planted. This was paid for by the Princes Street proprietors and they demanded exclusive use, keys could be purchased at a cost of 4 guineas a year and by 1861 there were 361 subscribers. Tough regulations were in place to stop the lending of keys. Gentlemen were only allowed to smoke cigars, bath chairs and perambulators were banned in case invalids spread disease. This rule was relaxed in 1870 but only for those who could produce a medical certificate. In 1876 ownership passed to the council and the gates were opened to the public. Developers wanted to build on the site and it took an act of parliament to prevent them.

Mound

When the building of the New Town was started there was no access and one man who lived in the New Town and had business in the Old Town used pieces of wood and earth to make a path and this became known as Geordie Boyd's mud brig. Digging the foundations for the new town 1,800 cart loads a day of rubble were dumped. Assuming it took five minutes to unload and ten could unload together it would be a fifteen hour day.

During bad weather there were a number of accidents and it was decided to install an electric blanket under the road. Completed on 23 October 1959 it utilised 47 miles of wire and alleviated the problem for many winters but became unreliable and although still in place it is never used. The bollards on the garden side of the road were situated there to prevent tramcars which had become derailed from dropping onto the railway line below, although it is difficult to see how they could have prevented this

According to the head of the highways department they were never stress tested as this was unheard of at the time and it is doubtful if they would have been effective. Fortunately this was never put to the test.

The Craigentinny Marbles

The large mausoleum like edifice in Craigentinny Crescent was erected by William Henry Miller at a cost of £30,000 as his own tomb. He purchased the land and bequeathed money with instructions for the tomb to be erected after his death, which occurred in 1848. The ground is soft and the foundations go down 40ft to where he is buried. The architect was David Rhind of Edinburgh and the marbles, sculpted by Alfred Gatley of Rome, are unique, one side shows the Pharaoh in the Red Sea, and the other the Israelites entering the Promised Land.

South Bridge

The foundation stone was laid on 1 August 1785. The bridge is 1,000 feet in length and has 19 arches only one of which is visible, the Cowgate. It opened for pedestrians in July 1798 and cost £6,446 to build.

The bridge dips from Nicholson Street to Chambers Street and then rises more slowly upwards towards the High Street. the reason for this is that the Lord President Dundas had a house which was in Adam Square (where Chambers Street is now) and if the gradient had been level his front door would have been six feet below the bridge. In deference to his exalted position a dip was made which was to be the bane of carters' lives for years. A few months after the bridge was opened he sold his house as the district was becoming too commercial.

McKenzie Mausoleum

Sir George MacKenzie of Rosehaugh died in 1692. Known as 'Bluidy McKenzie' he was a judge who showed the Covenanters no mercy.

After the battle of Bothwell Bridge in 1679, he condemned many to be executed. His mausoleum is in Greyfriar's Churchyard.

About 1750 James Hay escaped from the Tolbooth prison and hid in his tomb. A secret society of Heriot's schoolboys required a new candidate to climb the wall into Greyfriar's Churchyard and rap on the tomb door and call out 'Bluidy McKenzie come oot if ye daur, lift the sneck and draw the bar' and then run away in case he did come out. Imagine the shock when James Hay answered. He was an ex Herioter and the boys fed him for three weeks until it was safe for him to go to Leith and escape on a ship.

Medical Building, Teviot Place

The Italianate design of the medical faculty building is not perfect; the towers at either end are of different heights. Originally it was intended to build a clock tower 250ft high on the east side, but the treasury would not authorise the usual grant for this and proposed a hall. Sir William McEwan stepped in and provided the money for the hall, but the clock tower was postponed and a temporary roof was put on in place of the 'campanile' which has now become a permanent feature after so long. The building dates from about 1880.

Thistle Court

The first house built in the New Town was in Thistle Court in 1767, behind what is now the George Hotel. The owner, James Young, was offered £20 as an inducement before he agreed to build. Other concessions were given to New Town residents in the form of rates reductions etc. The circular well in the forecourt was essential before piped water was available, and may have influenced the decision to build here.

Leith Provost's Chain

In 1920 when Leith was absorbed into Edinburgh the Provost's chain and mace were given to Leith Dock Commission to be used by the chairman. In 1967 when Forth Ports took over, the old regalia was to be given to Trinity House where the Provost's chain was on display but the mace was missing until discovered in 1977 still in a box in a storeroom in the old dock offices, no one being aware of its location. Bill McKelvie photographed the mace in the boardroom on discovery.

Gabriel's Road

This was the old road from Mutries Hill at the East End of the Lang Dykes to the ford over the Water of Leith at Stockbridge. The path at the side of new Register House went by the east end of Abercromby Place, where the wall at Queen Street Gardens east shows the angle of the old road, to the steps from Saxe Coburg Place to Glenogle Road, signposted as Gabriel's Road until recently.

North Charlotte Street

Before the Moray Place development the Earl of Moray would not allow buildings within 40ft of his boundaries, consequently to avoid any infringement of the Moray properties the western end of Queen Street (Albyn Place) was bevelled slightly at North Charlotte Street instead of making a right angle as Craig's plan originally required.

Charlotte Square

Robert Adams' Charlotte Square is one of Europe's major achievements of civic architecture of the period, spacious, elegant and harmonious. There are forty-four separate houses built here at different times between 1792 and 1820, but all conforming in style, the doors, windows, pilasters, pediments, balustrades, festoons, decorations etc. Unfortunately there are a few later additions of dormer windows, altered doors and fanlights not originally intended, but the north side is nearly perfect. Each block of houses is completely unified to a symmetrical design but without fussiness, a restrained perfection of design texture and detail.

The east side has a block of seven houses on each side of George Street, each block has a centre house with pilasters and pediments flanked by three adjoining houses, but on the west side each block on either side of St George's church, (now West Registrar House) has only six houses, so the centre piece is at the join between two houses. To balance the high dome of the church Adam designed a large window effect as the centre piece on these side blocks, but this feature masks the dividing wall between the two houses, so the middle window on each block here is false. The illusion is perfected by facing it with glass, but note the two windows behind the fanlight at the top and the blank centre porch with a doorway either side.

Torch Extinguishers

At the north side of Charlotte Square are still preserved the torch extinguishers in the railings at the entrances to the houses, these were used by linkboys who accompanied carriages and sedan chairs. At the edge of the pavement are the stone steps to allow access to carriages, and also the covers of the coal chutes which allowed coalmen to deliver coal to the cellar.

Watch Tower

At the corner of Lothian Road and King Stables Road in St Cuthbert's churchyard this round tower was used to house watchers over the graves during the 'body snatching' era around 1825.

Dr Knox of the university required bodies up to three days old for medical research, so relatives of the deceased had to keep watch for three days and nights after a burial. Other methods used were an iron grating over the grave known as a mort safe or a flat tombstone. Burke and Hare are erroneously referred to as body snatchers. This is not true, they were murderers who sold the bodies of their victims to Knox.

At Duddingston Church there is a watch tower and a 'louping on stane' – which allowed ladies to mount side saddle, and the iron jougs or collar hanging from the wall, were designed to provide punishment for such offences as drunkenness, adultery, blasphemy and failure to attend Sunday worship. The victim would be chained to the collar for a while, then go into church to ask God's forgiveness.

Royal Yacht Britannia

Built at John Browns yard on the Clyde she was launched on April 16 1953 by her Majesty Queen Elizabeth II and accumulated over 40 years Royal service. As well as serving her Majesty the ship was used as a hospital ship in the Falklands conflict. Deemed to be too expensive to maintain she was decommissioned in 1997 and Leith was fortunate to win the tender as her final berth.

Opened as a visitor attraction in 1998 it is now one of Scotland's top tourist attractions with over 300,000 visitors a year.

Braid Road

Opposite 66 Braid Road the setts in the road mark the site of the twin gallows used at the last execution in Scotland for highway robbery. In 1815 two Irishmen, Kelly and O'Neill robbed the Biggar carrier of four pound notes, twenty shillings in silver, a two penny loaf and a leather tobacco pouch. With other offences they were sentenced to hang where their last crime was committed. A great procession accompanied them from the Tolbooth in the High Street, including the Lord Provost, magistrates, police, high constables, halberdiers, clergymen and the executioner. The centre stones were the sockets for the gibbets.

St Anthony's Chapel

The ruins of St Anthony's Chapel in Holyrood Park were possibly connected at one time to St Anthony's hospital in the Kirkgate in Leith and the monks showed a light or beacon to guide mariners in the Forth. Nearby is St Anthony's well, a natural spring which appears to have dried up.

Boundary Stones

Edinburgh Castle and the Esplanade are crown property as distinct from civic property. The boundary extends from the extremity of the Esplanade northwards in a direct line across the railway to a boundary stone in the shrubbery. By the east footbridge it continues westwards behind the Ross Bandstand in a line with the shrubbery to the west foot bridge and back over the railway, there it follows round the castle rock to Kings Stables Road, to the back of the Grassmarket directly up Castle Wynd South, across Johnston Terrace, up Castle Wynd, north to the Esplanade to include all of the castle rock.

Abraham Lincoln

The statue of Abraham Lincoln in Calton cemetery commemorates the fallen in the American Civil War; it must be remembered that Scots fought on both sides. This was the first statue to an American

President to be erected outside America. Note the figure depicting a freed slave. Alongside is the David Hume monument containing his grave.

Town Walls

A plaque on the wall of the former married quarters in Johnson Terrace marks the position of the King's Wall of 1450 which started at King David's Tower (half moon battery), went down towards the Grassmarket then along the side of the ridge halfway between the High Street and the Cowgate to the Netherbow Port and then down to the eastern end of the Nor Loch. The later Flodden Wall of 1513 enclosed a larger area going up the Vennel from the Grassmarket across behind Heriot's school to Greyfriar's Church and Bristo Port and east by the University (Kirk o' Fields) and Drummond Street to the Pleasance then up to the Netherbow. Much later the Telfer Wall enclosed Heriot's. Part of the Flodden Wall is well preserved in the Vennel running from Heriot's to the Grassmarket.

After Flodden, when Edinburgh's manpower was almost wiped out, this wall was hastily erected in anticipation of English raids, women and children being used as labour. Luckily these raids did not take place.

The plaque on the wall above Napier's shop at Bristo is wrongly dated, inferring as it does that this was the site of the 1513 Flodden Wall, actually this was a bastion of the Telfer Wall built in 1636 to include the extra area of land beyond the Flodden Wall to be within the city boundaries. The Flodden Wall crossed from Greyfriars Churchyard at Bristo Port 100 yards north near the top of Candlemaker Row.

The Buckstane

The Buckstane was originally some 200 yards north of its present position on Braid Road at Mortonhall golf course and it marked the boundary where the buckhounds were released during royal hunting beyond the Burgh Muir.

Some also claim that at this site the Lairds of Penicuik secured tenure of their property in return for three blasts of the hunting horn when the King passed by. The ancient reddendo in their charter includes the motto 'free for a blast.'

Cart Slide

On Calton Hill is one of the cart slides once common in Edinburgh on steep hills. The Carter placed a wide iron or wooden wedge under one wheel as an extra brake and slid this wheel down the slide.

Tram Lines

At the foot of Waterloo Place a section of the old cable car rails are preserved, showing the centre slot through which the cable was hooked. Edinburgh's first trams were horse drawn and were operated from 1871 on a route from Haymarket to Bernard Street. In 1888 cable cars were introduced on a route between Hanover Street and Goldenacre. In cable car operations a wire rope was wound through the streets between the tramlines, the driver would then lower a gripper onto the cable to start the car and retract it to stop. Leith town council decided to invest in electricity as their preferred method of power, using overhead wires. So for 25 years it was impossible to make an uninterrupted journey to Leith, passengers had to switch trams at the boundary and this became known as the 'Pilrig muddle'.

Edinburgh and Leith amalgamated in 1920 but it was not until 1923 that an electric tram could journey up to Princes Street. The network was eventually extended to cover 48 route miles. The trams operated from four depots, Tollcross, Leith Walk, Portobello, Gorgie with Shrubhill being the main engineering depot. The last tram ran on the 16 November 1956, a white liveried tram number 224, toured what was left of the system and a parade of ten trams left the Braids terminus at 7.45 p.m. The last tram, number 217, met at The Mound and made its way to Shrubhill. Thousands turned out to watch 85 years of tram transport come to an end.

Hitching Post

In front of the former GPO building is an old hitching post with a ring on top where the post corporal from Peirshill Barracks used to tether his horse when he collected the mail. It may have been used when extra trace horses were unhitched from horse drawn trams.

Wellington Statue

The statue in front of Registrar House honours the victor of the Battle of Waterloo in 1815. By Steele, the Edinburgh sculptor, it weighs 7½ tons and was cast in a foundry in Grove Street. It is effectively balanced on its hind legs and tail and Steele regarded it as one of his best works, cast in bronze it was erected in 1852. The name of his horse was Copenhagen.

Wellington was known as the Iron Duke because he had iron shutters put on his house in London so that meal mob rioters could not break in. During the unveiling a severe storm soaked the crowds and the next day the *Scotsman* published the story with the couplet:

'Mid lightning's flash
And thunders peal
Behold the Iron Duke
In bronze by Steele'

Fire mark

In the days before municipal fire brigades each insurance company had its own private fire engine and these plaques were to show which company the building was insured with. Possibly a house showing a rival fire mark would be left to burn. Certainly there was trouble when rival fire engines tried to connect to the same hydrant. There are a few fire marks at various locations round town.

Merchants Hall

This building at the corner of Hanover Street and Rose Street was earlier the Edinburgh office of the Glasgow Bank, which expired in 1866. The hall occupies only half of the building the other half, which housed the Chamber of Commerce, was built at a much later date (1902), but the detailed structure and stonework is so perfectly matched that it is impossible to notice any difference, or to see the join, apart from the portico. The original Merchants Hall was in Hunters Square, which became a branch of the Royal Bank of Scotland, now demolished and the Ibis Hotel now occupies the site.

Edinburgh Academy

Sir Walter Scott, Lord Cockburn and others did not like the education they received at Royal High School, then in Infirmary Street. They raised money and built Edinburgh Academy, to provide a more classical education. A map will show that this building lies at the termination of Frederick Street – if that street had continued north. G. Scott Moncrieff writes that the Town Council commissioned Wm. Playfair to build St Stephen's Church in 1828 to obstruct the view of the Academy from the foot of Frederick Street. The church has the longest pendulum in Europe and, with the slope of the ground, entry by the main entrance is to the gallery.

Duddingston Manse

The Reverend J. S. Thomson of Duddingston Church was an artist of note in 1880, and his paintings are on display in the National Gallery on the Mound, his studio was on the shore of Duddingston Loch at the bottom of the manse garden. He named this building 'Edinburgh' so that his maidservant could honestly tell callers that he 'was away to Edinburgh' to save him being disturbed while he worked. At that time there was an upper storey on the little building which received the light necessary to an artist.

St Cuthbert's Church

St Cuthbert's Church was the parish church of Stockbridge, the old Kirk Loan remains with us in Church Street and Church Lane, renamed Gloucester Street and Lane, up which parishioners tramped to worship. This lane continued up Wemyss Place but is lost in the New Town development of Queen Street and Charlotte Square, it reappears between Princes Street Gardens and St John's church leading down to St Cuthbert's, here the cobble stones are the original surface of the old road.

St John's Highland Tolbooth Church

While James Gillespie Graham was the architect of the Highland Church, A. W. Pugin is credited with the impressive spire, completed in 1844 and sited at the apex of Hanover Street. When viewed from the north, it is not generally realised that there are two buildings contributing to this view. In 1847 William Playfair designed the twin towers of the new college to frame the spire when viewed from Hanover Street. Services were held in Gaelic and when the church closed the congregation moved to Greyfriar's. Now called the Hub it is the administrative headquarters of the Edinburgh Festival.

Gudeman of Ballengreigh

King James V in disguise as the Gudeman of Ballengreigh was attacked by robbers at Cramond Brig in 1532. Jock Howeson, a farm worker, came to his assistance, and was granted the farm at Braehead in return for supplying a basin, towel, and ewer of water whenever the Sovereign passes. This service was offered to the Queen some years ago.

The statue by Robert Forrest is in the courtyard of the old farm now home to the SSPCA.

Royal High School

The first reference to the school was in 1519 and in 1529 James V granted to the headmaster the sole privilege of instructing the youth of Edinburgh at this school. In 1554 Cardinal Beaton's house in Blackfriar's Wynd was used for a short time before moving to High School Wynd in 1555. In 1567 the Town Council resolved to build a new school on the grounds of the Blackfriar's monastery and it received the royal patronage of James VI who gave it the title of *schola regia edinensis*.

The school was run jointly by the city and the presbytery, and after the first year the pupils spoke only Latin. The Royal High had a monopoly to teach Latin and pupils from other schools, e.g. George Heriot's were sent to the High School for classes in this.

In 1595 Bailie MacMorran was shot dead by a pupil during a sit in protest in demand of a holiday. The school met six days a week from 6 a.m. to 6 p.m. and the only holidays were saints days and one week in May and one in September.

In 1777 the foundations for a new school were laid at High School Yards (now the foot of Infirmary Street).

In 1825 work started on a new school at Calton Hill to a design by Thomas Hamilton and based on a Greek temple. When the new building opened in 1829 the old building became the surgical house of the Royal Infirmary and is now part of the university.

When the Royal High decided to go co-educational in 1969 a new school was built at Barnton and the Calton Hill building was used as a civic art centre. In 1977 work started to convert it for the proposed Scottish Assembly, but it was unpopular with politicians and Donald Dewar, the first minister, picked the site at Holyrood.

Leith Walk

In the seventeenth century the main road from north Leith to Edinburgh was by Bonnington Road, Broughton Village, the side of Calton Hill, by Leith Wynd to the Netherbow. There was also an 'Easter Road' beginning at south Leith, and a road at Restalrig.

In 1650, in defence against Cromwell, Leslie built a great trench and a mound from the Kirkgate to Calton Hill which successfully defied Cromwell's cavalry and artillery. Cromwell later defeated Leslie at Dunbar.

This mound became a handsome gravel walk, over which no horses were allowed prior to 1770. It became fashionable for the ladies of Edinburgh to come out on the 'Leith Walk' to take the air and admire the view (notwithstanding the existence of a gallows) as there was a permanent gallows at Shrubhill, where criminals were left to rot in chains. It was the haunt of thieves and footpads by night.

With the building of the North Bridge a causeway was laid and Leith Walk became a main highway.

Leith in 1645

During the Great Plague which killed more than half the population, illness was notified by hanging a white sheet from a window, thereafter the inmates were locked in and were supplied with food daily by an official. After a death the survivors were isolated in large camps of wooden huts on the links and at Seafield. Many of these also died and were buried in trenches at Wellington Place and other sites nearby. Their houses were smoked by burning heather and straw, destroying many in the process. Their clothes and effects were purified by boiling

in cauldrons over open peat fires and smoked in kilns. The Doocot at
Logan's Castle at Lochend was used for this purpose.

The Standing Group

The Genius of Architecture Crowning the Theory of the Practice of
Art is the title claimed by some for this statue in West Princes Street
Gardens. Catherine Sinclair was the model and William Brodie RSA
was the sculptor and it was cast in 1880.

Sir William Gowans RSA, his son in law, writes of a pair of statues
in the grounds of his house 'Rockville' in Napier Road (since
demolished), which complemented each other entitled 'mother with
children' both by William Brodie. He claims that one is in west Princes
Street Gardens and the other one is lost, could this be one of the pair?

Lauriston Castle

The entrance to Lauriston Castle retains the heavy bollards, which
were positioned in many places to prevent the axle hubs of carriages
from scraping the walls.

Lothian House

Note the horse drawn barge on the frieze, which commemorates the
terminus of the union canal, which was in this vicinity in 1922.

Ramsay Gardens

The figure which looks like a cat on the roof of one of the houses
really represents 'Old Nick' and at one time had also wings and a tail,
these have since worn away. Originally there were two contemporary
figures on adjoining gables, an angel on the west gable and a sphinx
on the central gable. These figures have no historical significance and
were erected in 1894 by Patrick Geddes. They represented the riddle
of life.

Bank of Scotland, St Andrew's Square

The former British Linen Bank building was built in 1851 by David
Bryce, and the statues on the roof are by a Musselburgh sculptor,
Alexander Handyside Ritchie, and represent Navigation, Commerce,
Manufacture, Art, Science, and Agriculture. They are somewhat

elongated in height so that when viewed from ground level they appear in proper perspective.

Salvation Army Hostel

In 1789 the George Heriot Trust built some sixteen schools in addition to the well-known original hospital of 1628.

The building at the corner of the Cowgate and Pleasance which is now a Salvation Army lodging house is one still standing. Note the plaque and the turrets recognisable as similar to those in the earlier school.

Prudential Building

The building on the corner of St Andrew's Square and South St Andrew's Street was built for the Prudential Insurance Company and was designed by Sir Alfred Waterhouse, whose firm built most of the 'Pru' buildings in this country. Knowing Waterhouse's reputation the Town Council accepted the plans but were later astounded to learn that the building was to be red brick so they insisted that stone must be used to conform with the other buildings in St Andrew's Square. Waterhouse had to alter his plans but got his own back by using red Dumfriesshire sandstone. The style is early Renaissance and was built in 1895.

Playhouse Close

At 180 Canongate was the butcher's shop owned by John Johnstone. Each evening he would boil up the scraps of meat from the day's cuts and distribute it to the poor of the district. In 1895 he emigrated to Canada and shortly afterwards 'Bovril' came on the market. Every jar had the name 'John Johnstone' on the label until recently.

Dean Gallery

This was formerly the Dean orphanage and was designed by Thomas Hamilton in 1833. The clock was originally on the Netherbow Port which was demolished in 1764. First it was taken to the old orphan hospital at the West End of Calton Road and then transferred to the Dean in 1830. For many years the building was used as the Dean training college.

Abercromby Place

Built about 1804, this street was unique in the new town where all the streets had been planned on the strict gridiron design as straight streets crossed by others at right angles. But the owner of the ground, which is now Queen Street Gardens, would not sell, so the houses were built round his perimeter as a crescent and caused considerable amazement at the time. Subsequently crescents became quite common.

Queen Street Gardens

The dome shaped 'temple' in the gardens seen from Dundas Street is a gas regulator. Perhaps the Queen Street Gardens' proprietors insisted on a classical style building to conform to the surroundings after considering the hideous structure housing a water pump erected earlier by the water board on Calton Hill.

Nisbet of Dirleton

The house of Sir John Nisbet of Dirleton, Provost of Edinburgh, has been restored but with one regrettable omission, the sharp angled 'oriel window' to the west no longer includes the small side window from which the approach to the entrance door could be monitored. Over the door lintel the Latin inscription is, 'Peace on entering, safety on leaving'.

Heraldry

Above the forecourt entrance to Holyrood Palace are the arms of Charles II as Monarch of Scotland, showing the lion rampant on the shield encircled by the collar of the Order of the Thistle with St Andrew's badge, the crest is a lion sejeant holding a sword in the Dexter paw and a sceptre in the sinister paw. Both supporters are unicorns, which heraldic beast was associated with Scottish monarchy from the reign of James II.

The Arms of James V in Abbey Strand

In Scotland the arms of the Sovereign differ from England in that the shield shows the lion rampant in the first and fourth quarters, the lion and unicorn supporters on sinister and dexter sides – (the reverse in England) – the crest of a lion sejeant with a sword in Dexter and a sceptre in sinister paw, also the shield is encircled by the collar of the most noble Order of the Thistle, (in England the garter belt).

Therefore it was not correct for the Forth customs building in York Place, Granton Square, and the Exchequer at Parliament Square to display Scottish arms and supporters along with the garter belt of England. The Lord Lyon confirmed that this was an error and ordered the York Place and Granton Square devices to be removed. There is a similar error above James Gray in George Street.

Registrar House

The site was purchased for £2,698, and was to be built of Craigleith stone. Work stopped in 1778 and for six years remained 'the most magnificent pigeon coop in Europe'. Jacobite estates were confiscated and sold to raise money and the government gave £15,000 and work restarted, the final cost was £31,000. The alcoves in front that house, the clock and barometer, were used as sentry boxes in time of war.

Old School House

The old school house on Morningside Road opposite Falcon Avenue was built in 1823 as the village school for the district. The clock face is false, the works having been removed to the church which was later built opposite but after 100 years the movement has worn out. In its early days the schoolhouse was used as a place of worship, as the parish church was St Cuthbert's, a long walk from the district. The school closed in 1892 when South Morningside School was built.

Borestone

The story of the Borestone at Morningside Church is controversial. Legend has it that before marching to the battle of Flodden in 1513 the King raised his standard here and put his flagpole in a hole in the rock but there is no hole in the stone which could have taken a flagpole. It is known that the Royal Standard was not ready when James IV marched to Flodden, but had to follow on later. Some authorities claim that this stone was the 'hare stone' at Tipperlin where the Lairds of Penicuik blew their 'three blasts of the horn'.

Opposite an old milestone is embedded in the wall stating 'one mile from Tollcross'.

Martyrs Monument

The Martyrs Monument in Greyfriar's Churchyard commemorates the suffering of the Covenantors during their imprisonment there.

In an open space to the south west hundreds of men were confined in a closely packed area for weeks during the winter after the battle of Bothwell Bridge in 1679. Scores were executed in the Grassmarket because they would not sign a bond of allegiance to the king.

National Library

The 8ft high carvings on the centre block of the National Library on George IV Bridge are by Hew Lorimer whose father, Sir Robert, built the shrine at the Castle and also the Thistle Chapel in St Giles.

The carvings depict the arts and culture in various aspects with the figure on the right representing music and would normally be playing a lute or lyre in classical style, but being Scottish is playing bagpipes in the classical style with the drones of the pipes looking like flutes. Note also he is wearing a kilt.

On the wings of this building the pictorial relief panels by James Barr of Glasgow show aspects of teaching and learning, each panel shows two pupils acquiring knowledge. The panel on the left has one figure finger spelling the sign for 'A' and the other figure is spelling 'B' in the manual alphabet for the deaf.

The panel on the right of this wing shows one figure guiding the fingers of the other over a Braille tablet.

The building was opened by the Queen in 1956.

Mound Square

On the step at the east side of National Gallery there is a measurement of 100 feet, and at 66 feet a mark showing 100 links or one chain.

Leith Street

From St James Centre across to Calton Hill stretches the 'bridge going to nowhere' which cost £100,000. It was to cross over the projected dual carriage way coming from the south by way of the Pleasance, under the Royal Mile and connect with a vast roundabout at Broughton Street/Leith Street. When the motorway was abandoned the council tried to cancel but the builder wanted full cost compensation so the council decided, if they were going to pay he might as well build it. It was demolished in 2003.

Crawley Tunnel

As the New Town grew the water supply from Comiston springs was totally inadequate. Accordingly Telford and Rennie surveyed Crawley springs near Glencorse and led a 15ft pipe to a reservoir in Queen Street in 1822. As the water might have lost pressure if the pipe had gone over Castlehill, they tunnelled through the castle rock. The tunnel goes north in a straight line from the Grassmarket to the foot of the Mound. It is not a sewer but makes inspection of the pipe possible. At Hanover Street the pipe travels in an orthodox trench. The inspection manhole is in the middle of the road at the traffic lights at the foot of the mound.

The Balmwell

The Balmwell got its name because St Katherine in the 11th century was bringing holy oil from Mount Sinai to Edinburgh. She rested just outside the city at a well where she spilt some oil into the water. Ever afterwards this well was attributed with miraculous healing powers, as no matter how much oil was taken out there was always more oil on the surface. James VI attested to its powers and the oil was used to relieve many ailments. Cromwell destroyed the well but Charles II restored it and added the temple surround. Many pilgrimages claimed the curative power of the holy Balmwell. Only recently shale deposits were discovered through which the water seeped to feed the well. Analysis shows that the well has no medicinal value whatsoever.

Esplanade

The length of the Castle Esplanade is not accidental, David I decreed that no building should be erected nearer the Castle walls than one bow shot, accordingly no enemy could shoot arrows into the castle from behind cover.

At the drawbridge the figures of King Robert the Bruce on the left and Sir William Wallace on the right were unveiled in 1929.

The translation of the inscription over the gateway is 'No one touches me with impunity'.

Cannonball House

This building has two cannonballs embedded in the wall facing the Castle esplanade and there are two different stories as to how they got there. The first is that they were fired at Holyrood Palace when Bonnie Prince Charlie lodged there in 1745 after he had taken Edinburgh but not the Castle. Some historians maintain that this version is not correct, as the two cannonballs are embedded in cement and that they only serve to mark the height that the water in Castlehill reservoir can rise to, being fed by Comiston Spring. However the cannonballs fell out of the wall some 100 years ago and were then replaced with cement, the 1745 version is true and the water authorities confirm that the Comiston Spring's original cistern level is 60ft higher than the Castlehill reservoir.

Bulls Eye Windows

Before plate glass was run into a mould early glass was very expensive and windows had very small panes. Crown glass was spun and the centre had a 'bulls eye' where the holding rod had been attached.

Normally this glass was cut into squares and held by astragals, but only one square would be a bullion. Windows with more than one bullion are not likely to be genuine for this period.

Castlehill Reservoir

The Castlehill Reservoir was built in 1849 and closed in 1997 and held over 2 million gallons of water. It replaced an earlier building of 1672 which took water from Comiston Springs, the building now houses the tartan weaving centre.

Early water supplies were from stagnant lochs or draw wells which were generally contaminated. In 1681 the Town Council hired a German engineer, Peter Brusche, who realised that the four springs at Comiston, Swan, Fox, Lapwing and Hare were higher than the Castle Esplanade and using a lead pipe with 3ins bore fed the reservoir at Castle Hill – the first gravity fed water supply in Europe. From this cistern wooden pipes (elm) fitted together with tapered ends fed a series of five wells down the Royal Mile with fresh water.

When the day came to turn on the tap nothing came out and Brusche mounted his horse and rode out to find the problem and was never seen again and was not paid for the work. One of the workmen tapped the pipe with a hammer and the water flowed, it had only been an air lock in the pipe. As the water was only turned on for a few hours a day queues at the wells were commonplace and a group of men, usually highlanders, would fill barrels and deliver to houses. They were called 'water cadies' a corruption of the French word cadet, and it is from them that the golf term of caddy is derived.

Turnpike Stair

A turnpike stair ascended in a clockwise direction so that the house could be defended by a swordsman with a sword in his right hand. One famous family called Kerr who were predominately left handed were in great demand for their attacking abilities with a sword in their left hand, and holding the banister with their right hand.

This gives rise to the expression 'Corrie Handed' meaning left handed.

Gladstone's Land

Rebuilt by Thomas Gledstanes in 1617 it shows the original arched style of the Royal Mile. After Hereford's invasion of 1544 called 'the rough wooing' houses built of stone minimised the risk of fire and also enabled higher lands to be built. As the population grew owners built out over the roadway by seven feet at the first floor level leaving the footpath clear underneath, effectively reducing the width of the street by fourteen feet. Early on this would have been of timber from the Burgh Muir or the forest of Drumsheugh, but later it was stone.

The name Gledstane comes from the Scots word gled – a hawk or a kite.

During restoration work in 1935 painted ceilings were uncovered, the house is now the property of the National Trust and is decorated as a merchant's house of that period would have been. At the house is an excellent example of the forestairs that most houses had in the seventeenth century and in which the family pig was kept and was allowed to run free in the street during the day, causing obvious filth. Ladies wore iron pattens on their shoes when venturing out on the streets and young girls could run and skip surprisingly fast up and down the steep closes wearing these irons on their shoes.

Passing Railings

In Milnes Court is a fine example of the curved railings which were designed to allow two ladies wearing crinolines to pass in modesty.

Riddles Court

This was the home of David Hume the Philosopher at one time, and here he wrote part of his history of England. The inner courtyard housed Bailie MacMorran who was shot dead by a Royal High School boy in a dispute over extra holidays in 1508. The quaint outside stair is a much later addition after some reconstruction.

Hanging Setts

At the corner of George IV Bridge and High Street, three brass setts in the road mark the spot where stood the gibbet, last used in 1864. Deacon Brodie was hanged here in 1788 on gallows he himself designed. He was the inspiration for Robert Louis Stevensons *'Dr Jekyll and Mr Hyde'*.

Heart of Midlothian

The brass studs in the road mark the outline of the Tolbooth prison and the setts mark the site of the door. The prison was demolished in 1817 as it blocked the High Street, the prisoners being transferred to the new prison on Calton Hill. Immortalised by Sir Walter Scott in his novel *The Heart of Midlothian*, the door to the condemned cell and the key were presented to him and he incorporated them into his house at Abbotsford. It was the custom to spit on the heart for luck when passing.

St Giles

St Giles High Kirk, dedicated in 1150 was the first parish church in Edinburgh, but there has been a church on this site since 854.

In 1385 it was burned by Richard II leaving only four massive central pillars standing and was rebuilt in stone in 1454.

William Preston of Gorton presented a sacred relic, the arm bone of St Giles mounted in gold with a diamond ring on the finger.

In 1466 it became collegiate and the crown spire dates from 1490. John Knox preached here between 1560 and 1572.

Charles I elevated St Giles to Cathedral status but it reverted to Presbyterian High Kirk in 1688. Restoration work by Burn in 1827 spoiled the exterior.

Crown Spire, St Giles

St Giles has a curious outside tower attached to, and spoiling the symmetry of, the twelfth century crown spire (rebuilt 1490). It contains a spiral turnpike stair with an entrance at the base and another at the top giving access to one arch of the crown. This arch is crowstepped, all the others are castellated so that one may ascend to the central gallery of the steeple apex. A watchman may have been stationed there as a lookout or firewatcher in the times when most buildings were timber and St Giles' steeple was the highest point in Edinburgh. The steeple arches are firmly strapped across to each other.

Parliament Hall

Built in 1638 by the citizens of Edinburgh, as Charles I would not pay the cost as promised, it housed the Scottish Parliament until 1707, which earlier had met in the Tolbooth and later in the Castle banqueting hall.

The painted glass south window by a German artist in 1868 depicts the inauguration of the Court of Session in St Giles by James V in 1532.

After 1707 the hall became the seat of the law courts and until 1819 cases were tried in this hall – often two or three at a time competing with the babble of crowds walking up and down.

The roof, popularly called a hammerbeam, is strictly only barrel vaulted.

The old gothic frontage was spoiled in 1808 by Robert Reid to make a symmetrical façade of Parliament Square. Note the false windows outside the hall facing the square and also at the south east corner where there is nothing behind them.

Charles II Statue

Known as the Merry Monarch, this is the oldest lead equestrian statue in the country, dating from 1685. It was originally to be a statue of Cromwell but on the restoration of the Monarchy the city decided it should be Charles II instead. Note the second face between the shoulder blades, he is dressed in the garb of a Roman general and they used neither stirrups nor spurs in Roman times.

Just behind is the grave of John Knox who died in 1572.

Mercat Cross

The Mercat Cross was moved from its site in the High Street (now marked by cobblestones) to Drum House in Gilmerton in 1756. In 1885 Gladstone, the member of parliament for Midlothian, had it re-erected on its present site. Part of the shaft is original, but the base and gallery are modern. The old site is where sheriff's officers sold by auction the goods and effects of debtors who had been poinded; this was as recent as 1925. Royal proclamations are read here four days after they are announced in London, that being the time it took a horseman to ride with the news.

Quadrangle City Chambers

The statue of Alexander taming Bucephalus (bullhead) by Steele and dated 1884 was moved here from St Andrew's Square in 1916 to make way for a statue of Gladstone which in turn was moved to Coates Crescent.

In 350 BC Alexander of Macedonia was nine years old when a wild stallion was presented to his father, Phillip II. No one could manage the horse but Alexander tamed it by laying his hand on it. Thereafter he rode it into every major battle in his career.

Mary King's Close

During the great plague of 1645 all the people in Mary King's Close died.

The authorities, hoping to contain the disease, had the close sealed off to keep the pestilence inside. Nobody went in for 100 years and later the Royal Exchange (City Chambers) was built over the old close which still exists almost as it was. It can be entered at the High Street end. The old butcher's shop shows the hooks for hanging meat and the baker's shop still has the deep baker's oven visible.

Cockburn Street, formed in 1859 to give access to Waverley Station from the High Street, cuts through Mary King's Close which appears to finish one storey above the Cockburn Street entrance to the City Chambers, from here it disappears but the Nor Loch end is reputed to exist in the cellars of the Doric tavern in Market Street.

The close was reopened as a tourist attraction in April 2003 when researchers discovered hitherto unknown evidence of a sixteenth century murder. Records show that a resident of the close, one Alison Rough, killed her daughter Katherine's husband, Alexander Cant, with a pair of fire tongs in a row over the non payment of a £250 dowry. Both women were sentenced to death but Katherine's execution was deferred until the birth of her unborn child to her dead husband. When she escaped to Germany, Alison also escaped but was recaptured and was drowned in the Nor' Loch in 1536 a year after the murder.

Tron Church

In 1637 Charles I elevated St Giles Kirk to become an Episcopalian cathedral when he tried to impose the English form of service on the Scots. Thus the Tron Kirk was built to house the evicted Presbyterian congregation. Completed in 1648 as Christ's church at the Tron, the Tron being the weigh beam for salt at this spot. It was here that merchants had their scales checked and any found to be giving short measure were nailed by their ears to the beam and had to stay there all day until the town bell sounded when the commander of the town guard would come down the High Street brandishing his sword to cut them free.

The church was severely shortened when the South Bridge and Hunter Square were built in 1789 when Lord Provost Hunter Blair was in office.

Fire destroyed the steeple in 1824 and among the crowds gathered to watch the blaze was Sir Walter Scott who remarked 'mony a boring sermon I have heard below that'. A new spire was erected in 1828 and the church closed in 1952 and was bought by Edinburgh Corporation in 1954. During restoration work excavations revealed 'Marlin's Wynd' an old cobbled thoroughfare which ran from the High Street to the Cowgate and was named after the Frenchman who laid it.

For many years it was the place where Edinburgh folk went to celebrate the new year – to see in the bells – but although the spire has a clock it does not chime, the bells come from St Giles.

Warriston Close

While minister at St Giles, John Knox lived here until 1566 when he left Edinburgh. But this manse was covered by the guns of the castle when Kirkaldy of Grange held the castle for Mary Queen of Scots during her imprisonment by Elizabeth I. The Town Council put him in the well-known house in the High Street where he died three months later.

Netherbow Port

At the junction of St Mary's Street and the High Street brass setts mark the outline of the Netherbow Port, one of the main gates in the city wall, which was erected after the battle of Flodden. The passageway was very narrow compared to today's standards, but there were very few coaches in the city, most travellers being on foot, horseback or in a sedan chair. On the wall of the building north west of this spot is depicted the Netherbow Port in relief. It was demolished in 1764.

Morrocco Land

The Moor at Morrocco Land in the Canongate is reputed to commemorate the story of Andrew Gray, sentenced to death by Provost Sir John Smith early in the seventeenth century for taking part in some disturbance. Escaping from the Tolbooth he went abroad and served with the Sultan of Morrocco. In 1645 during the great plague, a pirate fleet appeared in the Forth and held the city to ransom, and the Provost's son as a hostage. As there were not enough able-bodied men to defend the city the authorities had to give in to the demand but informed the pirate chief that the Lord Provost did not have a son, only a daughter and she was dying of the plague. He cured her using an eastern remedy and then married her. He was Andrew Gray. He had been banished for life from the city so built a house on this site outside the city walls and erected a statue to his benefactor.

But it could have been just a shopkeeper's sign.

During the renovation of these buildings near the top of the Canongate a plinth was included to take the statue of the Moor, but members of the old Edinburgh club pointed out that it was in the wrong place so the Moor is now thirty yards nearer the Netherbow.

Chessels Court

This is a 1963 reconstruction of the original built in 1748 by Andrew Chessel as high-class mansion flats or apartments, to 'accommodate genteel families'. The south block was for a while the Excise office where Deacon Brodie committed his final burglary in 1788.

The red block on the west side was Clark's hotel, the earliest proper hotel in the old town, prior to this travellers were lucky to find accommodation in inns which were primarily stables for horses.

By this time hotels were being built in the new town and people with money and influence were moving there and Clark's hotel could not survive.

Blue Blanket

In 1481 Queen Margaret and her ladies embroidered the sacred 'Blue Blanket' which her husband James III gifted to the craftsmen and powerful guilds of Edinburgh, in recognition of their loyalty and the aid they had given in releasing him from restraint in the castle.

They were given the right to raise the banner in defence of king, country and their own privileges, thus every ordinary citizen was bound to rally and fight for its preservation.

All artisans and craftsmen owe allegiance to it, and it was raised before the battle of Flodden. It is now kept in the Trades Maiden Hospital in Melville Street under the care of the Deacon Convenor of Trades. The governors of the Trades Maiden Hospital consist of the convenors of the trade incorporations which still exist. For many years a pub known as the Blue Blanket (now Canons Gait) stood here and had a mural depicting various historical incidents connected with the banner which shows various Scottish emblems and heraldic bearings of the crafts.

St John's Cross

The cross in the road in the Canongate, below New Street is the cross of St John in the vicinity of the quarters of the Knights of St John Hospitalers. The authority of the Provost and Bailies of Edinburgh extended beyond the city wall into the separate burgh of the Canongate as far as St John's Cross where they used to meet processions coming up from Holyrood and escort them through the city gates.

At this cross in 1667 Charles II elevated the Provost of Edinburgh to become Lord Provost. Earlier, in 1617 James VI knighted Provost Nisbet of Dean and in 1634 Charles I knighted Provost Alexander Clark here.

Bible Land

This was the hall of the incorporation of Cordiners, who got their name from Cordova in Spain, famous for goatskin leather. Their Patron Saint was St Crispin, and annually on 25 October, King Crispin's day was celebrated when the new king was elected and drawn through the Canongate in a golden coach with heralds and outriders in full regalia. Above the door is a shield with an open bible showing the first verse of Psalm 133 and the shoemakers arms, a paring knife and crown. The interior has been renovated but the frontage is original.

Moray House

Built about 1628 for Mary Sutton, daughter of Lord Darnley and widow of the Earl of Home, she presented it to her daughter, wife of the 4th Earl of Moray. Charles I was a frequent visitor here and Cromwell had his headquarters here in 1648. In 1650 the chief guests at the wedding of Lady Mary Stuart, daughter of Lord Moray, to Lord Lorne assembled on the balcony to see the Marquis of Montrose, bound to a low cart and led up the Canongate to his execution at the Mercat Cross. Such was his calm demeanour that the spectators were silent in their admiration of a brave man (instead of throwing mud). Argyle, arch-enemy of Montrose was on the balcony with his son Lord Lorne and his bride, and it is said that she jeered and spat at Montrose.

It is interesting to note that Argyle and his son went up the same road to their executions.

Some signatures to the Treaty of Union were signed in the garden in 1707.

Huntly House

This is known as the 'speaking house' because of the sixteenth century plaques on the front of the building.

Antiqva tamen jvvenesco (I am old but renew my youth.)

Hodi mihi cras tibi cvr igitvr cvras 1570 (Today for me tomorrow for thee. Why therefore carest thou?).

Vt tv lingv ae tv ea sic ego mear avriv dominvs svm. (As thou art master of thy tongue, so also am I master of my ears.)

Spes altera vitae. (There is hope of another life.)

Built in 1570 for John Acheson, originally the front of the ground floor was a series of timbered archways making the corbelling more pronounced. Corbelling was a feature of closes and wynds in Edinburgh, and top floor residents could almost shake hands with their neighbours from their windows, and encroached on backs of mansion houses of Edinburgh which allowed covered approach of bandits and robbers of the day. The timbers came from the forest of Drumsheugh which covered the lower slopes of what is now Holyrood Park.

Restored in 1932 it is now a museum of local history.

Canongate Tolbooth

Built in 1591, it was here that tolls were collected. It has also served as a jail, courtroom and council chambers of the burgh of the Canongate.

The Latin inscription on the wall translates as the place of the seal of the burgh: For one's country and one's successors, 1591, King James VI. Justice and piety are the strong bulwarks of a prince. The coat of arms of the Canongate bears a stag's head with a cross between the antlers and the ancient motto *sic itur ad astra;* this is the path to the stars.

On the east side of the gable are embodied many oyster and clamshells to ward off witches, as traditionally witches could not cross water and were repelled by any connection with water.

Today it is a museum of local history called the 'People's Story'.

Banners

The banners erected during the Edinburgh Festival are authentic crests of families who lived in these parts in earlier times and they cost around £100 each.

Balfour Railings

Singing Jamie Balfour was a well-known character in the early nineteenth century, a gifted accountant and also a staunch Jacobite with a great repertoire of Jacobite songs. A clever businessman he could do three hours work in one hour and so never lacked work. but he only made money to spend it in Jenny Ha's tavern nearby. The wrought iron railings shows the diligent accountant and also the reveller by comparison.

Canongate Kirk

Built in 1688 it was to replace Holyrood Chapel as the parish church which had been taken over by James VII as his Thistle chapel, but it was not finished until the reign of William and Mary whose arms are shown on the front, (in escutcheon of golden lion rampant on blue field represents the House of Nassau). The arms below are that of Thomas Moodie of Saughtonhall who provided the money.

While the Kirk was being built parishioners used Lady Yesters church in Infirmary Street. Pews inside are designated for the Royal Family and the Governor of the Castle as both Holyrood Palace and the Castle are in the Canongate parish. Pews are also designated for the Duke of Hamilton, Keeper of the Palace, the Countess of Errol, Lord High Constable of Scotland, Duke of Argyle, great master of the Household, the Lord Lyon King of Arms, the Earl of Dundee the Royal Banner Bearer, the Captain General of the bodyguard, the Royal Company of Archers. The pews of the chaplain and the dean of the Chapel Royal have been donated by St Margaret's Chapel guild showing a further connection with the castle.

The inscriptions on the side stalls indicate associations with illustrious families in the Canongate. The needlework on the holy table was embroidered by two ladies of the church around 1970 and depicts the legend of the founding of Holyrood Abbey.

In 1128, against the advice of his confessor, David I was hunting on a holy day in the forest of Drumsheugh which covered the southern boundary of Edinburgh. He was separated from his attendants and was attacked by a fierce stag, a glowing cross appeared between the stag's antlers and King David was able to grasp it and frighten off the stag.

To acknowledge the miracle he ordered the building of the Abbey of Holyrood on the site. The arms of the Canongate show a cross between the antlers of a stag. On the roof is a real stag's head with a cross between the antlers. When it needs replacing the Monarch gives permission for a stag on the Balmoral estate to be shot.

In the churchyard many famous people are buried and at the entrance a board displays their names.

White Horse Close

The name White Horse Close is reputed to come from a favourite white palfrey belonging to Mary Queen of Scots which was stabled here.

William Dick, the blacksmith who founded the 'Dick Vet', lived here. This was where the stage coaches left for London. Departure was by Calton Road, the main road to London at that time being by Spring Gardens.

Girth Cross

The Girth Cross represented the extent of the sanctuary of Holyrood Abbey. Within this area which included the environs of Arthur's Seat no one could be apprehended by civil authorities in the Middle Ages.

Pursued down the Canongate the fugitive had to grasp the cross to be safe. Later on the bounds of sanctuary were defined closer to the abbey and brass sets in the roadway by Horse Wynd denote the limits until imprisonment for debt ceased in 1881. The residents were known as 'Abbey Lairds' and the last resident was John Bain, a lawyer. The present day building housing the shop once housed De Quincey when he was being hounded for debt and could have been imprisoned in the Tolbooth.

On a Sunday the fugitives were free to roam until midnight and many were chased down the Canongate, with offers of drink in Jennie Ha's to delay them.

Queen Mary's Bathhouse

The quaint little turreted building opposite Abbeyhill may well have been a bathhouse or a dressing room for the Royal tennis court which used to adjoin Holyrood Palace. In 1490 it was a gatehouse in the original wall with another at the south west corner, long since demolished. In 1797 a jewelled dagger was discovered inside which is thought to have a connection with the Rizzio murder.

There are two floors with an inside stair from the doorway with a recess near the ceiling in the west wall of the lower room and could have contained the Queen's bath.

Holyrood Palace

The Palace of Holyrood House was originally an 'L' shaped building.

Constructed by James IV for his Queen, Margaret Tudor of England, in the early sixteenth century, the north tower adjacent to the abbey and the frontage from it are of that period. Later Charles II added the south tower and raised the levels of the first storey as well as adding an imposing entranceway in 1680. To replace an unsatisfactory statue of Queen Victoria in the forecourt, Prince Albert caused the present fountain to be erected in 1859, it is modelled upon the ruined fragments of the James V fountain in Linlithgow Palace and is the most elaborate fountain in the City.

Designed by Mathieson, the feature of three faces with only four eyes between them was a humorous touch by the craftsmen who carved the figures, it has no significance. The other figures represent Holyrood personalities. The contractor was the father of Conan Doyle the author.

The statue of King Edward VII in the courtyard was executed by H. S. Gamley RSA. The original plaster model from which the statue was produced was in a Paris studio in 1930 and was brought back to this country by Gamley's nephew, Edward, and Bill McKelvie.

To avoid controversy the inscription reads 'Edward King of Great Britain' and not Edward VII as this King was the first Edward in Scotland.

The inner courtyard of the palace is often regarded as just another example of the classical style of the New Town of Edinburgh, but this part of the Palace was constructed in 1680 long before the New Town or the crescent in Bath were designed, this is one of the finest examples of the exact proportions of the Grecian classical Palladian architecture showing Doric, Ionic and Corinthian orders to perfection.

Waverley Station

Waverley station was built on the site of the physic garden which moved to Leith Walk in 1766, a plaque opposite platform 10 which was unveiled in 1978 confirms this. It is the second largest station in Britain covering 25 acres. Designed by the Chief Engineer of the North British Railway Company, James Bell, it was built over a period of ten years, 1892–1902. It had two signal boxes, the one in Princes Street Gardens, Waverley West, was one of the largest manual signal boxes ever constructed, 260 levers in one continuous frame. A tunnel carried trains north to Scotland Street and Granton Harbour between 1847–1877. The trains ran down by gravity and were pulled up by rope and horse. The tunnel was used as a control room during the war and since then to grow mushrooms. It is now derelict but can still be seen from Scotland Yard adventure playground.

David Livingston Statue

Explorer and missionary, this statue by Mrs D. O. Hill, wife of the famous photographer, was considered too small to be in the open.

Balmoral Hotel

Built as the North British Railway Hotel in 1902 it was designed by Sir William Hamilton Beattie. The clock faces are 13ft (4 metres) in diameter, the minute hand 6ft 3ins (1.9 metres), the hour hand 4ft 6ins. (1.4 metres) long, the clock tower is 195ft high. The clock is always kept three minutes fast so people will not miss trains.

Jenners

Designed by Sir William Hamilton Beattie in 1895 to replace the original, which was destroyed by fire, it was the first steel framed building in Scotland.

Charles Jenner and his friend Kennington were fired for taking a half-day to go to Musselburgh races so started their own business.

Pillars on the corner are carved as women as 'women are the foundation of our business'.

Scott Monument

The work of George Meikle Kemp, a young self-taught architect and Peeblesshire carpenter. Completed in 1844 at a cost of £16,000, the spire is 200ft high and a staircase of 287 steps leads to a balcony at the top. The founds are 50ft (15 metres) deep. The statue of Scott and his dog Maida is in Carrera marble and the sculptor was Sir John Steele. There are 64 characters out of Scott's novels on the monument. Meikle Kemp drowned in the Union Canal in 1844 and never saw it completed.

Dean Village

Prior to the Dean Bridge being built in 1832, traffic for Queensferry descended Bells Brae and crossed the bridge at the Water of Leith village now known as Dean Village (until stagecoaches required an easier route, now by way of Belford Bridge). This bridge was built of stone about 1784, but a wooden bridge of a sort existed here in 1573, although the ford 100 yards upstream was regularly used. Bell owned a flourmill here hence the name Bells Ford. There were 11 mills where Baxters (bakers) ground flour, a tannery and a colony of linen weavers.

Well Court

Sir John Findlay, proprietor of the *Scotsman* newspaper as an experimental community living scheme built the Well Court in 1884 for local workers.

Dean Bridge

When John Learmonth, Lord Provost of Edinburgh, acquired the estates of Nisbet of Dean House he decided a new bridge was needed to give access to his land which he intended to feu for private building. The Cramond Road trustees decided to contribute to the cost but only if there was no toll. It was designed by Thomas Telford. With four arches and a chamber under the road carrying water pipes and electric cables it is possible to walk across the bridge under the road.

Work started in 1829 and was completed in 1831; the man in charge was a civil engineer from Aberdeen named John Gibb, a hard taskmaster who was not above exchanging blows with the workforce.

The bridge was completed six months ahead of the contract date and Gibb refused to hand it over as he was charging sightseers 1d. each to walk across. Learmonth had to wait twenty years before the first houses were built, that being Clarendon Crescent in 1850.

The church on the north end was for many years the Holy Trinity Church, then an electricity transformer station and now a church again, which gives new meaning to the saying 'the power and the glory'.

Kirkbrae House

The building at the south end, at the top of Bells Brae is called Kirkbrae House or the Baxter's house of call, built in 1640 as an inn, it was for many years Stewart's cab office where 'Cabby Stewart' ran his business. It is said he could shout orders at the cab drivers who were ranked at Randolph Crescent. The name Stewart's Cab Office is still on the front step. It is now a private dwelling. Built into the north east wall is the baker's stone of 1619 showing the ripening sun, the wheatsheaves for plenty, the baker's peels (shovels) and the scales for honesty.

The north section on the building on the bridge is a much more recent addition.

National Monument

Built on Calton Hill to commemorate the Scottish dead in the Napoleonic Wars, it was originally to be a copy of the Parthenon in

Athens, but although £12,000 was raised by public subscription the expected Parliamentary grant was not forthcoming and the funds ran out when only twelve of the Grecian Doric columns had been erected.

The lintel stone is the largest single stone to be quarried in Britain. It came from Craigleith Quarry which is now a shopping centre at the junction of Queensferry Road and Craigleith Road.

Nelson's Monument

This 106ft high tower by Robert Burn and Thomas Bonnar, 1816, is built in the shape of an inverted telescope to commemorate Nelson's victory at the Battle of Trafalgar. On Trafalgar Day (21 Oct) it is decorated with flags spelling out his famous message 'England expects that every man shall do his duty'. The time ball on top dates from 1856 and is intended as a time signal for mariners in the Forth who could not hear the one o'clock gun, raised by hand winding at 12.58 GMT, it is triggered by a clock controlled by the Royal Observatory on Blackford Hill at 1 p.m. If the drop fails it is slowly lowered by hand after five minutes.

Other clocks controlled by the same circuit and maintained by James Ritchie & Son are at the University Quad, Registrar House, Waverley Station and City Chambers.

Dugald Stewart

The monument to Dugald Stewart on Calton Hill is in the style of the Temple of Lysicrates in Athens and designed by Wm. Playfair.

Dugald Stewart was one of Edinburgh's most famous philosophers and a friend of Burns.

This monument is often confused with the Burns Monument (in similar style), which is on the other side of Regent Road.

Burns Monument

In the base of Burns Monument there is a large room capable of seating over fifty people which used to contain relics and paintings which are now in Lady Stairs House. The Flaxman statue of Burns is in the Scottish National Portrait Gallery in Queen Street. The monument is by Thomas Hamilton.

Boundary Bar

Now called City Limits this bar at Pilrig was the boundary between Edinburgh and Leith. Prior to 1920 when the amalgamation took place the licensing laws were different in the two areas. A brass plate on the wall marked the boundary which drinkers had to move over when time was called in the other half of the bar.

Mother Aitken's

Seafield Baths, built in 1813 was also a hotel, with comfortable warm rooms. There is a fine Doric portico and a dome. The baths were an innovation in the district with hot and cold, showers and seawater, and superior vapour baths at a cost of one shilling. There was also a large plunge bath, the shape of which is still obvious inside the building. The hotel had a frontage to Leith Sands, the finest part of the beach where Leith horse races were held at this time.

Leith Docks

In order of their formation, Old Dock 1806, Queens 1817, Victoria 1852, Albert 1869, Edinburgh 1881, Imperial 1904. Prior to 1969 Leith Docks were tidal and ships could only enter when the tide was right. In 1969 the greater dock area was enclosed and the west dock lock constructed at the entrance allowing access at any time for all ships.

Leith Police Station

Leith Police Station was originally Leith Town Hall, built in 1828 after an act of Parliament defined the boundaries and arranged for proper cleansing, policing, lighting, etc. Edinburgh appointed three magistrates annually, chosen from a list of nine presented by the retiring Bailies, which allowed Leith some measure of choice. These three, together with the masters of incorporations – mariners, maltmen & brewers, trades and crafts, merchants and trafficers comprised the council – hence the wording on the town hall pediment.

Leith became a parliamentary borough in 1823 with a Town Council of sixteen; this lasted until 1920 when Leith was absorbed into Edinburgh.

Lamb's House

Andrew Lamb's house was where Mary Queen of Scots dined and remained until the evening in 1561. She arrived from France some two weeks earlier than expected and no preparations had been made at Holyrood.

This is the finest specimen of old Leith architecture still standing, although the present building is an early seventeenth century restoration.

Newhaven

James IV founded Newhaven in 1504 to house workers who were building the *Great Michael* which was the biggest vessel at the time. Local people quite erroneously claim that the anchor at Anchorfield is from the *Great Michael* but it actually came from a shipbreaker's yard in Inverkeithing (according to the city architects office) the anchor signifies the seafaring traditions of Newhaven. The anchor at Forth Yacht Club is often confused with the *Great Michael* anchor, but it belonged to an Elizabethan ship which was forced to cut the cable in escaping from Scottish and French ships after bombarding Inchkeith in 1564 and it was recovered in 1899.

Arms of Leith

The arms of Leith as matriculated by the Lord Lyon King of Arms in 1889 show the Madonna and Child surmounted by a blue cloud, but prior to this date there was a church canopy in place of the cloud.

The Marquis of Bute claimed that it was offensive to show the deified figures under a cloud, and took exception to the Lord Lyon's version. He further claimed that the arms of Leith should ascend from the old seal of the early Leith parish church, the collegiate church of Restalrig which features a canopy, but this does not show a galleon with Leith's seafaring connection. Both the town clerk of Leith and the Lord Lyon interpreted the old seal of Leith as showing a cloud.

Granton Slipway

In 1850 when the railway from the Waverley through Scotland Street tunnel extended to Granton, coal was transported to Burntisland by the first train ferry in the world. The ship was the *Leviathan* and by an ingenious method of cables and pulleys operating a movable bogie up and down a slipway trucks were wheeled straight on board at any state of the tide. The slipway at Granton is hidden by a wooden pier but can be seen at the Royal Forth Yacht club area on the middle pier.

Fishwives travelled from Newhaven to Edinburgh by train from the station at Trinity Bridge, they occupied the guards van with their creels of fish and were barred from the normal booking office window when buying tickets, instead they used the fishwife's window outside the booking hall. This window can still be seen although the building is a private residence.

Leith Tolbooth

The Leith Tolbooth was established by order of Mary Queen of Scots in 1565 and demolished in 1819 when a more commonplace jail was erected in its place. It stood approximately in the centre of the Tolbooth Wynd according to old maps.

Ten Commandments

The 1706 panel of the ten commandments was inside the old Tolbooth jail in the High Street. When the Tolbooth was demolished in 1817 the panel was transferred to Calton gaol. It is now in the chapel of Saughton gaol after the demolition of Calton prison in 1936.

Broughton Tolbooth

The Broughton Tolbooth stood where the three shops at the corner of Broughton Street and Barony Street now stand. There is evidence of the old cells in the cellars of these shops extending under the roadway. The Tolbooth was demolished in 1829.

Arms of Mary Queen of Scots

Before James VI ascended to the English throne the unicorns in the Scottish arms were not crowned, so the arms of Mary Queen of Scots in the little chamber in the castle where James VI was born should not show the unicorn supporters wearing crowns. Originally this painting would have the unicorns correctly uncrowned, with the crowns being mistakenly painted in later.

London Street

This was originally the drive leading to Bellevue House, the residence of Lord Provost Drummond to whom is due the credit for the vision and promotion of the new town of Edinburgh. In Drummond's time the house was called Drummond Lodge. It was demolished 1846 due to the building of Scotland Street railway tunnel.

Glassblowers Panels

In Holyrood Road the two plaques sculpted in stone are reminders of the city glassworks, or Holyrood glassworks, where the famous Edinburgh lead crystal was made and which closed in 1904. Not to be confused with the Edinburgh & Leith glass works in Norton Park (off Rossie Place) which is now the Edinburgh Crystal Glass Company and moved to Penicuik in 1969.

King's Landing

The plaque at the water's edge marks the spot where George IV landed in 1822 and the crown above it on the quay was where the Royal foot first touched Scottish soil -' O happy day'. Most Royal landings took place here, including Mary Queen of Scots, Mary of Guelders, Queen of James II, in 1449, Princess Margaret of Denmark, 1469 who married James III, the French princess Madeleine, first wife of James V in 1537. Mons Meg was also landed here in 1829 after having been in London.

King's Wark

The Kings Wark was built by James I and extended by James II as a Royal arsenal, citadel, palace and warehouse. Damaged by Hereford in 1544 it was rebuilt in the reign of Mary Queen of Scots. Stores for the castle garrisons were taken ashore here and warehoused and many cannons and military materials were forged here, it was the principal arsenal of Scotland in Stuart times. A doorway still standing bears the date 1711.

James VI gave the building to Bernard Lindsay who kept a tavern on what was called the Lang or East Sands where the sea began and now called Bernard Street after him. He rebuilt it in 1613 and in 1617 was made an honorary burgess on the occasion of a banquet given to James VI on his only visit to Scotland after becoming James I of England.

Peacock Hotel

In 1767 Thomas Peacock established an inn on wasteland, it became celebrated for fish dinners. The Town Council of Edinburgh had an annual oyster bed inspection from Newhaven, but if the weather was inclement they 'repaired to the Peacock and deemed the inspection successful'. In 1870 the hotel was extended by Mrs Clark who added reconstructed cottages, her daughter took over for twenty years.

Armada Stone

The origin of the Armada Stone in Newhaven is obscure; the lower half is similar to a stone at Trinity House in the Kirkgate and may have been on property owned by the mariner's incorporation in Newhaven.

Note the cross-staff which preceded the sextant and has been obsolete since William of Orange, and the other navigational instruments, the two globes, terrestrial and celestial were always used together in Elizabethan times. The top half with the Armada date, 1588, suggests the relief felt when the threat of Spanish tyranny was lifted. The Thistle and St Andrew's flag appear at the masthead.

Royal College of Physicians

No. 8, the first house to be built in Queen Street, now occupied by the Royal College of Physicians, was built in 1770 by Robert Adam for Baron Orde of the Exchequer. The Baron did not like his servants to cross the road in front of the house with bundles of washing to lay out on the bleaching grounds opposite, so he built a tunnel under Queen Street which is still there, although now blocked off by a brick wall inside. The garden's end of the tunnel is used by the gardeners for storage.

York Place

No. 47 York Place was the home of Alexander Nasmyth, the artist who painted the well known portrait of Robert Burns, and also designed the beautiful temple at St Bernard's Well. On the front of the building is a plaque which is the crest on the Nasmyth coat of arms. Notice the device of the broken hammer at the foot of the plaque. The heraldic pun is that he was 'nae smith'.

York Place Casino

The casino occupies the site of St George's Chapel, built in 1793 by James Adam, brother of the more famous Robert. This was one of the first Scottish Episcopalian chapels built after the repeal of the penal laws of 1718 against Jacobitism, which were in force in the early eighteenth century.

Prior to 1685 the Episcopalian bishops had taken the oath of allegiance to the Stuart James VII and so were Jacobites. After closure it was for many years John Glendinning & Sons plumbers' showroom.

Baxter's Place

No. 1 Baxter's place was the house of Robert Louis Stevenson's grandfather, where the young lad often visited and played on the slopes of Calton Hill at the rear.

Opposite, at the corner of Union Street, was the shop where he bought scenery for his toy theatre – 'Penny plain and Twopence coloured' per scene.

Great King Street

At the East End of Great King Street, Sir James M. Barrie (author of *Peter Pan*) lodged with Mrs Edwards while a student at Edinburgh University.

At the West End a plaque seems to commemorate the founder of the first Edinburgh Festival, but this was the Edinburgh Musical Society Festival, and had no connection with the modern International Festival of Music and Drama.

Colonies

The 'Colonies of Stockbridge' were built on the site of Glenogle House in 1861 by the Co-operative Building Company as accommodation for artisans. They consist of ten terraces – the upper and lower flats each enter from different terraces. On the gable end walls are plaques of various trades and crafts. There are six other sites of colonies in Edinburgh.

Hamilton Place

The public convenience was at one time the fire station, which housed small hand pulled appliances which could quickly be at the scene of local fires without having to negotiate the difficult hills of Edinburgh. The building alongside was the police station.

Canonmills

At the corner of Munro Place was the little known school run by a Mr Henderson, which was attended by the seven year old Robert Louis Stevenson. After a short while the school moved to India Street and the Stevenson family moved to Heriot Row and RLS continued at Mr Henderson's school until he went to Edinburgh University.

On the wall of Canonmills filling station is the stone 'The Baxter's Land 1686' which was taken from the old granary and mill which stood nearby.

Tie Stones

When building the hospital block in 1896 the Victorians proposed to improve, and make Edinburgh Castle more picturesque, by erecting a false bartisan tower with turrets and battlements on the restored curtain wall in front. This was abandoned after public objections were voiced, but the tie stones to anchor the project are clearly seen from Princes Street. Edinburgh Castle is a tourist attraction mainly because it was not built as a tourist attraction.

Greyfriar's Kirk

In Greyfriar's Kirk the heraldic window by James Ballantine, in memory of the scholar James Buchanan who died in 1582, shows what purports to be the arms of Mary Queen of Scots in the lower left corner. But this is the English version of arms first marshalled by James VI in 1603, and with the initials 'M' and 'R' (Mary Regina) must be the arms of Mary II, daughter of James VII and joint sovereign with William of Orange. Perhaps, when this version was selected in 1845 the initials 'M' and 'R' were mistakenly accepted as indicating that the arms were of Mary Queen of Scots.

West Parliament Square

In Parliament Square West, the line of the stones in the walkway to allow lawyers to cross dry-shod between the High Street and the law courts, was allowed to remain when the whole muddied area was cobbled over. The two brass studs marked C. S. 1 and C. S. 2 mark the cab stances; C. S. 3 and C. S. 4 are at the Thistle Chapel.

Abbey Strand

The Abbey Strand was the covered entrance to the Palace of Holyrood House. Known as the 'Foir Yett' or fore gate it was demolished in 1755.

Castle Rock

The wording on the metal plaque on the west face of the Castle Rock facing Castle Terrace car park reads,
'On this spot a bomb fell during the German air raid, 2 April 1916.'

Riddles Court

The plaque at Riddles Court seems to infer that Bailie John MacMorran, who was shot dead by a Royal High School pupil when trying to quell a riot in 1595, was present at the banquet entertaining James VI which took place in 1598. What is not well known is that Bailie John MacMorran left his house to his less famous brother, Ninian, who was himself a Bailie in 1598. (Note the incorrect spelling of Bailie).

In Bailie MacMorran's house the painted ceilings of 1897 commemorate the date of the house, 1592, and panels show various dates of University interest, also the occasion of the dinner given in honour of James VI, his Queen and the Duke of Holstein 'with great solemnitie and merriness'.

Bowfoot Well

On the Bowfoot Well at the East End of the Grassmarket are the arms of the Richardson brothers who restored it in 1861. A reference to the motto found in an old book 'virtute acquiritur honos', led to finding that Ralph Richardson was granted arms in 1836. The blazon is or on a fess engrailed azure, between a bull's head couped in chief, and a galley oars in saltire in base sable, two fleurs-de-lis argent, all within a bordure gules charged with eight bezants.

Royal Infirmary

The curved building in the centre of the Royal Infirmary complex is part of the original George Watson's hospital which occupied this site in 1738.

The school was removed to the building built in 1818 for the Merchant Maidens Hospital at the foot of Archibald Place in 1870 and finally moved to Myreside in 1931.

Scottish Parliament

The Architect was Enrique Morales, a Spaniard whose design based on upturned boats was controversial. The first estimate was £40 million, but as M. S. Ps kept changing the plans the cost had risen to £150 million by September 2001 and to £350 million by January 2003.

Deid Chack

Abolished by Lord Provost Wm. Creech in 1812, this was the meal eaten by Magistrates after attending an execution.

The Royal Society

On 22 April 1662 the Royal Society was constituted by Royal Charter from King Charles II.

The Maiden

Now in the Royal Museum of Scotland this was the Scottish guillotine and the prototype for the one designed by Dr Guillotine. Made in Halifax and brought to Edinburgh by Regent Morton it was used for executions between 1565–1710. It is somewhat ironical that Regent Morton was himself beheaded by the Maiden in 1581. In 1661 the Marquis of Argyle was beheaded.

Prestonfield House Hotel

Originally named Priest Field and owned by the Scottish Crown it was purchased by Sir James Dick in 1677. It was burned to the ground in a religious riot in 1680. He received £800 from the Crown towards rebuilding. The building was completed in 1687 to the design of Sir William Bruce. It became a hotel in 1958. One of the early owners staked the house in a card game, betting on the ace of clubs. When he won he had trees planted in the shape of the ace of clubs with the main house at the centre. To get a view of this it is necessary to climb Arthur's Seat from where it is plainly visible.

Society of Writers to the Signet

Originally, the Signet was the private seal of the early Scottish Kings, and the Writers to the Signet were those authorised to supervise its use and later, to act as clerks to the courts. The earliest recorded use of the Signet was in 1369, but the society did not take definite shape until 1594, when the King's secretary, as Keeper of the Signet, granted commissions to a deputy keeper and 18 other Writers.

The function of the Society has of course changed much since then, but every summons initiating an action in the court of session still 'passes the Signet' meaning that it is stamped with the Royal Seal. The present Signet was made by the Royal Mint in 1954.

Today the Society is consulted on many legal matters and is represented on the governing bodies of many organisations. There are now about 900 members, most being solicitors in private practice in Edinburgh.

The Society is particularly noted for its ownership of the Signet Library, one of the finest Georgian buildings in the country. The library contains about 65,000 books, of which almost half are legal, of the rest, a large number are of Scottish interest.

The library, begun in 1810 to the design of Robert Reid, with principal interiors by William Stark, originally comprised a lower library for the Society, completed in 1815, and an upper library for the Faculty of Advocates, completed in 1822, in time for the visit of King George IV to the City. The entrance hall and stair, originally by Reid, were reconstructed in 1819 by William Playfair, and again in 1834 by William Burn, after the Faculty had sold the upper library to the Society.

The cupola painting, by Thomas Stothard, depicts Apollo and the Muses, accompanied by the following poets, orators, historians and philosophers: Burns, Shakespeare, Homer, Milton, Virgil, Cicero, Demosthenes, Herodotus, Livy, Hume, Robertson, Gibbon, Newton, Bacon, Napier and Adam Smith.

Pneumatic Tyres

The idea of pneumatic tyres was conceived by Robert William Thomson in the 1840s but John Boyd Dunlop was the first to develop and patent a practical version of it after watching his son having difficulties riding his trike over cobbled roads in 1888. In ten years it had practically replaced solid tyres and had been implemented for use in automobiles by the Michelin Brothers. Robert Thomson is buried in the Dean Cemetery.

Sir Alexander Leslie

He was made the 1st Earl of Leven by Charles I in 1644, a brilliant general he outmanoeuvred Oliver Cromwell at Leith before being defeated at the Battle of Dunbar. A bent and crooked man he is the inspiration for the nursery rhyme 'There was a crooked man who had a crooked house' which is still evident at Balcomie Castle in Fife where the nursery rhyme is carved under the stair. He bought the estate in 1635 and died there aged 89.

S. S. Sirius

On 22 April 1838 the 703 ton *Sirius* built by R. Menzies and Son Leith, and carrying 90 passengers, reached Sandy Hook, New York to become the first ship to cross the Atlantic entirely under steam. Shortage of fuel forced the crew to burn doors and furniture to complete the 18 day voyage. Brunel's steamship the *Great Western* arrived a day later.

Ned Barnie

Born in 1896, in 1950 he was the first Scot to swim the Channel and in 1951 he was the first to swim the channel in both directions. A science teacher at Portobello High School he swam in the Forth every day and to celebrate his 70th birthday swam the two miles from Fisherrow in Musselburgh to Portobello. He died aged 87 on Christmas Day 1983.

Floral Clock

First created in 1903 it was the idea of John McHattie, the city's parks superintendent, with assistance from James Ritchie and Son clockmakers. Using 30,000 bedding plants it takes the gardeners four weeks to assemble and each year has a different theme, celebrating such events as the Queen's Golden Jubilee. To celebrate its centenary a replica was taken to Chelsea Flower Show where it won a gold medal. The display lasts from May until October, but following the success at Chelsea it is intended to have a winter display for the Christmas festival and Hogmanay celebrations.

Tour One:
Tour of Royal Mile

Castle Esplanade, Lawnmarket, High Street, Canongate, Abbey Strand.

Edinburgh Castle was probably an Iron Age fort at one time, but all buildings earlier than 1314 except St Margaret's Chapel were destroyed by Robert Bruce to prevent further English occupation and rebuilt 50 years later. It has changed hands many times: by permission, by being given as a ransom, besieged and bombarded into surrender, but has never been taken by open assault except by two Scottish attacks.

Sir William Kirkcaldy of Grange held the castle on behalf of the exiled Mary Queen of Scots when she was a prisoner of Elizabeth I of England against the Protestant Scots who claimed the baby James VI as rightful sovereign. Eventually after a five year siege, during which Elizabeth sent artillery to batter the walls, two of the three towers were destroyed and choked the great well. Kirkcaldy was forced to surrender through lack of water and was promised leniency. Regent Morton dishonoured the pledge and hanged the gallant soldier.

In 1313, while the castle was in English hands, Randolph Earl of Moray scaled the face of the castle rock with 20 men and captured the castle for his uncle Robert the Bruce. He had with him a soldier called William Francis who had been one of the earlier Scots garrison and who had discovered a secret route in and out of the castle which he had used to slip out to meet his sweetheart in the Grassmarket.

In one of the rooms, on 19 June 1566, Mary Queen of Scots gave birth to James (VI) of Scotland and (I) of England.

A time signal was first suggested in 1846 by a banker called Hewat who had seen one operating in Paris and the town council decided to send representatives to Paris to see for themselves. They came back saying that the gun was fired 12 times at noon. It is said however that the canny Scots decided that by waiting an hour they need only fire one shot thus saving 11 shots. The real reason for one o'clock being chosen is that mariners in Leith would see the signal because at 12 o'clock they would be too busy checking their sextants against the sun.

Before the time signal mariners would have had to take their chronometers in a wheelbarrow up to Calton Hill observatory and check them against the clock set in the wall. The clock was called a politician's clock as it was two faced, one inside the building and one outside.

The one o'clock gun was first fired in 1861 and is fired every day except Sundays, Good Friday and Christmas Day. It is a supplement for a time ball that has operated at a fixed time on top of the Nelson Monument on Calton Hill since 1851. The Astronomer Royal at the time, Professor Charles Paizzi Smyth, worked out how to link the time ball and gun. A fantastic feat of nineteenth century electrical engineering saw a 4000ft copper cable linking the time ball and gun. At the time this was the longest electrical wire in Europe. A chain connected to the castle clock was hooked to the gun's fuse and at one o'clock a weight dropped and the gun fired automatically. Some tour guides have been known to tell tourists that if the gunner's aim is correct the ball will fall 'but that he missed twice last week'. When the ball drops the gunner gets a round of applause.

Scottish National War Memorial

This contains the names of service personnel killed during the two world wars and has a bronze relief depicting every branch of the military. Children can be kept busy trying to find the animals which include a camel, a canary, a pigeon, a horse and a dog.

The Scottish regalia are also on display. They are the Scottish crown, the sceptre, and the Sword of Scotland and also the Stone of Destiny or as it is also known the Stone of Scone. It is alleged to be Jacob's pillow and was kept at Scone palace near Perth, where Scottish Kings and Queens were crowned including McBeth. The last Scottish king

to be crowned on it was Edward Balliol in 1292. It was stolen by
Edward I and for 700 years was kept under the coronation throne in
Westminster abbey. On Christmas Eve 1950 Ian Hamilton, a law
student at Glasgow University, assisted by three others stole the stone
back. When it was recovered it was returned to Westminster and on
30 November 1996 it was finally returned to Scotland.

Mons Meg

A romantic story claims that 'Mons Meg' was constructed in 1455
for the siege of Threave castle, by a Monnance blacksmith who named
it after his wife Margaret, but it is more likely that it was forged at
Mons in Belgium and brought to this country by James II in 1450.
It was in use until 1862 when it burst firing a salute at the castle in
honour of the Duke of York – later James VII. It was taken to London
in1754 and restored to Edinburgh in 1829 by Sir Walter Scott's efforts.

Firing a stone ball of 5cwt it had a range of about one and a quarter
miles. Two men with a wheelbarrow were employed to collect the
stones and return them to the castle. It became red hot after each
firing and required time to cool down. The gun carriage is
comparatively recent and is modelled on the design of a very old stone
one just inside the drawbridge entrance. At the drawbridge the figures
of Robert the Bruce on the left and Sir William Wallace on the right
were unveiled in 1929.

Robert the Bruce (1274–1329)

From a Norman family, Bruce was the architect of Scottish
independence from England. Crowned King in 1306 at Scone he
fought a guerrilla war against Edward I, after many setbacks he was
inspired to try again after watching a spider. He defeated a superior
English army at Bannockburn in June 1314. In 1328 Edward III
signed the treaty of Edinburgh with Bruce which recognised Scotland's
independence.

William Wallace (1270–1305)

A fighter for national independence he defeated the Earl of Surrey at
Stirling Bridge and was appointed guardian of Scotland. He was
defeated at the battle of Falkirk by Edward I and he went to France

to enlist the help of the French. On his return he was betrayed to the English and executed in London by hanging, disembowelling, and beheading, 'hung drawn and quartered'.

Sasine of Nova Scotia

To make money Charles I sold baronetcies of Nova Scotia in Canada, the new barons had to take sasine or possession on the actual terrain. To save a long and dangerous journey this part of the Esplanade was legally declared part of Nova Scotia by Royal Mandate. The number of baronets was to be limited to 150, each paying £3000 for the privilege. The first one was Sir Robert Gordon of Gordonstoun in 1625. In the next 24 years 64 baronets took sasine. In 1953 the Prime Minister of the province sprinkled a token handful of earth here.

Duke of York and Albany (1763–1827)

Erected in 1836 as the nursery rhyme says 'at the top of the hill' this refers to the Grand Old Duke of York of the rhyme. He was commander of the British army during the Flanders campaign of 1793 but a series of tactical blunders led to him being fired.

Duke of Albany's Own Highlanders

Commemorating men who died during the Afghanistan campaign 1878–80.

Originally raised as the Earl of Seaforth's regiment in 1778.

In 1880 a forced march of 300 miles was ordered, temperatures ranged between 130 at midday to freezing at night. For 22 days the army of 10,000 troops, 11,000 animals and 8,000 camp followers marched between Kabul and Kandahar.

On the 1 September they attacked the Afghan army, in the battle the commanding officer and one officer and eleven men were killed.

Gordon Highlanders

This commemorates the fallen in the Boer War of 1899–1902. At the siege of Ladysmith the Gordons were part of the British garrison 78th Highland Regiment (Indian mutiny). A Celtic cross in Redhall stone this memorial was the work of a local sculptor, S Hunter, the railings were constructed at Leith fort. According to the inscription 28 NCOs and 220 privates fell in India.

Kings Own Scottish Borderers

This commemorating the raising of the regiment on the 19th March 1689 by David Leslie the 3rd Earl of Leven when 1000 men were enlisted in 2 hours. The regiment was raised to defend lowlands against the Jacobite highlanders. At the battle of Killiekrankie Leslie's regiment was one of only two which did not run away before the highlanders' onslaught.

John Graham of Claverhouse 'Bonnie Dundee' won the battle but was himself killed. After the battle the Edinburgh regiment took the song 'Bonnie Dundee' as its regimental march.

To honour its achievement at Killiekrankie the magistrates of Edinburgh conferred on Leven's regiment the unique right of recruiting by beat of drum in the city and of marching through the city at any time with drums beating, colours flying and bayonets fixed.

Colonel Kenneth Douglas Mackenzie C. B. (1811–1873)

He served for 42 years in the 92nd Highlanders and on the staff of the army in many parts of the world.

Princess Louise's Argyllshire Highlanders

Later known as the Argyll and Sutherland Highlanders they were raised by the Duke of Argyll in 1794 following a request by George II in the aftermath of the French revolution.

Scottish Horse

In memory of the officers and men killed in action in the South African war (1901–1902) the regimental motto 'Nemo Me Impune Lacessit'('no one touches me with impunity)-the motto of Scotland.

Scottish Horse was recruited in South Africa mainly from men of Scottish descent. On 3 September 1902 Scottish Horse disbanded at Edinburgh castle. 100 men stayed in South Africa and joined the Natal mounted police.

Ensign Ewart

Under this granite block lie the remains of Ensign Ewart, a sergeant in the Scots Greys who at the battle of Waterloo captured the standard of the French single-handed.

Earl Haig (1861–1928)

Sir Dhunjibhoy Bomanji, an Indian Pharisee, gifted the statue.

Haig was Commander–in-Chief of the British army in the Second World War. He came under heavy criticism for his strategies which needlessly caused loss of life among British infantry. After the war he worked for the British legion in the after care of wounded veterans. He instituted the distribution of poppies for Remembrance Day.

Canonball House

Dated 1630, this building has two cannonballs imbedded in the west-facing wall; (facing Castle Esplanade) they are reputed to have been fired at Holyrood palace when Bonnie Prince Charlie lodged there in 1745 after he had captured Edinburgh but not the castle.

Ramsay Gardens

The poet Allan Ramsay built his house here in 1740 and because of its distinctive shape it was known as the 'Goose pie' house. His son Allan Ramsay the painter added a terrace of houses in 1768.

Castlehill Reservoir

Built in 1849 and closed in 1997 it held 2 million gallons of water. It replaced an earlier water house of 1672 which took water from Comiston springs.

Peter Brusche a German engineer brought the first gravity fed water supply in Europe here in a lead pipe of 3inch bore. He was to be paid a fee of £2,900 but at the opening ceremony an airlock formed in the pipe and when the tap was turned on no water appeared. Brusche rode out to find the fault, took fright, and never returned. A workman tapped the pipe with his hammer and the water flowed freely.

Earlier supplies were from stagnant lochs or draw wells which were generally contaminated. From this cistern wooden pipes (elm) fitted together with tapered ends fed the wells down the Royal Mile with fresh water. The building has now been converted into a Tartan-weaving centre. On the wall facing the Esplanade there is a small bronze well known as the Witches Well.

The Witches Well

Between 1479 and 1722 more than 300 women branded as witches were burned at the stake near this spot. The well shows the two faces of witchcraft – the serene and the evil – some of these women were not involved in witchcraft at all but were victims of the superstition and religious bigotry or personal vendettas brought about by local gossip. The mere ownership of a cat could be enough to arouse suspicion.

Castle Boundary Stone

Edinburgh Castle and Esplanade are Crown property as distinct from civic property. The boundary extends from the extremity of the Esplanade northwards in a direct line across the railway line to a boundary stone in the shrubbery in Princes Street Gardens. By the east footbridge it continues westwards behind the Ross bandstand in a line with the shrubbery to the west footbridge and back over the railway, thereafter it follows round the castle rock to Kings Stables Road into the Grassmarket and directly up Castle Wynd, south up to the esplanade again to include all of the castle rock. There are 23 stones in all.

Whisky Heritage Centre

This building used to house Castlehill School but now shows the whisky industry development over the past 300 years.

The Outlook Tower and Camera Obscura

On this site stood the town mansion of the Laird o'Cockpen. In the 1850s the building was bought by Maria Theresa Short, an optician, who added two floors and added the camera obscura as an experiment in optics. A superior lens was installed in 1945 and is still operational today. Sir Patrick Geddes the pioneer town planner took over Outlook Tower as a museum in 1891.

The Highland Tollbooth Church

Designed by James Gillespie Graham and built in 1842–44, at 73 metres the octagonal spire is the tallest in Edinburgh and the cross on top is the point that sentries at the castle entrance keep their eyes fixed on. The sevices were held in Gaelic and the congregation moved to Greyfriars Kirk in June 1981. It is now called the Hub and is headquarters for the Festival.

Church of Scotland General Assembly Hall

Built on the site of the palace of Mary of Guise, Queen of James V and mother of Mary Queen of Scots, this was demolished in1861 The General Assembly of the Church of Scotland takes place here each year. In 1999 it became the temporary home of the first Scottish Parliament since the union of parliaments in 1707.

In the middle of the road at the junction of Johnston Terrace and Lawnmarket stood the butter Tron weighhouse which was demolished in 1822 when the road was widened for the visit of George IV.

The Ambassadors of France, England and the Low Countries had their residences here. Also in the area was the home of Major Weir, commander of the town guard in 1649. He was never seen without his staff who it was said used to walk in front of him holding a lamp and to post letters for him. In 1670 he went to the magistrates and told them that he was in league with the devil and that he practised sorcery. Although there was no other evidence against him he was found guilty and hanged and burned at the stake. When his walking staff was thrown onto the fire it was said to have 'wriggled and writhed and to have taken on a life of its own.' His sister also pleaded guilty and was hanged in the Grassmarket. She ripped open her bodice to expose herself so that she could die with as much shame as possible. Their house lay empty for over a hundred years and neighbours told of strange noises and tapping sounds coming from the empty house. It was demolished in 1878. A favourite ghost story tells of a black coach pulled by black horses snorting fire driven by a headless man being seen hurtling down the Lawnmarket on the night before one of the residents died.

Mylnes Court

Built by Robert Mylne, the King's Master Mason in 1690 this was the first example of open court planning. Mylne also designed extensions to Holyrood Palace, the Castle and St Paul's Cathedral in London where he is buried.

One of the features is the 'passing railings' which are bent outwards at the bottom so that two ladies wearing crinoline dresses could pass each other with dignity. The buildings fell into disrepair through neglect and were restored in 1970 by the university and are now halls of residence for students.

James Court

Built between 1725–27 by James Brownhill after whom it is named, it has three entrances west, mid and east which fell into decline with the rise of the new town. Some of the original buildings were destroyed by fire in 1857 but were rebuilt shortly after.

Some notable residents were David Hume philosopher, Adam Smith author of the *Wealth of Nations*. James Boswell biographer of Samuel Johnson, entertained Johnson here. Boswell a notorious social climber rescued Johnson from his lodgings in a coaching inn. Taking him to his house they had to go down a flight of stairs and along a dark passage way, Boswell enquired if Johnson was following him without difficulty and Johnson replied that he could smell him in the dark. On entering the house Johnson could not understand how there was daylight coming in the windows as he thought they were underground. He did not know that the back of the building faced over what is the Mound today.

Gladstone's Land

Rebuilt by Thomas Gledstanes in 1617 it shows the original arched style of the Royal Mile. After Hereford's invasion in 1544 houses were built of stone to minimise the risk of fire and also enabled higher lands to be built. As the population grew owners built out over the roadway by seven feet at the first floor level leaving the footpath clear underneath. Earlier they had been built with timber from the burgh muir and the forest of Drumsheugh. This effectively reduced the roadway by fourteen feet. In 1935 restoration work uncovered painted ceilings. The name Gledstanes comes from the Scots word Gled meaning a hawk or kite, and at the first floor there is a gilded hawk with a rat in its claws.

On the left there is an excellent example of forestairs which most houses had in the seventeenth century (there is another example outside Moubary house). Generally pigs were kept under the forestairs and allowed the run of the street during the day, foraging for food and causing obvious filth.

The house is now a museum and is owned by the National Trust for Scotland.

Lady Stairs Close

This leads through to a courtyard in which stands Lady Stairs House which was built in 1622 by Sir William Gray who married Gidia Smith and, as was the custom, they had their initials and the date carved into the lintel above the door. In 1719 the widow of the 1st Earl of Stair purchased the house and it is after her that it is named. After her death in 1731 the house passed to her son the second Earl of Stair who married the widow of the first Viscount Primrose, a most beautiful woman who turned heads whenever she appeared. Her marriage to Primrose was a disaster, he was a cruel man who beat her regularly and on one occasion she jumped half-naked from a window to escape his murderous intentions, thereafter he fled abroad. Some time later a fortune teller visited the town and Lady Stair had him visit her. He had her look into a mirror, when the smoke cleared she saw a marriage ceremony taking place. When the minister asked if anyone knew of a reason why the marriage should not go ahead the door burst open and her brother came in brandishing a sword and stopped the ceremony. She told no one but recorded the details in her diary. When her brother returned from overseas she quizzed him about it and he confirmed that her husband had tried to enter a bigamous marriage. When he died in 1706 she vowed never to marry again. However she had not bargained for the determination of the second Earl of Stair, he was a great admirer of her beauty and had proposed marriage several times but she had always rejected him. However he bribed one of her servants to allow him to hide in her house overnight and in the morning appeared at the window wearing his nightshift and people passing by assumed he had spent the night with her. To save her reputation she agreed to marry him. One evening, returning home drunk after an evening spent drinking with friends they had an argument and he struck her. Next morning, realising what he had done he promised never to touch another drop of wine unless she herself poured it, a promise he kept until his death in 1747. The Earl of Rosebery acquired the house in 1895 and spent two years restoring it. He presented it to the city in 1907 and it is now the Writer's Museum dedicated to Scotland's three literary geniuses, Robert Burns, Sir Walter Scott and Robert Louis Stevenson. The house features an early form of burglar alarm known as a 'trip stair'.

The trip stair was a feature of many Edinburgh houses, one or more steps were made higher than normal, the occupants were familiar with them but the intruder would stumble and betray his presence.

Riddles Court

In the courtyard stands the house of Bailie Macmorran who was killed in 1595. The boys of the high school rioted and barricaded themselves in a dispute over reduced holidays. Bailie Macmorran was called to negotiate but as he approached the door he was shot and killed. The perpetrator was William Sinclair, son of the Chancellor of Caithness. Macmorran's family wanted retribution but as the Sinclairs were wealthy he went unpunished. Sinclair persuaded James VI to use his influence on the magistrates to allow his son to go free. David Hume lived here before moving to James Court.

In 1598 James VI and his Danish Queen attended a banquet here.

The plaque at the entrance seems to infer that John Macmorran was present at the banquet but what is not so well known is that Bailie John Macmorran left his house to his brother Ninian who was himself a Bailie in 1598. Note the incorrect spelling of bailie on the plaque.

Turnpike stairs ascended in a clockwise direction so that a house could be defended by a swordsman with a sword in his right hand. One famous family called Kerr were taught to attack with swords in their left hands giving rise to the expression corrie handed.

Brodie's Close

Home of Francis Brodie, a highly skilled, well respected Deacon of the incorporation of Wrights; his work was much in demand and his business flourished. His only son William, who was also a highly skilled craftsman was a playboy, waster, and dissolute gambler who had two separate families both unknown to each other, preferring the company of drunkards, gamblers and other low lifes who frequented the drinking and gambling dens. After his father's death William inherited the business but instead of obtaining lucrative work in the growing new town Brodie preferred gambling and was soon heavily in debt and needed money quickly. He turned to crime, robbing houses where he had done work by simply taking a wax impression of the key and returning at night to rob the premises.

Brass studs in the road at the corner of George IV Bridge and High Street mark the site of the public gallows, the last public execution took place in 1864 when a murderer named George Bryce was hanged. William Burke was hanged here on 29 January 1829 and Deacon Brodie on 1 October 1788.

David Hume Statue (1711–76)

Philosopher and historian and man of the enlightenment, so radical were his ideas that he ran the risk of prosecution and he failed to secure any academic post. He did not dare publish his 'Dialogue concerning natural religion' during his lifetime. Academics now acclaim him as one of the most influential philosophers of his time. The monument was commissioned by the Saltire Society to mark its 60th anniversary in 1996 and was unveiled on St Andrews's Day 1997 by Sir Stewart Sutherland, Principal of the University of Edinburgh, and was designed and sculpted by Alexander Stoddart, an Edinburgh man.

Well in the Street

Out of ten originals this is one of five in the old town which supplied water which was gravity fed through hollowed out elm trees (elm being water resistant) from Castlehill Reservoir, it was then carried to houses for a half penny a cask. The people who carried it were known as water cadies, a corruption of the French word cadet, and were a forerunner of today's golf caddies.

In west Parliament Square the line of the stones is the walkway which allowed lawyers to cross dry shod between the High Street and the law courts, this has been allowed to remain when the whole muddy area was cobbled over. On the walkway there are two brass markers CS 1 and CS 2 they mark the site of the cab rank, there are two further marks CS 3 and CS 4 on the east facing wall of St Giles.

Heart of Midlothian

Causey stones laid out in the shape of a heart and immortalised by Sir Walter Scott, in the Waverley novel of that name mark the site of the door to the Tolbooth prison which was demolished in 1817 as it blocked the High Street. It still is the custom to spit on it for luck when passing the spot.

The brass setts in the roadway mark the outline of the prison. When it was demolished the key and the door to the condemned cell were presented to Sir Walter Scott and he had them incorporated into his house at Abbottsford.

5th Duke of Buccleuch (1806–84)

Dressed in the robes of the Garter, this is the design of Dr Rowland Anderson. Six panels showing historical incidents in the Buccleuch family are by Clark Stanton. Six figures representing the virtues of the Duke are by Birnie Rhind, while six panels by Stuart Burnett depict incidents in the Duke's life.

He paid for the erection of Granton harbour and breakwater out of his own pocket at a cost of £500,000. Queen Victoria landed there in 1842.

High Kirk of St Giles

Saint Giles was a Greek hermit living in the forest of Nîmes in France about 600 AD. During a royal hunt a wounded hind took refuge in his cave and was given sanctuary, which was respected by the hunting party, but in the confusion an arrow was shot into the cave which penetrated St Giles' hand. The figure above the west door of the church shows St Giles with the hind and the arrow through his right hand.

Inside there are some coloured glass windows showing the arrow through his left hand. Although it has not been a cathedral since 1688 it is still commonly known as one.

St Giles, dedicated in 1150, was the first parish church in Edinburgh but there had been a church on this site since 854.

In 1385 it was burned by Richard II leaving only four massive central pillars standing and was rebuilt in stone in 1454. William Preston of Gorton presented a sacred relic, the arm bone of St Giles mounted in gold with a diamond ring on its finger. In 1466 it became Collegiate and the crown steeple dates from 1490. John Knox preached here in 1560 as minister until 1572. In 1637 Charles I elevated St Giles to a cathedral but it reverted to the Presbyterian High Kirk in 1688. The restoration by Burn in 1829 was known as 'sacrilegious misdeeds', except for the tower the whole exterior dates from this time. In 1633 the church was turned into an Episcopal Cathedral and in 1637 Jenny Geddes threw her stool at Dean Hanna as he attempted to conduct a Episcopal service, with the words 'wha daur say mass in my lug'. In 1639 episcopacy was abolished. Sir William Chambers planned to restore the church but died before it was finished. St Giles has a curious outside tower attached to, and spoiling the symmetry of, the twelfth century Crown spire, it contains a spiral turnpike stair with an entrance at the base and another door at the top giving access to one of the arches of the crown. The arch is crowstepped, all the others are castellated, so that one may ascend to the central gallery of the steeple apex. A watchman may have been stationed there as a lookout or firewatcher in the times when buildings were constructed of timber and St Giles' steeple was the highest point in Edinburgh.

In 1912 the clock, which was installed in 1585, was removed from the tower leaving the bell, which today still confuses people when rung as they think it belongs to the Tron Kirk. In 1911 Sir Robert Lorimer designed the Thistle Chapel. The most ancient and most noble Order of the Thistle is the highest order of chivalry in Scotland which was founded by James III in the fifteenth century. There are only sixteen Knights of the Thistle and the order is a personal appointment by the sovereign.

All the materials used in the construction of the chapel came from Scotland. The woodwork is carved oak by the brothers W. & A. Clow of Edinburgh. The floor is granite from Ailsa Craig with small squares of marble from Iona, the stone is from Cullalo quarry near Aberdour.

On each stall is a stall plate showing the coat of arms belonging to the present occupier and also the predecessors.

Signet Library

This has probably the finest example of interior design in the old town.

The Society of Writers to the Signet was formed in 1594, and in 1722 decided that Scots law books and statutes be purchased, and opened a library in Writers Close. In 1809 the society decided to move to buildings which would be built closer to Parliament Hall. The new buildings were completed in 1815 and the upper hall was purchased in 1826. The halls are used to assemble the procession of the Knights of the Thistle for the short walk to the Thistle Chapel.

Parliament Hall

Built in 1638 by the citizens of Edinburgh, as Charles I would not pay the cost (£11,000) as promised, it housed the Scottish Parliament until 1707 which earlier had met in the Tolbooth and the Castle banqueting hall. After 1707 the hall became the seat of the law courts and until 1819 cases were tried in the hall, often two or three at a time, competing with the babble of the crowd walking up and down, a practice still followed today by lawyers as they cannot be overheard whilst discussing the strategies of their cases.

In the corridor there are a number of wooden boxes with the name of the lawyer on them and they contain their legal documents tied up with pink tape. This is the origin of the saying 'tied up with red tape'.

A painted glass window depicts the inauguration of the Court of Session in St Giles by James V in 1532. The spectacular roof popularly called a hammerbeam roof is wrong, as this is strictly barrel vaulted. The old gothic frontage was spoiled in 1808 by Robert Reid to make a symmetrical façade of Parliament square, note the false windows outside the hall facing the square and also at the south east corner where there is nothing behind them. Underneath is the laigh or low parliament hall which Oliver Cromwell used as a stable.

Statue of Charles II

This statue of Charles II is the oldest lead equestrian statue in the country, dating from 1685. Originally this was to be a statue of Oliver Cromwell but on the restoration of the monarchy the city decided that it should be Charles II instead. He is dressed in the garb of a Roman general but has stirrups and spurs, neither of which were used in Roman times. Between the shoulder blades there is a second face which may suggest that the king was devious. A translation of the inscription on the statue is: 'To Charles II, most august, most magnificent, the invincible ruler of Britain, France and Ireland, upon whose birth, providence smiled at the very moment when a star was conspictious in the noon day sky and who after a youth spent in arms under his father and after the latter in the end had been beheaded, maintained his own right for two years with energy indeed, but without success: for unable to cope with a rebellion that was too often victorious he was compelled to change his country for almost a decade .... Abroad however despite the pacts, the wiles, the threats and military power of the usurper, he was defeated and protected by the power of heaven, and at length emerging like the sun all the brighter from the clouds that enveloped him he returned to his own realms without any shedding of blood and simply through recognition of his lawful claim. Whereupon he established, enlarged, strengthened and confirmed the church, the state peace and commerce. Then winning fame by his war with Holland he became the arbiter of peace and war with his embattled neighbours. Finally when the old rebellion showed signs of recrudescence he checked the basilisk while it was still in embryo, crushed it and trod it underfoot by sheer sagacity and not by force of arms. To him therefore, a prince of marvels in a season of profound peace and at the height of his glory this monument is erected.'

Somewhere behind the statue is the grave of John Knox who died in 1572.

Mercat Cross

From the fourteenth century this is the scene of the most important proclamations celebrations and executions. One story tells of the night before the battle of Flodden, ghostly heralds appeared at the cross and read out a list of names that would be killed in the battle. A merchant named Richard Lawson was walking down the High Street when he heard the announcement, the sky glowed dark red and the first name was that of the King. Lawson was terrified when the twelfth name was called out, as it was his. He dropped to his knees and prayed to God for help, his prayers were answered when he was the only one named in the list that returned from the battle.

The Mercat Cross was removed from its site in the High Street (now marked in the cobblestones) to Drum House in Gilmerton in 1756. In 1885 the famous Member of Parliament, William Ewart Gladstone, had it re-erected at its present site. Part of the shaft is original but the base and the gallery are modern. The old site is where sheriff's officers sold by auction the goods and effects of debtors which had been poinded, this was as recent as 1925.

It is still used to announce Royal Proclamations. Four days after they are announced in London the Lord Lyon and his court assemble to read the news, four days being the time it took a horseman to ride from London with the news.

Luckenbooths

Built around 1460 these were seven timber fronted tenements four to six storeys high. The ones on the ground level sold meat and bread and most of the merchants lived in the flats above. Behind the luckenbooths and St Giles was a narrow passage called the 'Krames' where merchants who owned no property could sell their wares, leatherware and hardware but mostly toys and cheap trinkets, Lord Cockburn described it as a paradise of chidhood. In 1726 Allan Ramsey set up the first circulating library in Scotland. In 1786 William Creech bookseller and publisher took over the premises and many famous people came to his premises. The luckenbooths were demolished in 1817.

City Chambers

Designed by John Adam and built in 1753, at a cost of £31,500 it was intended as a Royal Exchange but was ignored by the merchants who preferred to conduct their business in taverns or on the street where they could catch people who owed them money. It became the City Chambers in 1811. It was built over three Closes, Stewart's, Pearson's and Mary King's which was abandoned during the plague in 1645 and was discovered intact in later years. Many strange stories are told about the close, some more fanciful than others. The building is deceptive when viewed from the High Street as it has 12 storeys and is one of the highest remaining buildings in the old town. In the quadrangle the statue of Alexander and Bucephalus is by Sir John Steele and was cast in 1883 and shows the taming of Bucephalus, a wild war horse, and represents the mind over strength.

In 1927 the stone of Remembrance was laid beneath the central arch.

Under the left-hand arch is a plaque stating that in 1567 Mary Queen of Scots spent her last night in Edinburgh in the house of Sir Simon Preston before being imprisoned at Loch Leven Castle.

Fishmarket Close

A market operated here from 1592 and it was described as a 'stinking ravine'. George Heriot lived here for a time as did Daniel Defoe, author of *Robinson Crusoe*, who acted as a spy for the English Government at the time of the Union of Parliaments in 1707.

Anchor Close

Named after the Anchor Tavern which was operating in 1715.

Sir Walter Scott's parents lived here and Robert Burns' publisher, William Smellie, had his premises here where he printed the first edition of *Encyclopaedia Brittanica* which sold for 6d (2½p). Smellie introduced Burns to the 'Crochallan Fencibles' club which held its meetings in the tavern.

North Foulis Close

Named after an Apothecary named John Foulis who owned property here in the eighteenth century. At the entrance to the close James Gillespie of Colinton, snuff manufacturer and tobacconist, had a shop. Gillespie was the founder of Gillespie's school, and a wit of the day observed that as all good schools had a motto theirs should be, 'Wha would have thocht, it noses have bocht it'.

Old Stamp Office Close

The Stamp office operated from here between 1779–1821. Flora MacDonald who helped Bonnie Prince Charlie to escape to France after the Battle of Culloden in 1746 attended school to learn English here. The Royal Bank of Scotland, which was constituted in 1727, had an office here until 1753. A famous resident of the close was the Countess of Eglinton who with her seven beautiful daughters lived here in the early part of the eighteenth century … When they were going to the dancing assemblies in Old Assembly Close they would go in a sedan chair each accompanied by six link boys dressed in sky blue livery with silver piping and carrying a torch.

Old Assembly Close

A hall built in 1720 which was used for dancing assemblies and balls. The balls were held weekly over the winter until they transferred to premises in the High Street. The Assembly Hall was destroyed in the great fire of 1824.

Town Guard House

The Town Guard raised in 1648 comprised of sixty men split into three companies. They were armed with a musket and bayonet through the day and a lochaber axe at night, they also had rattles to attract help in the event of fire. They were old Highland soldiers and were paid 15 shillings a month. They were also known as the 'Toun rats'. Their guardhouse was demolished in 1785 and they were disbanded in 1817 to be replaced with a police force.

Tron Church

Named after the Tron weighing machine on which merchants had their scales checked, any found to be short were nailed by their ears to the beam and had to stay there all day until the town bell sounded.

Cockburn Street

On the eastern corner between High Street and Cockburn Street is a basement that is known as the Union Cellar. In 1707 whilst out collecting signatures for the Treaty of Union, the Marquis of

Queensberry, who had taken a bribe from the English Government to sway the vote, was pursued by an outraged mob and had to take refuge in the cellar until they had dispersed.

South Bridge

Built between 1785–88 it is 1075ft long and has 22 arches all hidden in the buildings along its length except for the one over the Cowgate. The bridge dips from Nicholson Street to Chambers Street and rises slowly towards the High Street. The reason for this is that the house of the Lord President Dundas was in Adam Square, about where Chambers Street is now, and if the gradient had been level his front door would have been about six feet below the bridge. In deference to his exalted position the dip was made much to the annoyance of future generations of carters. A few months after the bridge was opened Dundas sold his house, as the district was becoming too commercial.

North Bridge

Built to open up the way to Leith, work started in 1763 but due to incorrectly dug foundations part of it collapsed in 1769 killing five workmen. It was completed in 1772 and altered in 1876 and demolished in 1896 due to increased traffic. The present day bridge is made of iron and was built in 1896 and opened in 1897.

Currubbers Close

Named after a Bailie of Edinburgh, John Spottiswood, Archbishop of St Andrews, had a house here, it was he who crowned King Charles I at Holyrood in 1633.

Allan Ramsey the poet, wigmaker and bookseller opened a theatre here in 1736 but the magistrates closed it down the following year. The building was occupied in 1858 by the atheist club known as 'the celebrated cathedral of the prince of darkness'.

On 30 April 1858 it became Currubbers Close Mission and in 1865 Sir James Young Simpson, discoverer of the anaesthetic properties of chloroform, ran a dispensary as part of the mission's work.

Holiday Inn Crowne Plaza

Built as the Skandic Crown hotel and opened in April 1990 it is built in twentieth century Scots baronial style and the architect was Ian Begg, a local man. On the front of the hotel are the names of the old closes that it replaces.

Paisley Close

'Heave Awa close' as it is known was named in 1679 after Henry Paisley who owned the property. In 1800 Sir William Fettes, Lord Provost and founder of Fettes College, lived here. On Saturday 23 November 1861 a shopkeeper complained to a policeman who lived in the close that he could not get his door to shut properly and another one was stuck shut. On Sunday morning 24 November the building collapsed killing 35 occupants including the policeman's family. When rescuers were digging in the rubble they heard the shout 'heave awa lads I'm no deid yet' and doubling their efforts rescued Joseph Mcivor, a twelve year old boy. It was due to this incident that the authorities decided to employ Sir Henry Littlejohn as medical officer of health, a post he held until 1908. Edinburgh was the first city in Europe to appoint someone to this post. His reforms included a bye-law that all infectious diseases must be notified but it was 18 years before Parliament made this law. A bye-law was also passed that closes and stairs were washed weekly.

Moubary House

This is one of the oldest houses in Edinburgh, dating from 1462. George Jamesone (1588–1644) the portrait painter lived here, he studied under Reubens and was a fellow student of Van Dyck.

In 1710 Daniel Defoe edited the *Edinburgh Courant* from here.

John Knox House

It is not certain that the reformer lived here.

Built around 1472 and reconstructed in 1556 by James Mossman (goldsmith to Mary Queen of Scots) it has Mossmans initials and those of his wife Maria Arras on the front of the building. Above the ground floor windows is the legend 'lufe god abufe all and yir neighbour as yiself'. On the corner is a plaque showing Moses receiving the tablets from God, and God is shown in three different languages.

John Knox was born in 1513 and was a Roman Catholic priest; in 1545 he changed to the Protestant faith and led the struggle for reformation in 1559. His plans for the education of the poor were to his credit but he was also a harsh critic of Mary Queen of Scots. John Knox died in 1572 and is buried behind St Giles.

Tweedale Close

The mansion was built for the first Earl of Lothian's daughter, and wife of Lord Hay of Yester, Dame Margaret Kerr. The house became the head office of the British Linen Bank and in 1806, a girl returning from getting water at the well opposite stumbled across the body of William Begbie a bank messenger who had been murdered and robbed of £4,392. The murderer was never caught but some years later during demolition work at Broughton some of the banknotes were found in a wall.

Oliver and Boyd, the publishers, took over the building in 1817 and remained there until 1973. The building was restored in the 1980s and now houses the Scottish Poetry Library.

The original iron gates are still in use, as is part of the town wall, there is also a sedan chair shelter.

World's End Close

The last close in the safety of the Flodden Wall it was considered to be the end of the world. Formerly known as Stanfields Close this was the town residence of Sir James Stanfield who had a wool mill at Haddington. His son Philip spent money excessively and the two fell out, and the father disinherited the son. Their quarrels were well known, and when in 1687 the Colonel's body was found in the River Tyne at Haddington it was assumed he committed suicide, but suspicion fell on the son when it was discovered that he had been strangled. In the times of superstition it was believed that the body of a murdered person bled at the touch of the murderer's hands and was known as the laying on of hands. This was considered evidence at the trial of Philip Stanfield and he was found guilty and hanged on 24 February 1688. His head was displayed on the east port in

Haddington, this being the nearest spot to the scene of the crime, as was reported at the time

'Young Stanfield touched his father's corpse
When rose a fearful wail;
for blood gushed from the winding sheet
And every face grew pale.'

This was to be the last time the laying on of hands was to be used.

The World's End pub is the scene of one of Edinburgh's mysteries. In 1978 two young girls were having a drink when they disappeared, their bodies were later found in East Lothian and no one has been arrested yet.

Netherbow Port

Brass studs in the roadway mark the location of the Netherbow port or gate in the Flodden Wall of 1513 and demolished in 1764. This gate marked the end of the old Town of Edinburgh and the separate burgh of the Canongate. It was through this gate that Bonnie Prince Charlie gained access to Edinburgh in 1745 when the Jacobite army was camped at Slateford. Emissaries went to discuss the position but when they returned the Jacobites jammed a cart under the gate making it impossible to close it, allowing the Jacobite army to walk in.

Burgh of the Canongate

In 1128 King David I, against the advice of his holy advisors went hunting in the forest of Drumsheugh (an area stretching from Holyrood Park to Gilmerton). A stag broke from the undergrowth and caused the King to be thrown from his horse. It was about to gore him when a glowing cross appeared between its antlers. The startled animal fled leaving the King unharmed. On his return to the Castle he ordered that an abbey should be founded on the spot where his life had been spared and that it should be called the Abbey of the Holyrood. So Augustinian Canons were brought in to do the building work and the King gave permission for them to build along the path they took to reach the Old Town, this became known as the Canon's Gait or walk. It was a separate burgh from Edinburgh with its own rules and taxes and its own Tolbooth and its own coat of arms, a

Cross between a Stag's Antlers which can still be seen on various buildings in the Canongate. With the building of the Palace of Holyrood House the gentry had houses here so as to be close to the Palace, but with the Union with England and the building of the New Town the area fell into decline, it was absorbed into the Royal Burgh in 1856. The wheel has turned full circle, with the building of the Parliament building it is once more a much sought after area to live in.

Mid Common Close

Also known as Morocco land this being where Andrew Gray had his house which is marked by an effigy of the Sultan of Morocco.

A young Edinburgh lad, Andrew Gray was condemned to death for leading a riot during the reign of Charles I, escaped from the Tolbooth Prison and made for Leith where he boarded a ship which was later captured and he was taken prisoner. He entered into service with the Sultan of Morocco and became a great favourite. During a visit of the plague in 1645 he returned to demand a pardon for his unjust treatment and held the city to ransom and demanded the Provost's son as a hostage. As there were not enough able bodied men to defend the city the council had to give in to his demands, but on being informed that the Provost did not have a son but a daughter and she was dying of the plague, he offered to cure her using a secret eastern remedy. A few days later she was cured, he won his pardon and they married and lived in a house on this site as he had been banished from the Royal Burgh.

Chessels Court

Built by Archibald Chessel in 1748, this is where the Excise office was that Deacon Brodie and his accomplices were disturbed in whilst carrying out a robbery in 1788.

The building in the right hand corner was built as a hotel –the first in Scotland, up till then only coaching inns offered basic accommodation. Restoration work was carried out in the 1960s.

180 Canongate

Where John Johnson butcher had his shop and it was here that he boiled up the left over cuts of meat to feed the poor and so invented 'BOVRIL' much loved by generations of football fans.

Playhouse Close

The Canongate Theatre opened in 1747 and was capable of taking £70 a performance. The boxes were half a crown = 12½p, stalls 1s 6d, so it is obvious that it was very popular and the patrons were prone to riotous behaviour leading to the Magistrates closing it down.

The Reverend Home's play *Douglas* was first performed here, when one member of the audience got quite carried away and called out 'Whaur's yer Wullie Sheakspear noo'.

St John Street

Situated in the roadway is the cross of St John where Provosts of Edinburgh came to meet visitors and where Lord Provosts were knighted.

Moray House

Lord Darnley's daughter, Mary, and widow of the 1st Earl of Home had the house built in 1628 for her daughter Margaret, wife of the 4th Earl of Moray

King Charles I was a frequent visitor and Oliver Cromwell made it his headquarters in 1648. After the wedding of the daughter of the 4th Earl of Moray to Lord Lorne in 1650 the wedding party congregated on the balcony to watch the Marquis of Montrose bound to a low cart make his way to Parliament House to receive the death sentence which was carried out three days later (21 May) at the Mercat Cross. Legend has it that the bride spat in Montrose's face.

It was in the garden that the Treaty of Union was being signed in 1707 when an angry mob chased the signatories forcing them to take refuge in the Union cellar in the High Street, among them the Marquis of Queensberry.

Canongate Tolbooth

Built in 1591 the dormers and clock were added during later renovations. It was here that tolls were collected and it also served as a courtroom and jail until 1818 when the prisoners were transferred to the new Calton jail on Regent Road. Inscriptions on the front of the building read 'The place of the seal of the burgh. For one's country and one's successors, 1591' 'King James VI. Justice and Piety are the strong bulwarks of a Prince' the coat of arms of the Canongate and the motto '*Sic itur ad astra,*' This is the path to the stars. There is also a war memorial listing Canongate men who fell in two wars.

On the east side of the tower there are oyster shells stuck into the wall, this was a device used in earlier times to prevent witches entering the building as it was well known that witches cannot cross water or anything to do with water. The building is now a museum called The People's Story telling the story of local people's lives over the last hundred years.

Huntly House

Known as the Speaking House because of the four sixteenth century Latin inscriptions carved into the stonework, the fifth one was added in 1932 when the building was restored.

Built in 1570 for John Acheson it is now a local history museum and among the exhibits are the National Covenant of 1638 and Greyfriars Bobby's collar.

Acheson House

Built in 1633 for Sir Archibald Acheson, Secretary of State for Scotland under King Charles I. For many years it was the Scottish Craft Centre, bought by the City Council in the 1990s it is now part of Huntly House museum. In the courtyard at the rear, entered through Bakehouse Close, the family crest and motto is carved above the door. During a census in 1851 it was found that 230 people lived in Bakehouse Close.

Canongate Kirk

When James II decided to convert the church of Holyrood House to a Chapel Royal the congregation had nowhere to worship and with funding by Thomas Moodie the church was built in 1688.

Inside there is the Royal Pew where the Queen worships when she is resident at Holyrood Palace; unlike in England where she is head of the church, in Scotland she is a member, no different from anyone else.

On the apex of the roof is the coat of arms of the Canongate, it is a real stag's head from the Queen's estate at Balmoral. The board inside the gate displays the names of many famous people who are buried in the churchyard, Adam Smith, author *Wealth of Nations*, Mrs Mary McLehose who was 'Clarinda' to Robert Burns 'Sylvander' and the poet Robert Fergusson to whom Burns referred as 'my brother in the muse' and paid for the erection of a headstone which is inscribed with Burn's own verse, and George Drummond six times Lord Provost and the moving force behind the New Town development.

Panmure Close

Panmure House was the residence of the 4th Earl of Panmure, Baron Maule, in the early eighteenth century.

Adam Smith lived here from 1778 until his death in 1790. The poppies on the gate are a reminder that Lady Haig's Poppy factory occupied premises here from 1931–65 when they moved to Logie Green Road. It was also home to Canongate boys club and is now a training centre for young people.

Jenny Ha's Tavern

Janet Hall was the landlady for a time in the tavern which stood here from 1600–1857 and was famous for her claret which was drawn straight from the barrel and was reputed to 'glue the drinker's lips together'. A plaque at the east end of the building showing the coat of arms of John Paterson commemorates 'Golfer's Land', a tenement which was built in the seventeenth century by John Paterson with his winnings from a game of golf in which he partnered the Duke of York, later King James VII, against two English nobles. The bronze plaque is a copy of the stone carving on the original building.

Paterson chose as his motto 'Far and Sure'(now adopted by golfer's everywhere) and his coat of arms depicts a hand holding a golf club and has the words 'I hate no Person' which is an anagram of his name. It may be noticed that there is no 'I' in John Paterson but it must be remembered that there was no 'J' in the Scots alphabet at that time and an 'I' was used instead.

Queensberry House

This was built in 1681 by the 3rd Earl of Lauderdale, who sold it to William, 1st Duke of Queensberry.

As Lord Lieutenant of Dumfriesshire the 2nd Duke had to reside in Dumfriesshire while his Parliamentary duties compelled him to live in Edinburgh; accordingly in 1706 this house was legally designated as part of Dumfriesshire to solve the problem.

During negotiations for the Union of Parliaments in 1707 the Duke, who had taken a bribe of £12,325 to push through the treaty, was out collecting signatures when he was attacked and chased by a angry mob and had to take refuge in the union cellar until the mob dispersed. Returning home he found that his idiot son Lord Drumlanrig who was kept locked in the attic had escaped, murdered a Canongate kitchen boy, roasted him on a spit and was eating his flesh.

Jacobite soldiers wounded at the Battle of Prestonpans in 1745 sheltered here.

The Duke sold it to the government in 1801. It was used as a barracks, a hospital and in 1906 as a House of Refuge for destitute women and a home for inebriate women. After the war it became a home for the elderly until the late 1990s when it was closed and was to be demolished to make way for the new Parliament building but such was the outcry that it had to be incorporated into the new buiding. Sir John Sholto 8th Marquis of Queensberry (1844–1900) was known as 'Old Q', and in 1867 laid down the rules for boxing. His son had an affair with Oscar Wilde which led to the latter's imprisonment.

Whitefoord House

Built for Sir John Whitefoord in 1766, in 1910 it became a residence for 240 war veterans and today it has accommodation for 103 former Armed Forces personnel.

In front of the Bowling Green is the Balfour Railings. 'Singing' Jamie Balfour was a well-known character in the nineteenth century. A gifted accountant and a clever business man he could do three hours work in one hour and so never lacked work, but he only made money to spend it in Jenny Ha's.

A staunch Jacobite he would entertain his friends with his vast repertoire of Jacobite songs.

The wrought iron railings show the diligent accountant with his ledgers and quill pen and also the reveller with a tankard of ale and his golf clubs by comparison.

White Horse Close

The White Horse Inn built in 1623 and named after Queen Mary's white palfrey was situated here and it was from there that the stagecoach left for London by way of what is now known as Calton Road and Spring Gardens. During Bonnie Prince Charlie's occupation of Edinburgh in 1745 his officers used the Inn as their headquarters. William Dick, blacksmith and founder of the Edinburgh Veterinary College (Dick Vet), was born here in 1793. After falling into disrepair the close was restored in 1965

The Girth Cross

Now a circle of cobblestones marks the spot where the cross once stood. It was the site of many executions and proclamations were read out. People seeking sanctuary from their debtors had to grasp the cross to gain sanctuary.

Queen Mary's Bathhouse

The small quaint building in the Palace grounds may well have been a bathhouse or a tennis pavilion.

Legend has it that Queen Mary bathed in milk but this arose because bath salts that she brought back from France turned her bath water white. She is said to have had a bath twice a year which was twice more than anyone else. During repair work a jewelled dagger was found embedded in the roof and is thought to have been used in the murder of Rizzio.

Abbey Strand

Three brass 'S' on the roadway mark the sanctuary line.

The buildings on the left hand side were the Abbey Sanctuary buildings in which aristocratic debtors lived, they were known as the 'Abbey Lairds' and they could not be arrested and imprisoned for debt as long as they stayed inside the boundaries of the Abbey which included Holyrood Park. Only on a Sunday were they free to visit family and friends without fear of arrest but they had to return by midnight.

The people who were owed money would waylay the debtors and try to induce them to visit Jenny Ha's for a refreshment so that they would be late in returning.

Imprisonment for debt was abolished in 1880 and the last resident was a lawyer named Bain.

The buildings are now used as residences for court officials when Royalty is in residence at the Palace.

On the door of the shop is an example of a 'Tirlin Pin' which was an early form of door knocker. It consists of a piece of iron with a serrated edge over which a iron hoop is run, the door acting as a sounding board carried the noise inside the house, there is an original example on the door of Canonball House and in the children's rhyme this is what 'Wee Willie Winkie' was doing at the door.

Wee Willie Winkie runs through the Toun
Upstairs and doonstairs in his nichtgoon
Chappin at the windaes tirlin at the lock
Are the bairns in their bed?
It's past 8 o'clock.

Queens Gallery

The building on the corner of Abbey Strand and Horse Wynd was built in 1850 as the Holyrood Free Church and was later used as workshops for Palace maintenance staff. In 2002 it was converted into a gallery to exhibit works of art belonging to the Royal Family and not normally seen by members of the public.

On the wall of the Abbey Courthouse is the heraldic panel showing the cypher and arms of King James V. The building is now used by the High Constables of Holyroodhouse.

Holyrood Abbey

In 1128 King David I ordered that the Abbey be built as thanks for his escape from death.

It has been used for Royal weddings and James V was crowned

there in 1524 and was buried there in 1542. It was damaged in 1544 and 1547 during Hereford's raids which became known as the 'Rough Wooing'. In 1688 a Presbyterian mob ransacked the Royal Vault and scattered the bones.

A new roof was put on in 1758 but collapsed ten years later leaving the ruin pretty much as we see it today.

Holyrood Palace

Originally used as a guesthouse for travellers to the Abbey, King James IV extended it to become a Royal residence. King Charles II had extension work carried out by Robert Mylne the Kings Master Mason over a five-year period in the 1670s.

While Mary Queen of Scots was in residence in 1566 her secretary David Rizzio was dragged from her chamber and stabbed to death.

King Charles II commissioned the Dutch artist, Jacob DeWitt, to paint Scottish Monarchs and the paintings are displayed in the Picture Gallery. There are one hundred and eleven portraits and it would have been impossible for DeWitt to capture a likeness so he used men from the Canongate as models.

Charles Edward Stuart ('Bonnie Prince Charlie') held dancing levees during his stay in 1745.

The Palace is the Queen's official residence in Scotland although it is reputed to be her least favourite.

Tour No. 2

St Andrew's Square, George Street, Charlotte Square, Lothian Road, West Port, Grassmarket, Holyrood Road, Horse Wynd.

Royal Bank of Scotland.

Built as Sir Laurence Dundas' house in 1773 at a cost of £30,000, and designed by Sir William Chambers it was later lost in a card game to General John Scott. Dundas was allowed to keep the house after agreeing to build Scott another one elsewhere.

On Craig's plan of the New Town this was to be the site of a church, but Dundas got wind of the New Town plan and got in first. The Royal Bank took over the House in 1820.

The statue in front is of the Earl of Hopetoun by Thomas Campbell in 1834. Hopetoun who was in the Gordon Highlanders took command of the army at the Battle of Corunna after the death of Sir John Moore, he later became a Governor of the Royal Bank. The statue is out of proportion as the male figure is taller than the horse and was intended to portray Hopetoun as a big man, however legend has it that because it is out of proportion Campbell was never paid.

Bank of Scotland

Designed by David Bryce in 1851 as the head office of the British Linen Bank, it later merged with the Bank of Scotland in 1971. The statues on top represent Navigation, Commerce, Manufacture, Science, Art and Agriculture and are the work of Musselburgh sculptor Handyside. The statues are one and a half times normal size so that when viewed from the street they appear normal size.

Prudential Insurance Company Building

Sir Alfred Waterhouse, whose firm built most of the 'Pru' buildings in this country, designed this. Knowing Waterhouse's reputation the Town Council accepted the plans but later were astounded to learn that the building was to be red brick. They insisted that stone be used to conform to the other buildings in the Square. Waterhouse had to alter his plans, but got his own back by using red sandstone. The style is early Renaissance and was built in 1895. The ground floor is now licensed premises.

Melville Monument

Henry Dundas, (1742–1811), the first Viscount Melville, was born in Edinburgh and trained as a lawyer. In his twenties he was Solicitor General for Scotland. William Pitt made him Treasurer of the Navy. He became First Sea Lord of the Admiralty and Secretary for War. He gained complete control over the electoral system in Scotland and was known as 'King Harry' the 9th Uncrowned King of Scotland'.

In 1805 he was charged with embezzling Navy funds but as his party was in power he was acquitted. The wags of the day said the reason he was up so high was to keep his hands off their money and the reason he is facing west was that he turned his back on Holyrood Palace.

No. 21 St Andrew's Square

This was the birthplace of Henry Brougham who became an advocate in 1800, an MP in 1810 and was Lord Chancellor 1830–34, and popularised the carriage named after him, 'The Brougham'. In 1859 Brougham Place was named after him.

Standard Life Building

The pediment is by Sir John Steele and depicts 10 virgins. On the extension Gerald Laing's frieze illustrates the parable of the 5 wise and 5 foolish virgins. On the right the five foolish virgins do not know where salvation lies and have no cohesion, while the wise virgins on the left are perfect, identical and equal, they are looking towards the Christian faith represented by a secret sign of the Christians in Roman times. This cryptogram is a word square of which various examples have been discovered dating around A. D. 70–180. The translation was meaningless to the Romans 'Arepo the sower guides the wheels with care' but in 1920 the device was translated, it is an anagram of the letter's 'Paternoster' twice arranged as a cross with only one 'N' taking that as a centre 'A' and 'O' twice, Alpha and Omega being the first and last letters of the Greek alphabet translates as 'Our Father, the beginning and the end'.

    ROTAS
    OPERA
    TENET
    AREPO
    SATOR.

St Andrew's Church

Designed by Major Frazier, Royal Engineers, in 1785 it is unique in that it is the only church designed by a member of Her Majesty's armed forces. The 168ft spire was added four years later by William Sibbald. The nave is unusual in that it is oval, there being no corners for the Devil to hide round. It should have been built in St Andrew's Square but the site planned was already occupied.

On the 18 May 1843, 470 ministers of the Church of Scotland, led by Thomas Chalmers, angry at the way in which the Church appointed Ministers walked out of the General Assembly, in protest at church law which gave the right of patronage to landowners to appoint ministers regardless of the wishes of parishioners. These ministers then formed the Free Church of Scotland. This became known as 'The Disruption'.

16 George Street

The plaques on the wall are known as 'Fire Marks'.

In 1771 insurance companies formed fire fighting crews to protect the property of their clients. Ill trained and ill equipped they would only protect premises insured by their employers and displaying the company fire marks. Often they would stand and watch as premises insured by other companies burned to the ground.

In 1820 six companies saw the logic of contributing to fire fighting on a shared basis, and in 1824 James Braidwood took charge and revamped the whole operation introducing many innovative practices. This was the first local authority controlled fire fighting force in Europe and was the forerunner of today's Lothian and Borders Fire Brigade.

Thistle Court

The first house built in the New Town was Thistle Court in 1767, behind what is now the George Hotel. The owner, James Young, was offered £20 as an inducement before he agreed to build. The circular well in the forecourt was essential before piped water was available, and may have influenced the decision to build here. Other concessions were given to New Town residents in the form of rates reductions, etc.

Royal Society

The Charter for the Royal Society was granted by King George III in 1763. Originally intended to serve both science and literature equally, however, the literary side has disappeared. The building was originally the premises of the Commercial Union Insurance Company, and designed by J. M. Dick Peddie in 1908. The building is unusual in that Portland Stone was used in the construction, the first building in George Street to depart from Craigleith Stone. The figure on the dome is 'Prudence' by Percy Portsmouth.

King George IV Statue

The statue was designed by Chantry and unveiled in 1831 to commemorate the King's visit in 1822. This was the first visit to Scotland by a reigning monarch since Charles II in 1650, George IV Bridge is named in his honour. The events were stage managed by Sir Walter Scott.

Hanover Street (looking south): The Merchants Hall

Charles II granted the Charter of Incorporation of the Company of Merchants in 1681.

Now headquarters of the Merchant Company, it was earlier the Edinburgh office of the City of Glasgow Bank and was designed by

David Bryce Jun. in 1865. The hall half of the building is at the corner of Hanover Street and Rose Street. The other half which housed the Chamber of Commerce was built at a much later date (1902) but the detail in structure and stonework is so perfectly matched that it is impossible to notice any difference, or to notice the join. The original Merchants Hall was in Hunters Square. The Merchant Company moved here in 1879.

New College and Assembly Hall

Designed by William Playfair in 1845, it was built as a church and Theological College. The towers of its gatehouse are sited to frame the spire of St John's Highland Tolbooth Church (now the Hub) on Castlehill, making it appear to be part of the building. This is the home of the General Assembly of the Church of Scotland.

In 1999 it became the temporary home of the first Scottish Parliament since 1707.

Assembly Rooms

By John Henderson, it was opened in 1787 at a cost of £2,000 and was the centre of social life in the New Town for dancing assemblies. The portico was added in 1818 to the design of William Burn. It was here on 23 February 1827 that Sir Walter Scott first publicly admitted authorship of the *Waverley Novels*.

Here in 1867 the Freedom of the City was granted to Benjamin Disraeli.

The Music Hall was built behind in 1843 and designed by David Bryce and William Burn. During both World Wars it was used as a recruiting centre.

William Pitt (the Younger) 1759–1806

By Sir Francis Chantry in 1784. Pitt was Prime Minister on two occasions: 1783–1801 and 1804–06 and at the age of 25, the youngest ever, he was responsible for the introduction of Income Tax at 6d. in the pound. (2½pence)

The huge public debt that he inherited when he became Chancellor of the Exchequer in 1782 was reduced by policies based on the ideas of Adam Smith author of *The Wealth of Nations*.

He solved the crisis created by the Irish rebellion in 1798 by uniting Britain and Ireland.

Frederick Street

Named after the son of George II and father of George III, he was the Duke of York and Albany. As Commander of the British Army in France in 1793, he started well but a series of tactical blunders led to his recall in December 1794. In 1799 he was again Commander, this time in Holland, where he was joined by 10,000 Russian troops who misunderstood the orders and advanced too eagerly, causing an unexpected encounter on unfamiliar ground with the enemy, resulting in humiliating negotiation and withdrawal. These events and popular derision resulted in the nursery rhyme 'The Grand Old Duke of York'. A statue was erected to him on the Castle Esplanade, ironically at the top of the hill. Arthur Wellesley (later the Duke of Wellington) who was a young soldier during the campaign later admitted that 'I learned what one ought not to do and that is always something'.

Frederick Street (looking north): St Stephen's Church (1828)

The Town Council commissioned W. H. Playfair to design and build the church to obstruct the view of Edinburgh Academy from the foot of Frederick Street. Playfair made the most of the steep descent as you enter the church on the gallery. It has the longest pendulum in Europe.

Freemasons Hall

The home of Grand Lodge of Scotland was founded in 1858 at 98 George Street and moved into the present premises in 1911. A. Hunter Crawford of the Baking family designed the building in 1910. The figure above the door is St Andrew by H. S. Gamley.

Thomas Chalmers Statue (1780–1847)

By Sir John Steele, erected in 1878, Chalmers led the Disruption in 1843 and became the first Moderator of the Free Church.

The placing of the statue is somewhat ironic facing as it does down Castle Street towards the statue of Reverend Thomas Guthrie. The two fell out over funding of 'Ragged Schools' and could not stand the sight of each other.

As it was put at the time 'They can spend eternity looking at each other'.

Castle

When building the hospital block in 1896 the Victorians proposed to improve and make the Castle more picturesque by erecting a false bartisan tower with turrets and battlements on the restored curtain wall in front. This was abandoned after public objections were voiced, but the tie stones to anchor the project are clearly seen.

Sir Walter Scott's House

No. 39 North Castle Street is where he wrote some of the *Waverley Novels*. A small copy of the statue under the Scott Monument is visible in the fanlight above the door. Kenneth Graham, author of *The Golden Age* and *Wind in the Willows*, was born at 32 Castle Street in 1859.

Tontine Building

Henry Duncan House, Lloyds T. S. B. this was originally a cavalry barracks. Thirteen people put up the money to build it and the last one alive owned it outright.

127–129 George Street

When an American company bought London Bridge, (in the mistaken belief that they were buying Tower Bridge) they had it shipped to Nevada where it is now a tourist attraction. The Edinburgh company of stonemasons, McGlashens of Canonmills, bought the stonework from the retaining walls for use in making gravestones. However it was Craigleith stone from the now closed Craigleith Quarry, the same quarry which had provided stone used in the building of the New Town and was now in demand for restoration work. When this building was refaced in the mid seventies this was the stone used. Craigleith Quarry stood at the junction of Queensferry Road and Craigleith Road and is now the site of a supermarket.

133 George Street

Home of Sir John Sinclair, compiler of the First Statistical Account of Scotland from 1815–35.

He was a very tall man, over six feet, as were his fifteen children, so the pavement outside his house became known as the Giant's Causeway.

Charlotte Square

The four sides of the Square designed by Robert Adam in 1791 are one of Europe's major achievements of civic architecture of the period, spacious elegant and harmonious, there are forty-four separate houses built at separate times between 1792–1820, but all conforming in style, doors, windows, pilasters, pillars, pediments, balustrades, festoons, decorations, etc. Unfortunately there are a few later additions of dormer windows, altered doors and fanlights which are not as originally intended, but the north side is nearly perfect.

Each block of houses is completely unified to a symmetrical design but without fussiness, a restrained perfection of design texture and detail.

At the north side of the square are still preserved the torch extinguishers in the railings at the entrances to the houses, these were used by 'Linkboys' who accompanied the carriages and sedan chairs.

The manhole covers in the pavement gave access for deliveries of coal and the oblong stones in the gutter were to enable passengers easy access to carriages.

The Square has been home to many famous people. On the North Side No. 5 is the headquarters of the National Trust for Scotland. No. 6 is Bute House, the official residence of the First Minister, No. 7, The Georgian House is a domestic museum showing how the interior would have looked at the latter end of the eighteenth century, the upper floors are the official residence of the Moderator of the General Assembly of the Church of Scotland.

At No. 9 Joseph Lister, pioneer of antiseptic surgery, lived from 1870–77

No. 13 Sir William Fettes, founder of Fettes College lived in 1810.

No. 14 Lord Cockburn Lived.

No. 17 Viscount Haldane Secretary for War, who remodelled the British Army between 1905 and 1912, was born here.

At No. 24 Douglas Haig was born to a wealthy whisky distiller ('Don't be vague ask for Haig') and it was he who led the remodelled Army to victory in the First World War. As Commander in Chief he was severely criticised for the heavy loss of life among his men due to his tactics. After the war he worked for the British Legion supporting and giving work to men injured in the conflict. He was instrumental in establishing the poppy works which provides poppies for Remembrance Sunday. He received the Freedom of the City on 28 May 1919 but as word of his tactics leaked out this is never admitted to.

Albert Memorial

In memory of Albert Prince Consort (1819–61)

The base is Aberdeen granite with a bronze statue of Albert in Field Marshall's uniform and stands over 17ft high at a cost of £16,500. The sculptor was John Steele and it was unveiled by Queen Victoria on 17 August 1876. After the unveiling ceremony Queen Victoria knighted Steele at Holyrood Palace.

West Register House

Originally St George's Church with a dome 160ft high it is a scaled down copy of St Paul's Cathedral in London. Robert Adam submitted a design but it was rejected on the grounds of cost and Robert Reid adapted Adams' design, and the cheaper version was preferred. Reid made a rash verbal estimate of £18,000 but when it opened in 1814 the cost was £33,000. *Scots Magazine* said when it opened 'It is certainly a pity that the Adam design was not used.' It closed when dry rot was discovered in the dome and repairs would have been too costly for the congregation. It was taken over by the Government and is now an annexe of the Scottish Record Office.

31 Charlotte Square (south side)

Note the diamond shape on the wall, this is the mark remaining when the support bracket for overhead tram wires was removed. The last tram ran on 16 November 1956, bringing to an end 85 years of transport covering three types of power, Horse, Cable and Electricity.

Dummy Windows

In Edinburgh many people believe that 'Dummy Windows' were blocked out to avoid the window tax of 1707–1851, but on examination many of these could not have been real windows, they were constructed thus to maintain a façade where there was a fireplace or chimney flue on the other side or perhaps in front of an interior partition wall between rooms, or on a corner site where windows on both walls would have been cold or weakened the structure. In the case of Parliament Hall and Charlotte Square it was to make the buildings symmetrical. It would be very difficult to find a Dummy Window directly attributable to Window Tax in Edinburgh today.

Window Tax is the origin of the saying 'Daylight Robbery'.

North Charlotte Street

Before the Moray Place development, the Earl of Moray would not allow building within 40ft of his boundaries, consequently to avoid any infringement of the Moray properties the western end of Queen Street (Albyn Place) was bevelled slightly at north Charlotte Street instead of a right angle as Craig's plan originally required.

Catherine Sinclair Monument

Catherine Sinclair (1800–64) was a novelist and benefactor, she set up missions and was the first to set up a public fountain in the city; she took a special interest in cab drivers and became known as their patron saint. She was the first person to guess the identity of the author of the *Waverley* novels. Hundreds lined the streets in tribute as her funeral passed on its way to St Johns Church where she is buried.

Alexander Graham Bell House

At 16 South Charlotte Street the inventor of the telephone was born in 1847. He spent one year at a private school and two years at the Royal High from which he graduated aged 14; he was largely family trained and self taught. His invention of the telephone grew out of research into ways to improve the telegraph. On 7 March 1876 the U. S. Patent office granted him patent no. 174,465 governing the method of transmitting vocal or other sounds telegraphically. After inventing the telephone, Bell continued his experiments in communication, which culminated in the Photophone – transmission of sound on a beam of light, a precursor of today's optical fibre systems. In all 18 patents were granted in his name. In 1888 he founded the National Geographic Society.

Statue of Sir James Young Simpson (1811–1870)

Professor of Midwifery and discoverer of Chloroform as an Anaesthetic at his home at 52 Queen Street in 1847.

After dinner he passed round a small bottle of chloroform to his assistants, 'immediately an unwanted hilarity seized the party; they became bright eyed, very happy and very loquacious. The conversation was of unusual intelligence and quite charmed the listeners, but suddenly all was quiet, and then crash'. He attended Queen Victoria at the birth of Prince Leopold. He also founded the modern practice of gynaecology. The statue is the work of William Brodie and was unveiled in 1876.

St John's Episcopal Church

By William Burn in 1817 at a cost £18,000, and the interior modelled on St George's Chapel at Windsor.

Many famous people are buried here: Sir Henry Raeburn, portrait painter, Sir Walter Scott's mother, James Donaldson, founder of Donaldson's Hospital, Catherine Sinclair novelist, and McVey Napier producer of the seventh edition of *Encyclopaedia Britannica*.

St Cuthbert's Church

This was the Parish Church of Stockbridge. The old Kirk Loan remains with us in Church Street. Church Lane, renamed Gloucester Street and Lane, up which parishioners tramped to worship. This lane continues up Wemyss Place but is lost in the New Town development of Queen Street and Charlotte Square. It reappears between Princes Street and St John's Church leading down to St Cuthbert's. Here the cobblestones are the original surface of the old road.

Lothian Road

About 1790 Sir John Clerk of Penicuik took on a bet, that in one day between sunrise and sunset, he could build a road twenty paces wide and nearly a mile in length between the Lang Dykes (Princes Street) and Tollcross.

This was just after the Highland Clearances and he organised hundreds of unemployed Highlanders into gangs, some to cut down trees, some to bring earth and rubble to fill hollows, some to demolish sheds, barns etc.

He provided whisky, porter, bread and cheese, and as the sun rose they started work and before sunset Sir John drove his horse and carriage over the new road, now called Lothian road.

Kays Portraits relates the tale of a poor woman who had a cottage and a cow, and on this day rose early, milked her cow, lit her fire and made some tea, she smoked her pipe and put on a pot of sheep's heid kale to simmer while she went to town with her daily wares. When she returned there was,

'Neither cottage nor byre
Nor cow, nor fire
Nor pipe, nor pot
Nor anything on the spot.'

Watch Tower

This round tower was used to house watchers over graves during the body-snatching era, around 1825.

Supply of corpses matched demand but then a surge in anatomy meant more were required, so ressurectionists, as they were called, sold bodies to the Medical School, who required corpses up to three days old. Bereaved families would spend three days and nights watching over the grave until the body was of no use for medical science. Other methods to deter the grave robbers were an iron grating (known as a Mort Safe) over the grave; (many have since been removed by vandals) or a flat tombstone. The tower is now an artist's studio.

Usher Hall

Andrew Usher, brewer and distiller, donated £100,000, in 1896. After a lot of wrangling it was finally built in 1910–14. J. Stockdale Harrison was the architect. In front is the Bell Clock Tower, a gift to the city from another distiller, Arthur Bell of Perth, in 1962.

In front of Festival Square is the statue 'Woman and Child' by the Aberdeen sculptress Ann Davidson. It was unveiled on 22 July 1986 by Mrs Suganya Chetty of the African National Congress, and commemorates South African Freedom Fighters against apartheid.

The Castle

Looking up at the Castle from Castle Terrace, can clearly be seen the Postern Gate where James Graham of Claverhouse (Bonnie Dundee) had a conference with the Duke of Gordon, Governor of the Castle in 1689 who held the Castle to uphold the Stuart cause against William of Orange. Graham of Claverhouse agreed to bring reinforcements to strengthen the Castle garrison but was killed at the Battle of Killiecrankie and the Castle had to surrender. Further round to the north, Randolph, 1st Earl of Moray, with 30 men was led up the Castle Rock by one of his men who knew a secret path, which he had used to visit his lady friend whilst stationed in the castle.

They scaled the walls with a scaling ladder and took the garrison of two hundred by surprise and thus regained the Castle for his Uncle Robert Bruce in 1312.

A plaque on the rock above Kings Stables Road records that the castle was bombed by a Zeppelin on 2 April 1916.

West Port

This was the main approach into Edinburgh from the West and South.

Grassmarket

There was a regular weekly market here from 1477–1911 selling meal, corn, horses and cattle. Jousting tournaments were held here.

The White Hart Inn, which claims to be the oldest pub in Edinburgh, started out as a coaching inn and in 1810 as many as 80 coaches a week arrived and departed. Guests here included Robert Burns and William Wordsworth.

Opposite is the Vennel where can be seen part of the Flodden Wall of 1513. At the foot of the West Bow the public gallows stood until 1784 where common criminals died in their hundreds, along with Covenantors of whom at least a hundred martyrs who had signed the National Covenant were executed to 'Glorify God in the Grassmarket' between 1661–88. They are remembered in the memorial in the small walled enclosure which marks the site of the gallows and is marked by a St Andrew's cross in rose coloured cobblestones and the words 'For the Protestant faith on this spot many martyrs and Covenanters died'. The tenements offered a good view of the executions and could be rented out (the first grandstands). The victims were taken into a bar for a drink before execution and it was said to be 'The last drop before the last drop'.

The Porteous Riot

In 1736 the most famous of disturbances occurred, in an expression of discontent with the Union with England.

The presence of English customs officers was a conspicuous sign so it follows that smugglers were popular heroes. When two of them, Robertson and Wilson, were condemned to death feelings were on their side.

The common practice was to take condemned men to St Giles on the last Sunday before execution, but Robertson escaped with the passive help from the crowd. At the execution of Wilson Captain Porteous of the Town Guard became alarmed at the sympathetic murmuring of the crowd. He ordered his men to fire a warning shot but several people were killed. Porteous himself was arrested and charged with murder, brought to trial, found guilty, and condemned to death. The authorities in London looked on this as a defiant act of a rebellious people against a man who was only doing his duty. Queen Caroline, who was acting as regent, granted a respite of execution for six weeks until the King returned. This was too much for the long-suffering people of Edinburgh. In a way that was riotous, orderly and systematic they seized Porteous from prison and duly carried out the sentence against him. They purchased a rope from Bell's Rope shop in the West Bow for a guinea and hanged him from a dyer's pole.

Half Hangit Maggie Dickson

Margaret Dickson was a High Street FishWife whose husband deserted her. Making her way to Newcastle she stopped in the Borders where she became pregnant to her landlady's son, one William Bell. Her attempts to conceal her pregnancy resulted in the child being born prematurely and it died a few days later. She hid the body in the grass at the side of the River Tweed where it was discovered by a local fisherman who notified the Magistrates. Maggie was eventually traced and sent to Edinburgh where she was charged under the Concealment of Pregnancy Act of 1690. She was found guilty and sentenced to death by hanging.

Several thousand turned out to see her execution on 2 September 1724. Friends brought a cart and a coffin to give her a decent burial. As the body was cut down by the hangman a group of medical students tried to take the body for dissection at the Surgeons' Hall. The crowd were outraged and gave the medics a severe beating. Her friends took her body and set off for Musselburgh where she was to have been buried. Stopping for refreshments at the Peffermill inn they heard groans coming from inside the coffin, raising the lid they were astonished to find that she was still alive. In a few weeks she made a full recovery, but the question was, would she be tried again? Top legal brains considered that she had been tried, convicted, hanged, pronounced dead and that the sentence against her had been carried out and she would therefore have to go free. She went on to live for another 40 years carrying the name of 'Half Hangit Maggie'.

The Bowfoot Well

One of the original wells to be built by Robert Mylne, King's Master Mason in 1680.

The Cowgate

So named, as this was the way people used to take their animals to graze on the Burgh Muir.

Magdalene Chapel

Founded in 1547, it contains the only surviving example of pre-Reformation stained glass in Scotland. Windows show Royal Arms of Scotland, the emblems of the Queen Regent, Mary of Guise (mother of Mary Queen of Scots) and of the founder Michael MacQuan and his widow Janet Rhind.

It was taken over by the incorporation of Hammermen of the Canongate in 1614, they added the spire in 1622, which contains a bell dated 1632. It was used as a morgue for people executed in Grassmarket.

Tailors Hall

Now home to the pub 'The Three Sisters' it was here in 1638 that 300 ministers of the Church of Scotland drew up the National Covenant.

Gilded Balloon Nightclub

At the foot of Blair Street was the scene of one of the worst fires seen in Edinburgh. In early December 2002 a blaze started in the buildings, it soon spread upwards destroying buildings on the South Bridge. The damage was so bad that the street was shut for months to allow demolition of the buildings.

This is the only exposed arch of the 19 that form the South Bridge.

St Cecilia's Hall

The work of Robert Mylne in 1763 it was the venue for dancing assemblies in the 1760s. It fell into disuse in the nineteenth century and was restored by the University in 1966 and today houses the Russell collection of early keyboard instruments. It has an oval concert hall and the building is said to have perfect pitch.

Cardinal Beaton's House

A stone tablet on the corner of Cowgate and Blackfriars Street marks the site of a house built in 1512 by James Beaton, Archbishop of Glasgow, and afterwards the palace of Cardinal Beaton, who crowned Mary Queen of Scots at Stirling in 1543.

Effectively the last Archbishop of St Andrew's he was opposed by John Knox and was murdered by Protestant reformers.

Salvation Army Hostel

The badge on the wall facing down Holyrood Road shows that this was one of Heriot's Hospitals, now a shelter for the homeless.

Pleasance

Looking up the Pleasance from the corner of St Mary's Street is the site of the Flodden Wall, which would have run up St Mary's Street to the Netherbow Port.

Begun after the defeat of the Scottish Army at the Battle of Flodden in 1513 it defined the boundaries of Edinburgh for over 250 years. It started at the East End of the Nor Loch and travelled over the High Street at St Mary's Street down to the Cowgate and up the Pleasance along Drummond Street and College street, through the site of the Museum in Chambers Street, enclosing Greyfriars Churchyard but excluding Heriot's Hospital (now George Heriots School), down the Vennel to the Grassmarket and up to the Castle Rock. There were six gates or ports in the wall; they were New, Netherbow, Cowgate, Potterrow, Bristo and West.

St Johns Street

This street was named after the Cross of St John which stood in the Canongate.

The Knights of St John, an ancient order of chivalry, had their houses in the street. A house built for the Wemyss family in 1730 is now occupied as the Chancery of the Priory of Scotland of the Most Venerable Order of the Hospital of St John of Jerusalem.

The Order of St John is a charitable religious body with the twin aims of supporting the Christian faith and of working for the good of mankind. The Order supports an ophthalmic hospital in Jerusalem, holiday and respite homes in this country and a canal barge named the *St John Crusader* for taking disabled people on trips from Ratho.

Many famous people have lived in the street including Tobias Smollett who wrote *Humphrey Clinker* in 1766.

Lord Monboddo was an eccentric High Court Judge who, if it was raining would hire a sedan chair to carry his wig while he walked alongside. He also believed that man was descended from monkeys, and when women from the Canongate were in labour he would hang about outside the house until he heard the baby cry and then burst into the room hoping to catch the midwife cutting off the tail.

In 1780 Lady Betty Charteris, a relation of the Earl of Wemyss, was jilted at the altar of the Tron Church and was carried home in a sedan chair, she took to her bed where she stayed for twenty six years until she died.

The oldest building in the Street is the Canongate Kilwinning Masonic Lodge, of which Robert Burns was a member and where he was Poet Laureate. It claims to be the oldest Masonic Chapel still in use in the world. The chapel was built in 1735 and contains an organ of 1757.

On the wall of the Holyrood Hotel are the Glassblowers plaques, these were on a tenement building which was demolished in the 1990s as part of the re-development of the area. The plaques are a reminder of the city glass works, or Holyrood glassworks where the Famous Edinburgh Lead crystal was made which closed in 1904. This is not to be confused with the Edinburgh & Leith Glassworks in Norton Park (off Rossie Place) which is now the Edinburgh Crystal Glass Company and which moved to Penicuik in 1969.

Arthur's Seat

Height 823ft (251 metres). This is an extinct volcano of red igneous rock and is probably named after King Arthur after a revival of Arthurian legends in the fifteenth century.

James Hutton (the father of modern Geology) whose studies of Salisbury Crags allowed him to define how the earth was formed, caused an outcry as his theories went against the teachings of the bible.

In June 1836, 17 miniature coffins (of which 8 are in the National Museum of Scotland) were discovered by boys out hunting rabbits. The coffins and the figures inside are carved from wood and the reason for their existence is unknown. It may have been witchcraft representing victims to be harmed, or a custom practised by seafaring folk who buried their menfolk in effigy if lost at sea.

Scotsman Building

Scotland's leading newspaper moved here from its old home on the North Bridge in 1999, the new building being opened on St Andrew's Day, the 30 November. The architects were the Comprehensive Design Group and the building cost £18 million.

Scottish Parliament Building

Enrico Moralles, the Spanish architect whose design is based on upturned boats, is at the centre of a sorry saga of political bickering over the cost which has spiralled four times over the original estimate and the completion date seems to be unknown. It was originally cost at £50 million with a completion date of September 2001. In February 2000 the cost had risen from £109 million to £200 million with a completion date of 2003. At the end of 2003 this figure rose to £400 million, still with no opening date.

Dynamic Earth

In 1988 Scottish and Newcastle Brewers gifted the site of their former Holyrood brewery to the people of Edinburgh on condition that a building would be created for the benefit of the community.

Construction work began in 1997 with sponsorship from the Millennium Commission, City of Edinburgh Council and British Gas. The building, known as the William Younger centre, designed by Michael Hopkins and Partners, cost £15 million and was opened in June 1999.

It tells the story of how the planet was formed from the 'Big Bang'. It is appropriate that it should be sited here, as this is where James Hutton (1726–97) the Father of Modern Geology lived and worked during the eighteenth century. He formulated theories on how the Earth was formed by Fire and Ice, and was one of the leading figures of 'The Enlightenment'.

Horse Wynd

The Queen's Gallery, opened in 2002 to exhibit some of the works of art held in the Royal collection.

Tour No. 3

Queen Street, Dundas Street, Canonmills, Inverleith Row, Inverleith Place, Ann Street, Dean Bridge, Moray Place, Doune Terrace, St Stephens Street.

National Portrait Gallery

Founded in 1882 and housing a large library of photos and engravings it was originally based in the premises opposite and moved in 1999.

The present building was formerly the National Museum of Antiquities.

It is fourteenth century Gothic, designed by R. Rowand Anderson and built in 1890, the erection of it was made possible by a donation of £30,000 from J. R. Findlay, owner of the *Scotsman* newspaper. Sculptures are by Birnie Rhind in 1892–3. Other figures are by C McBride, D. W. Grant Stevenson, John Hutchison, and Pittendrigh MacGillivary and depict figures from Industry, Religion, Fine Arts, and Sciences. The stone is red Dumfriesshire sandstone.

No 8 Queen Street

This was the first house to be occupied in Queen Street and is now the home of the General Medical Council; it was built in 1770 by Robert Adam for Baron Orde of the Exchequer.

The Baron did not like his servants to cross the road in front of the house with bundles of washing to lay out on the bleaching grounds opposite, so he had a tunnel built under Queen Street which is still there, although blocked of by a brick wall inside the house. The garden end of the tunnel is used by the gardeners for storing their tools.

No 9–10 Queen Street

Home of the Royal College of Physicians designed by Thomas Hamilton in 1844. The statues on the façade are of Hippocrates, Aesculapius, and Hygeia.

No 52 Queen Street

This was the home of Sir James Young Simpson, Professor of Midwifery and pioneer of anaesthetic (chloroform). He died here in 1870.

There is a story told of a young lady who went to Simpson to have an abscess under her arm lanced and he used his new found discovery on her as an experiment. She made a full recovery and later became Queen Victoria. She attended Simpson's funeral.

Queen Street Gardens

The dome shaped 'temple' in the gardens is a gas regulator.

Perhaps the Queen Street Gardens proprietors insisted on a classical style building to conform to the surroundings, after considering the hideous structure housing a water pump erected earlier by the water board on Calton Hill.

Abercromby Place

This should really be spelt Abercrombie as it is named after Sir Ralph Abercrombie, a General in the Napoleonic Wars. He became an MP for Clackmannanshire, returned to the army as a Major General to fight the French and died as a result of his wounds in Egypt in 1801.

This street was built about 1804, and was unique in the new town where all the streets had been planned on the strict gridiron design as straight streets crossed by others at right angles. The owner of what is now Queen Street Gardens would not sell his land so the houses were built round his perimeter as a crescent and caused considerable amazement at the time. Subsequently crescents became quite common.

At the east end of the gardens runs Gabriel's Road which was the old road from Multries Hill at the east end of the Lang Dykes (Princes Street) to the ford over the Water of Leith at Stockbridge. The road ran through Saxe Coburg Place to Glenogle Road.

Heriot Row

The second new town was built on land owned by the Heriot Trust and is named after George Heriot, who was goldsmith to James VI and his Queen, Anne of Denmark. He became very rich and had the nickname of 'Jinglin Geordie'. When he died he left his fortune to found Heriot's Hospital and school. Henry McKenzie (1745–1831) author of a *Man of Feeling* lived at No. 6.

Robert Louis Stevenson lived at no. 17 and it was there that he got the inspiration for *Treasure Island* from the ornamental pond in Queen Street Gardens. On a brass plate on the railings is his poem 'The Lamplighter'. The street is now a popular address for members of the legal profession.

Great King Street

J. M. Barrie, author of *Peter Pan* had lodgings at no 3 and is reputed to have used his landlady Mrs Edwards as inspiration for a character in his play 'The Old Lady Shows Her Medals'.

On the corner of Great King Street and Dundas Street stood the last sedan chair plying for hire until about 1870. The badge of the chairmen showed two of them carrying a chair and their motto 'Honesty is the best Policy' round the border topped by a crown. Their tariff for 1810 was, hired from 10 a.m. till midnight, seven shillings and sixpence (38 p).

9 a.m. till 4 p.m. three shillings and sixpence (18p).

The sedans were wooden boxes with a door at the front and a hinged roof for easy access, the carrying poles passed through rings on each side of the chair and were carried by Highlanders who survived the Jacobite war and came to Edinburgh to find employment.

Scotland Street

Northern entrance to Scotland Street Railway tunnel which ran to Waverley Station and closed in 1868, it is now the home of Scotland Yard adventure playground, the first one to be designed for handicapped children. The cost was £300,000 of which £200,000 was donated by BBC Television's Children in Need Appeal, the rest by private donations.

Henderson Row

The Scottish Life Assurance Company building was rebuilt in 1991 but retained the façade of the 1888 building which housed the Edinburgh Northern Tramways Company who ran cable cars from Princes Street to Stockbridge and Goldenacre until 1920. On the east facing wall two iron wheels used in the operation are to be seen and there is an inscription which reads, 'This pulley unit was part of the equipment installed by the Edinburgh Northern Tramways Company to carry the cables for cable tramcars operated from the depot on this site from 1888 until 1920'.

The building was used as the police garage for many years and as the Cab Office between 1979 and 1986 when they moved to Murrayburn Road.

Edinburgh Academy

Designed by William Burn and opened in 1824 it was always surrounded by controversy. When the building of a new school was being considered by the Town Council this site was considered inappropriate and the site on Calton Hill was chosen but Sir Walter Scott and Lord Cockburn and the original subscribers decided to build on this site in defiance of the Town Council. The building contractor ran out of money and the building was not finished until 1829 at a cost of £24,200.

The Deaf and Dumb Institute which was founded in 1819 was built on a site to the west. This later became part of Donaldson's School for the Deaf as their nursery and infant department, the building was sold to Edinburgh Academy in 1977. During the filming of Muriel Spark's book *The Prime of Miss Jean Brodie* in 1968 the building was used as the Marcia Blaine School for Girls.

Glenogle Road

For two hundred years, on the site of the Barratt houses at Ettrickdale Place and Liddesdale Place, stood the whisky distillery of the Haig family whose motto was 'Don't Be Vague Ask For Haig' until it was demolished in the early 1970s.

This was the scene of the 'meal mob riots' in 1783. Due to a bad harvest there was a shortage of food and when stories began to circulate that vast amounts of potatoes and oats were being bought by the distillery, an angry crowd assembled and were intent on wrecking the distillery, employees were issued with firearms and the sheriff read the riot act. The mob returned a few days later but were driven off by the military.

Canonmills

When King David I granted the building of Holyrood Abbey to the Augustine Order in 1128 he granted them land in this area and built them a mill on the Water of Leith. The name has nothing to do with 'Cannons' as suggested by the housing development called 'Cannons Court' and displaying a large cannon.

Canonmills Clock

By L. Graham Thomson 1947.

In 1842 Queen Victoria and Prince Albert visited the city for the first time and it was intended to present the keys of the city to her at a triumphal arch at Canonmills, then the city boundary, but owing to a mix up the Royal party landed at Granton unheralded and neither the Lord Provost, James Forrest, the Bailies, the Royal Company of Archers nor the High Constables were in position when she passed through the arch.

In the plan, when the Queen's ship passed Dunbar a beacon would be lit. This would be seen on Calton Hill and a flag would be raised, this would be seen from the Castle and a double gun salute would be fired to warn the Town Council. However, due to a storm she passed Dunbar in darkness and arrived at Granton unexpectedly. The Duke of Buccleuch sent a runner to the Castle to inform them and also a runner to Archer's Hall to warn the Royal Company of Archers. A double gun salute was fired from the Castle and the Town Council, thinking they had plenty of time, went to the City Chambers for a leisurely breakfast. The Royal Company of Archers running down Dundas Street met the Queen en route to Dalkeith. She arrived at Dalkeith Palace before the welcoming party caught up with her. She graciously agreed to receive the keys at the Mercat Cross the next day. This led to the singing of a song called 'Hey Jamie Forrest are ye waukin yet' based on the tune 'Johnnie Cope'

Hey Jamie Forrest are ye waukin yet?
Or are your Bailie's snorin' yet
If you are waukin I would wit
ye'd hae a merry, merry mornin!
The Queen she's come tae Granton Pier,
Nae Provost and nae Bailie's here:
they're in their beds I muckle fear
sae early in the mornin'
The Queen she's come tae Brandon Street
The Provost and the keys tae meet
and div ye think that she's to wait
till ye're waukin in the mornin'.

Canonmills Service Station

On the gable wall can be seen an old lintel stone with the inscription 'the Baxters land 1686' which was rescued from an earlier building when it was demolished. On the front of the baker's shop just opposite the garage can be seen a hitching post for dogs while their owners are inside.

Warriston Crescent

At No 10 Chopin lodged on a visit in 1848. A plaque on the wall commemorates this.

No. 8 Howard Place

Robert Louis Stevenson was born here on 13 November 1850.

Royal Botanic Gardens

One of the finest in Europe, specialising in flora from the Himalayas and South West China. It has been here since 1836, but there has been a Physic Garden in Edinburgh since 1670 and claims to be the second oldest in Britain. The large Palm House designed by Robert Matheson and built in 1858 is the largest greenhouse in Britain at over 70ft high. In the grounds stands Inverleith House built in 1773 by James Rocheid, which for many years housed the Scottish Gallery of Modern Art before it moved to Belford Road.

Fettes College

By David Bryce in 1864. The Merchant, Sir William Fettes, who died in 1836 had left £166,000 for the establishment of the school, the main building cost £150,000 including accommodation for fifty foundationers. Ian Fleming's character, James Bond, went to school here, as did Tony Blair the Prime Minister.

Ann Street

Built between 1815–25, designed by Sir Henry Raeburn, portrait painter, and named after his wife this was the first street in Edinburgh built with gardens.

Holy Trinity Church

Designed by John Henderson in 1838, the church closed and for many years was an electricity sub station. Now in use as a church again it gives new meaning to the phrase 'The power and the glory'

Dean Bridge

Paid for by John Learmonth, Lord Provost, to open up access to his Learmonth estate, and designed by Thomas Telford in 1832. The bridge is hollow to carry water pipes and electric cables. The bridge was completed three weeks early and the builder refused to hand it over until the contract date, and charged people 1d. a time to walk across. The parapets were made higher in 1912, making it more difficult to jump off.

Moray Place

Designed by James Gillespie Graham in 1822 it has twelve sides but only two at a time can be seen. Lord Moray lived at No. 28. No. 36 is the Queen's House and used as a Grace and Favour residence.

Doune Terrace

Designed by James Gillespie Graham in 1822. No. 1 was the home of

Robert Chambers the historical writer and co-founder with his brother William of the publishing firm W. & R. Chambers.

Duncan's Land

The building is 18th cent. A door lintel reading 'Fear God Only 1605' was rescued from an Old Town building.

St Stephen's Church

By Wm. Playfair in 1827, allegedly to hide Edinburgh Academy from the New Town. It has the longest pendulum in Europe.

Tour Four

Holyrood Palace, Holyrood Park, Duddingston Village, Craigmillar Castle Road, Kingston Avenue, Liberton Drive, Braid Hills Road, Biggar Road, Oxgangs Road, Swanston Road, Redford Road, Colinton Road, Balcarres Street, Morningside Road, Holy Corner, Bruntsfield Place, Tollcross, Lauriston Place, George IV Bridge.

Palace of Holyrood House

Originated as a great house for the Abbey, the present Palace was begun in 1498 by James IV who died at the Battle of Flodden in 1513, the Palace was completed by his son James V between 1528–32. Severely damaged by the English during what was known as 'The Rough Wooing' in 1543, and again by fire during Cromwell's occupation in 1650 it was restored in 1658 but all the work was pulled down in 1671 when construction of the Palace as we know it today, was begun by Charles II, who carried out James I's idea of two matching towers. The cupola clock dates from 1680. The fountain is a copy of the one at Linlithgow Palace designed by John Thomas in 1859 and replaces a statue of Queen Victoria with which she was not amused. The 1633 sundial is by Robert Mylne.

Mary Queen of Scots' secretary, David Rizzio, was dragged from her chamber and stabbed to death on 19 March 1566. After Bonnie Prince Charlie left in 1745 it was unused for fifty years until Count D' Artois, later Charles X of France sheltered here during the French Revolution.

It is the Queen's official residence in Scotland, although it is said to be her least favourite.

St Margaret's Well

Dates from fifteenth century and was originally in Restalrig but was moved due to the construction of St Margaret's railway engine depot, now the site of St Margaret's House and Meadowbank House.

St Anthony's Chapel

This small ruin dates from the early fifteenth century and may have belonged to the Knights Hospitallers of St Anthony at Leith to watch for the arrival of ships and to hang up a guiding light.

Mushchat's Cairn

In 1720 Nichol Muschat, a surgeon, cut his wife's throat after attempts to divorce and poison her failed because it is said that she was 'very free with her favours'

The cairn was moved here from Hunter's Bog for the visit of King George IV visit in 1822, and is mentioned in Scott's *Heart of Midlothian*.

Dunsapie Loch

Built as part of Prince Albert's plan to beautify the Park it is artificial and just over 4 metres deep.

Radical Road was built at the instigation of Sir Walter Scott to provide work for the unemployed after the Napoleonic Wars so that they would not be swayed by radical orators and so it was named The Radical Road. A children's quiz poses the question,

'Round and round the Radical Road.

The radical rascal ran

If you can tell me how many 'R's' are in that

I'll call you a clever wee man.'

The answer being there are no 'R's'in 'that'.

The last private owner of the park the Earl of Haddington allowed quarrying in the early nineteenth century to pave the streets of London.

Duddingston Loch

Duddingston Loch is the only natural loch in Holyrood Park and is now a bird sanctuary as part of Scottish Wildlife Trust's Wildlife

Reserve, but it was not always so. Weavers living in Duddingston Village harvested the reeds from the loch and wove them into a coarse fabric called 'Duddingston Hardings'. The Duddingston Curling Society was founded in 1795 and produced a set of rules which are now used throughout the world but the society disbanded in 1948.

Duddingston Kirk

Duddingston Kirk dates from 1120 but has had many alterations over the centuries although it has retained its Norman charm. At the gates there are stone steps known as 'Loupin on Stane' which enabled lady riders and obese gentlemen to mount their horses after the service, and were also used to rest the coffin on the way to a burial. Embedded in the wall is an iron ring known as 'The Jougs' which was used to punish parishioners who were found guilty of moral crimes such as drunkenness, blasphemy, adultery, the offender being chained to the wall until the service started then made to sit on a stool in front of the congregation and swear before God not to repeat the offence. During improvements a hole was discovered in the wall and is said to be a 'Lepers Squint', enabling lepers from a nearby colony to witness the service without mixing with the congregation. The most famous of the ministers at Duddingston was the Reverend John Thomson who was minister from 1805 until his death in 1840 aged sixty two. He always referred to his flock as 'My Bairns' which gives rise to the expression 'We are all Jock Tamson's Bairns' used by Scots all over the world and meaning that all men are equal. He was a famous landscape artist and was a member of the Royal Scottish Academy. He had a studio on the shore of the loch which he named Edinburgh so he could paint uninterrupted by unwelcome visitors, as his servants could truthfully say to callers that 'He had gone to Edinburgh'.

Today the village has the attraction of Dr Neil's garden which although only open at certain times has raised money for charity.

The Sheep Heid Inn

The Sheep Heid Inn is one of the oldest pubs in the city as it has been in business since the fourteenth century and was a favourite of King James IV who presented it with a silver snuff box mounted in a sheep's head. The skittle alley is the oldest in Scotland and is home to the 'Sheep Heid Trotters'.

In the Causeyway is the building known as Prince Charlie's house where Charles Edward Stuart stayed on the 19 September 1745 before defeating General Cope at the Battle of Prestonpans.

The Innocent Railway

The Innocent Railway is now a cycle path but was originally a railway line to transport coal from Dalkeith to Edinburgh at St Leonards. It did not have steam engines and all trains were pulled by horses and acquired the nickname because they never had an accident and no-one was killed or injured. This novel form of transport appealed to the public and soon they were going for outings on Sundays until the Company was transporting over three hundred thousand passengers a year and were making as much money from passengers as coal. The railway closed in 1968 under the Beeching cuts.

Craigmillar Castle

Sir Simon Preston bought the Castle in 1374, and it was burned by Hereford during the 'Rough Wooing' in 1544. Mary Queen of Scots was a frequent visitor and came here after the murder of Rizzio in 1566. Restoration work was carried out in 1951.

Little France

There is a dubious story that this area got its name from Mary Queen of Scots' French courtiers who lived here while the Queen was in residence at Craigmillar Castle.

The clubhouse of Liberton Golf Course was built as Kingston Grange and designed by Robert Adam in 1785.

Liberton Village

Liberton is believed to be a corruption of Lepertoun so named from a leper colony in the area.

The lands were granted to the monks of Holyrood by King David I in 1143. The parish church is by Gillespie Graham in 1815, replacing an earlier one.

Liberton House was built for the Littles of Liberton in 1675. Liberton Tower was built for the Dalmahoys of Liberton in the fifteenth century.

Royal Observatory

Designed by W. W. Robertson in 1896 it is an important station for recording earthquakes and nuclear explosions. It also is linked to telescopes in Hawaii and Australia.

Braid Hills Golf Course

The first children's golf course in the city, work started spring 2003.

Braid Hills Golf Course is believed to be among the finest public golf courses in the world. It was opened in 1889 and a second 18-hole course was opened in 1922.

The Buck Stane

Marks the spot where the buckhounds were unleashed when Royal Parties went hunting in the area. Legend has it that the Clerks of Penicuik had to blow three blasts on a trumpet when the King went hunting, to retain ownership of the land.

On Biggar Road opposite the Fairmile Inn stood the Bowbridge cottage which was the last illicit still in Scotland.

Caiystane View

The Caiystane, a standing stone, marks the site of a prehistoric battle and is now the property of the National Trust for Scotland.

Swanston Cottage

The summer residence of Robert Louis Stevenson, the village is mentioned in his novel *St Ives*, the story of a French prisoner during the Napoleonic Wars who escaped from the Castle.

The Hunters Tryst Inn

An eighteenth century inn much modified which was the meeting place for the Six Foot High Club all of whose members had to be over six foot tall although exceptions were made, namely Sir Walter Scott and James Hogg.

Dreghorn Castle

Nothing now remains of what was once Colinton's finest house. Built for Sir William Murray, the castle had many owners including Alexander Trotter who purchased it in 1797 and sold it to R. A. Macfie. It later became a private school before being purchased by the Government for use by the War Department. Poor maintenance and neglect led to the demolition by the Army in 1955 in what must be considered a gross act of vandalism, first by using flame throwers to destroy the interior then explosives to flatten the shell. All that remains are the two lodge houses, one next to the Hunters Tryst Inn, now converted into houses and the other on Redford Road at the bridge over the Braidburn.

Oxgangs

Takes its name from the old Scots measure of land, namely 13 acres, which was the area that could be ploughed by an ox drawn plough in a year.

The Covenantors Monument on Redford Road was constructed by R. A. MacFie using columns from the old Royal Infirmary which was demolished in 1884

At the junction of Redford Road and Colinton Road stands the 'Sixpenny Tree' where the Guild of Papermakers are reputed to have met to pay their Guild Dues, the tree was replaced in the 1980s.

Henry MacKenzie's Cottage

The plaque reads 'In this house lived Henry MacKenzie Author of A *Man of Feeling.* Born 25 August 1745. Died 14 January 1831'.

Colinton Village

Has been in existence for over nine hundred years and among its famous residents are the Rev. Lewis Balfour, Robert Louis Stevenson's maternal grandfather who was minister of the parish from 1823–1860, and James Gillespie who lived in Spylaw House which he had built in 1773.

James and his brother John owned a snuff mill on the Water of Leith and while James concentrated on the running of the Mill his brother ran the retail side from a shop in the High Street. They never married and when James died on 8 April 1789 he left his fortune to found a school for poor boys, which today is on Lauderdale Street, for which the wit the Hon. Henry Erskine suggested as a motto 'Wha wad hae thocht it, that noses had bocht it'.

In Spylaw Street the row of cottages which were once owned by Gillespie for his workers are now owned by the Merchant Company and are granted free of rent to deserving pensioners.

Malcolm Cant in his *Villages of Edinburgh* relates the story of an inscription of a tombstone reputed to be in the Graveyard 'Here lyes the banes o' Cuthbert Denholm, if ye saw him noo ye wouldna ken him'.

The last passenger train service was on 30 October 1943 although the line remained open for goods traffic serving the mills on the Water of Leith until the Beeching cuts of the 1960s. It is now part of the Water of Leith walkway.

Merchiston Castle School

Stands in the grounds of the ruined Colinton Castle which dates from the sixteenth century. The school was founded in 1828 by Charles Chalmers, whose brother Thomas led the Disruption of 1843, and was owner and headmaster until 1850. In need of more space he leased, in 1833, Merchiston Tower on Colinton Road which had been the home of the Napier Family. Again short of space he tried to have extensions done but this was not possible. When Colinton House came on the market he sold Merchiston Tower to the Merchant Company and purchased Colinton in 1924 with the first pupils registering in 1930.

Redford Barracks

This was built by Colin MacAndrew and Partners in 1909 who laid a railway line from their premises in Dalry to convey the building materials.

Craiglockhart Hydropathic

This Italian style villa was built in 1877 by Peddie and Kinnear but in the nineteenth century Hydropathics were not profitable and it was used during the First World War as a military hospital for officers suffering from shell shock which earned it the nickname of 'Dottyville'.

Two of the most famous patients were the war poets, Siegfried Sassoon and Wilfred Owen, who came here to recover from the traumas of the trenches. Sassoon was a very brave man winning the Military Cross and being wounded in 1917 and returning to England. Owen returned to the front line where he was killed a week before the Armistice.

In 1920 the Society of the Sacred Heart purchased the building and used it as a convent and training college for Roman Catholic teachers. In 1965 it became Craiglockhart College of Education and in 1986 became part of Napier College.

Bruce Street

Tommy Armour lived here as a boy. He became a member of Lothianburn Golf Course and fought in the First World War as a tank commander where he was gassed and wounded in the head causing him to lose the sight of one eye. After the war he emigrated to America where he won the U. S. Open in 1929 and the U. S. P. G. A. in 1930 and The Open when it was first held at Carnoustie in 1931. He became known as 'The Silver Scot'.

23 Balcarres Street

Where Robert Louis Stevenson's nurse Alison 'Cummy' Cunningham to whom he dedicated A Child's Garden of Verse lived in 1893. She died aged 91 and was buried in Morningside Cemetery.

'The Canny Man's'

So called as the proprietor James Kerr would tell his customer's to 'Ca Canny', it is probably Edinburgh's most unique pub with a varied collection of relics and where sawdust is still used on the floor. It has been in the Kerr family since 1871 and its proper name is 'The Volunteer Arms' as the Edinburgh Volunteers would call in after shooting practice on the Braid Hills. The signpost outside shows a kneeling rifleman on both sides and was painted by Sam Brough R. S. A., possibly to pay a bar bill.

Cannaan Lane

On the right hand side is Goshen Bank House where Reginald Johnston was born in 1874. He became the tutor to the last Emperor of China. Johnston died in Edinburgh in 1938.

Peter O' Toole played the part of Johnston in the film *The Last Emperor*.

Church Hill Theatre

Formerly the Morningside Free Church it became vacant in 1960 following a merger of congregations with Morningside Parish Church. It was purchased by the Council for £6,000 and a further £67,000 was spent on conversion to a theatre where many amateur dramatic companies staged productions. It became the Churchhill Theatre in September 1965 and is now a venue during the Festival.

George Watson's College

Founded by first accountant of the Bank of Scotland in 1723 and moved here in 1930.

Napier College

Napier College now surrounds Merchiston Castle, a fifteenth century building which was acquired by the Napier family in 1438 and was the birthplace in 1550 of John who is credited with inventing logarithms. His tables were published in 1614, three years before his death. He is also the inventor of 'Napier's Bones', an early form of calculating machine.

The Borestone

On the wall of the former Morningside Parish Church is located a boulder where legend has it the Royal Standard was planted by James IV on the Burgh Muir when the Scottish army mustered before the Battle of Flodden.

Holy Corner

So named for the churches on each corner.

The former North Morningside Church is now home to the Eric Liddell Centre.

Eric Liddell was born in China where his parents were missionaries, he attended boarding school in Edinburgh and entered Edinburgh University in 1920 where he played rugby for Scotland. As a runner he qualified for the Olympic Games in Paris in 1924 where he won a gold Medal in the 400 metres and a bronze in the 200. He passed up the chance of another medal when he would not run in the qualifying heats which were held on a Sunday. He graduated from University in 1924 with a science degree.

He went to China to work as a missionary in 1925 and in 1941 sent his family home but, against Foreign Office advice, he elected to stay. During the Japanese occupation of China he was placed in an internment camp where he died of a brain tumour in 1945.

The actor Ian Charleston played him in the film *Chariots of Fire* which told the story of his part in the 1924 Olympics.

Bruntsfield Links

One of the earliest places where golf was played. Edinburgh Burgess Golfing Society and Bruntsfield Links Golf Club both started here. There is still golf being played today over the Short Hole Course known as Pitch and Putt.

It was here that the Scottish Army mustered in 1513 and during the outbreak of the plague in 1645 was used to bury many of the victims.

Golf Tavern

One of the oldest pubs in city.

Barclay Church

Designed by F. T. Pilkington 1864, its 250 spire can be seen from Fife.

King's Theatre

Built 1906. Foundation stone laid by Andrew Carnegie.

Fire Museum

The headquarters of the Fire Brigade designed by City Architect Robert Morham in 1897, it houses early forms of fire appliances.

Edinburgh College of Art

By J. M. Dick Peddie in 1906 with extension by Ralph Cowan in 1961 it has large sized windows to let in light.

Chalmers Hospital

Designed by Peddie and Kinnear in 1861 and paid for by George Chalmers 1773–1836, a Canongate plumber, who died and left £30,000 for the purpose.

Royal Infirmary

The site was agreed in 1867 and work began in 1872 by David Bryce, completed by his nephew, it follows the principles laid down by Florence Nightingale and her approval was obtained. It was built to replace the old building in Infirmary Street. In front of the central entrance is a statue to George II who granted a charter to the infirmary in 1736. The sculptor was James Hill in 1759; the statue was brought from the old hospital. The infirmary moved to a new site at Little France in May 2003.

George Heriot's School

Built between 1628–1660 with money left by George Heriot ('Jinglin Geordie') Goldsmith and court Jeweller to King James V. The clock tower and statue of Heriot were added by Robert Mylne in 1693. The building has 200 windows no two of which are alike.

Between 1650 and 1658 the unfinished building was used as a hospital by Oliver Cromwell's troops wounded in the Battle of Dunbar. The school opened for thirty boys in 1659.

The perimeter wall contains parts of the Flodden Wall of 1513

Edinburgh University Medical School

Designed by Rowland Anderson and built in 1878 at a cost of £300,000.

Greyfriars Kirk

Built in 1612 and opened for worship in 1620. The National Covenant was signed here in 1638. It was used as a barracks by Cromwell's troops.

In 1679 after the Battle of Bothwell Brig over two hundred Covenanter prisoners were confined in the open air for five months. In 1718 the old tower which was being used as a gunpowder store blew up and a new church was built alongside in 1721. The old church burned down in 1845 and was rebuilt by David Bryce in 1857. It continued as two separate churches until 1938 when the dividing walls were removed.

In 1979 when the Highland Tolbooth church closed down the congregation moved to Greyfriars where the services on a Sunday afternoon are held in Gaelic.

Buried in the churchyard are many famous people including James Craig, architect of the New Town, George Watson, founder of School, Regent Morton, James Gillespie Graham architect, John Porteous captain of Town Guard and hung in Porteous Riot and Sir George Mackenzie of Rosehaugh ('Bluidy MacKenzie') Founder of Advocates library and persecutor of the Covenantors and at whose crypt the boys from Heriots would call out, 'Bluidy MacKenzie come oot if ye daur, lift the sneck and draw the bar'

Greyfriars Bobby

When his master Jock Grey died in 1858 and was buried in Greyfriars the dog refused to leave his grave and slept there for 14 years. It was given the freedom of the city and when it died Queen Victoria suggested that it be buried beside his master. Baroness Coutts of the banking family raised the money to pay for the statue which was sculpted by William Brodie and unveiled in 1873.

Royal Scottish Museum

Designed by Captain Fowke of the Royal Engineers in 1861 the foundation stone was laid by the Prince Consort, the last public duty before his death. It is the largest general museum in Britain with further extensions in 1990s.

National Library

Built in 1956 and designed by Robert Fairlie on a site previously occupied by the Sheriff Court between 1868 and 1938 when it was demolished to make way for the Library. The building has two storeys on George IV Bridge and a further nine below. It is a copyright library and as such it is entitled to receive a copy of every book published in Britain, and has over 3 million books. It is not a lending library; all books must be read on the premises.

On the front are sculptures by Hew Lorimer representing the Arts and Sciences and at each end cherubs learning Braille and sign language.

Central Public Library

Founded on a gift from Andrew Carnegie it was designed by Sir George Washington Browne and houses the Edinburgh Room where the staff with their encyclopaedic knowledge have helped many researchers. The Highland Institute, built in 1836 and one of the first buildings on the bridge, became part of the library as a Music Library.

Tour 5

Waverley Bridge, Calton Hill, Royal Terrace, Leith Walk, Constitution Street, Shore, Salamander Street, Portobello High Street, Joppa, Milton Road.

Statue of David Livingston (1813–73)

By Mrs Amelia Hill, wife of the photographic pioneer David Octavius Hill. It was thought that this statue was too small to stand the rigours of the open air. David Livingston was born in Blantyre and studied medicine in London. He became a missionary in 1840 and worked in Bechuanaland (now Malawi). He married in 1844. He explored the Zambezi River, discovering the Victoria Falls which he named after Queen Victoria. He returned home in 1864 and in 1866 returned to Africa, this time to Zanzibar. He lost contact with the outside world while searching for the source of the Nile. *New York Herald* editor Gordon Bennett sent out Henry Morton Stanley to find him. When they met it was with the now famous quotation, 'Dr Livingston, I presume'. When he died his body was brought back to Westminster Abbey for burial.

Scott Monument

By George Meikle Kemp, a Peeblesshire carpenter and self taught architect, completed in 1844 at a cost of £16,000. The height is 200ft, a staircase of 287 steps takes you to the top. The foundations are 50ft (15 metres) deep.

The statue of Scott and his dog Maida was carved out of a block of Carrera marble by the sculptor Sir John Steele. There are 64 characters out of Scott's novels on the Monument. Meikle Kemp never saw the monument completed as he drowned in the canal in 1844.

Jenners

Designed by Sir William Hamilton Beattie in 1895 to replace an earlier building destroyed by fire, it was the first steel framed building in Scotland. Charles Jenner and his friend Kennington were fired for taking a half-day holiday to go to Musselburgh races. As a result they started their own business. The pillars on the façade are carved in the shape of women, as 'Women are the foundation of our business'.

Balmoral Hotel

Built for the North British Railway Company in 1902 and designed by Sir William Hamilton Beattie, named the 'North British' and known affectionately as the 'N. B.' The clock tower is 195ft high, the clock faces are 13ft in diameter, the minute hands 6ft 3ins (1.4 metres) long, the hour hands are 4ft 6ins (1.4 metres) long. The clock is always kept three minutes fast so that passengers will not miss their trains.

Burger King

For many years an F. W. Woolworth's store and occupying the site of the first house to be built on Princes Street.

John Neale a silk merchant was induced in 1769 to move here from the Old Town only after the Town Council agreed to waive his rates.

Register House

Designed by the brothers Robert and James Adam, it is the Public Record Office for Scotland. This was the first major work to be started in the New Town and was funded by the proceeds of forfeited Jacobite estates, some £12,000.

Work started in 1774 and it opened in 1789, still uncompleted, at a cost of £80,000 and earned it the nickname of 'The most magnificent pigeon coop in Europe'. It was not finally finished until 1827. It houses the Declaration of Arbroath and the Treaty of Union, and also the Court of the Lord Lyon King of Arms. The former sentry boxes in front now house a clock and barometer.

Duke of Wellington

The twelve-ton bronze statue was cast in a foundry in Grove Street. The victor of the Battle of Waterloo on his favourite horse, Copenhagen, liked the statue so much that he had a copy made for his own house in London. At the unveiling in 1852 there was a violent thunderstorm and the *Scotsman* reported the proceedings the next day as, 'Mid lightning's flash and thunders peal, behold the Iron Duke in bronze by Steele'. He earned the nickname 'The Iron Duke' not because of his military exploits, but as a result of having steel shutters put on his house to protect it from rioters.

North Bridge

Lord Provost George Drummond pushed to open the land to the north as part of his plan for the New Town.

The Nor' Loch was partly drained in 1763 for the foundations of the bridge to the design of William Mylne, and the foundation stone was laid by Lord Provost Drummond. Due to faults in the founds an arch of the bridge collapsed in 1769 killing workmen. The bridge reopened in 1772 and due to increased traffic was widened in 1873.

In 1874 the bridge was demolished for the construction of the present bridge and the foundation stone was laid in 1896. The new bridge like the old one has three arches, is 525ft (160metres) long and is an ironwork structure by William Arrol of Forth Bridge fame. It was opened in 1897.

Standing on the site of the old Theatre Royal, the building at the corner of North Bridge and Princes Street is the former General Post Office, designed by Robert Matheson, the foundation stone was laid by Prince Albert on 23 October 1861. It took five years to complete and cost £120,000. Due to reorganisation of the Post Office the building is presently empty and undergoing major renovation work. In front of the building is a Hitching Post where the Post Corporal from Peirshill Barracks would tether his horse whilst collecting the mail.

At the junction of Princes Street and Waterloo Place is the last remaining section of cable car tramlines. Tram cars ceased running in 1956.

Regent Bridge

Built in 1816 the bridge was designed as a memorial to celebrate the victory of the Battle of Waterloo. The architect was Archibald Elliot and the engineer Robert Stevenson and it was the first 'flyover' in Scotland, crossing as it does Calton Road below.

Calton Cemetery

The Martyrs Monument is an obelisk designed by Thomas Hamilton in 1844 and commemorates the memory of five men, Thomas Muir, Thomas Fyche Palmer, William Skirving, Maurice Margarot and Joseph Gerald who were charged with treason and sentenced to transportation for advocating Parliamentary Reform in 1793. The philosopher, David Hume's grave is marked by a memorial by Robert Adam in 1777. The statue of Abraham Lincoln was the first statue to an American President to be erected in Britain. Unveiled in 1893 it is in memory of Scots who died on both sides in the American Civil War.

Rock House

Between 1843–69 it was the house and studio of David Octavius Hill, portrait painter and pioneer of photography.

His wife Amelia Hill sculpted the statue of David Livingston. At the foot of the staircase leading to Rock House are three medallions commemorating three Scottish Tenors, Kennedy, Templeton, and Wilson.

Calton Jail

In 1808 work was begun on the Calton Jail which was to replace the Tolbooth prison. It opened in 1817 and closed in 1925 when Saughton Prison was opened. It was demolished in 1937 to allow the building of St Andrew's House.

All that remains is the Governor's house which was built in 1815 to a design of Archibald Elliot. At the time of opening it was described as 'A piece of undoubted bad taste to give so glorious an eminence to a prison'.

St Andrew's House

Government Offices built by Thomas Tait in 1939 on the site of Calton Jail. The bronze doors carry a bas-relief of the Scottish Saints Andrew, Ninian, Kentigren, Columba and Magnas by Walter Gilbert and represent 'I will make you fishers of men'.

Royal High School

Designed by Thomas Hamilton in 1829 at a cost of £24,000, it is a copy of a Greek temple.

The High School was founded in 1128 and is one of the oldest schools in Britain. Originally it was in High School Yards but former pupils including Sir Walter Scott and Lord Cockburn decided a new building was required. They had a disagreement with the Town Council and decided to build their school at Canonmills (Edinburgh Academy). The school moved to Barnton in 1969 when it went co-educational. The building was proposed as the home of the Scottish Parliament but was deemed unsuitable. Part of it is now used as an artists co-operative.

Nelson Monument

Built to commemorate his victory at the Battle of Trafalger it is in the shape of an upturned telescope which represents his famous act of raising his telescope to his blind eye and remarking 'I see no ships'.

Designed by Robert Burn in 1816 the tower is 106ft high and carries a time ball that is linked to the one o'clock gun and is a time signal to ships in the Forth. Above the door is a sculpture representing the stern of Nelson's ship *San Joseph*. On Trafalgar day the Monument has flags spelling out his message to his fleet before the battle 'England expects that every man will do his duty'.

National Monument

Intended to be a memorial to the Scottish soldiers and sailors who died during the Napoleonic Wars and to be a copy of the Parthenon, the original design was by C. R. Cockerell and the architect was W. H. Playfair and to be funded by public subscription. £12,000 was raised and the foundation stone was laid 27 August 1822. Each of the twelve Doric columns is built of blocks of Craigleith stone weighing ten to fifteen tons each, and costing £1000, but money ran out and the work was never completed, leading it to be named Scotland's Pride and Poverty or Edinburgh's Disgrace.

The lintel stone at 140 yards is the largest single stone quarried in Britain.

Dugald Stewart Memorial

By W. H. Playfair in 1831 it is a copy of the Lysicrates monument in Athens and is in memory of Dugald Stewart, Professor of Moral Philosophy at Edinburgh University between 1786–1828.

City Observatory

The work of James Craig, who planned the New Town. Work was started in 1776 but due to financial difficulties it was not completed until 1792 when it was discovered that there was no money left to buy a telescope (a handy thing for an Observatory). A group of interested parties formed the Astronomical Institution and commissioned W. H. Playfair to design a new observatory, this he did modelling it on the Temple of the Winds and erected in 1818. The old observatory became the Astronomers house. Set into the south facing wall is Playfair's monument to his uncle, Professor John Playfair, (1748–1819) Philosopher and Mathematician who was President of the Astronomical Institution.

Burns Monument

By Thomas Hamilton and erected in 1832 it is, like Dugald Stewart's memorial, a copy of the Greek Temple of Lysicrates.

Regent Terrace

Built around 1825 it was to be the first part of a New Town stretching from Calton Hill to Leith and designed by Playfair. There is a wrought iron balcony running the entire length of the street.

Royal Terrace

'Whisky Row' as it became known was the home of a number of whisky distillers and ship owners who could watch for their ships arriving in Leith Docks. It has the longest continuous frontage in the city with 17 sections, 7 of them colonnaded with a Corinthian columned section in the middle and a quarter of a mile in length. It was built between 1821–1860.

Haddington Place was once the site of the Botanical Gardens between 1763 and 1820 when it was moved to Inverleith.

A popular name for the street running from Princes Street to Great Junction Street is 'Leith Walk' but in fact Leith Walk only extends from Great Junction Street ('the foot of the walk') to Pilrig Street. A common expression for anyone looking sad and forlorn is 'Having a face as long as Leith Walk'.

In the seventeenth century the main road from North Leith to Edinburgh was by Bonnington Road, Broughton Village, the side of Calton Hill by Leith Wynd to the Netherbow Port. There was also an 'Easter Road' beginning at South Leith and a road at Restalrig. In 1650, in defence against Cromwell, General Leslie dug a great trench and built a mound of earth 30 yards wide and a mile in length from the Kirkgate to Calton Hill which successfully defied Cromwell's cavalry and artillery. Cromwell later defeated Leslie at the Battle of Dunbar. Leslie was the inspiration for the children's nursery rhyme 'There was a crooked man'.

The mound became a handsome gravel walk, over which no horses were allowed prior to 1770. It became fashionable for the ladies of Edinburgh to come out on the 'Leith Walk' to take the air and admire the view (not withstanding the existence of a gallows where criminals were left to rot in chains) as there was a permanent gallows at Shrubhill.

It was the haunt of footpads and thieves at night. With the building of the North Bridge a causeway was laid and Leith Walk became a main highway.

Pilrig Church

French Gothic design by Peddie and Kinnear, built in 1862 and noted for its Rose window by Ballantine and Son.

This was the boundary between Edinburgh and Leith until the amalgamation of the burghs in 1920.

At the boundary stood a public house appropriately called the

'Boundary Bar' (now 'City Limits') where the boundary was marked on the bar by a brass plate. The bar had two doors, one in Leith and one in Edinburgh and with different licensing laws in the Burghs the door in the Edinburgh area had to be closed while the one in Leith remained open and the drinkers inside had to move over the boundary mark to remain drinking.

This was also the scene of what became known as the 'Pilrig Muddle'. In 1895 when the two burghs were considering changing from horse drawn trams to cable cars Edinburgh went ahead and changed while Leith prevaricated, so passengers had to change vehicles to continue their journey. It continued when Leith opted for Electric Trams and was not stopped until after the amalgamation. Edinburgh adopted electric trams in 1922.

'The Foot of the Walk'

Traditionally where Leithers met to celebrate Hogmanay it was from here that the Leith Volunteers (Scots Guards) set out to fight in the Boer War. Also from here in 1915 during the First World War the men of the 7th Battalion Royal Scots (Leith's Own) marched to Waverley station en route to France. Their train was involved in a rail crash at Quintinshill (Gretna Green) and three officers, twenty nine N.C.Os and one hundred and eighty two soldiers were killed in the crash and the resulting fire. Their bodies were brought back to Pilrig Cemetery for burial.

Queen Victoria Statue

Designed by John Rhind in 1907. When Lord Rosebery performed the unveiling 20,000 attended. When the statue was moved for restoration in 1985 a casket was found containing Leith newspapers dated 1907. When the statue was replaced a copy of the *Edinburgh Evening News* was put in the casket along with a mint set of 1985 coins. The statue was moved a few yards to the east in 2002.

Leith Central Station

Leith Central Station opened in 1903 to cash in on the 'Pilrig Muddle' and the five-minute journey to Waverley known, as the 'Penny Jump' became very popular. Passenger traffic declined and after the Second

World War the station was closed. In the 1950s it was transformed into a diesel maintenance depot, the first in Scotland. The depot closed down in 1972 and the building was demolished to make way for a leisure complex and shopping centre, all that remains is the clock tower at the corner of Duke Street.

Trinity House

In the Kirkgate stands Trinity House, the headquarters of the Company of Master Mariners, which was founded in 1380 to help Mariners who had fallen on hard times and to teach mathematics in schools. In 1680 they employed a professor of mathematics to teach maths and navigation to the sons of the members. The present building dates from 1816 and the architect was Thomas Brown. The vast collection of maritime artefacts collected over centuries was put on public display in 2003.

South Leith Parish Church

Founded by the Trade Incorporations in 1483, it was looted during the Rough Wooing in 1544 and destroyed by English Artillery in 1560. It was rebuilt in 1846.

Leith Council Chamber

Built by R. & R. Dickson in 1828, the council chamber contains a painting by Alexander Carse of King George IV landing at Leith on 15 August 1822, his only state visit to Scotland. The ceiling painted in 1892 has heraldry Coats of Arms of families who are connected to Leith, although it must be pointed out that there are a few errors.

The Council Chamber has not been used since the amalgamation in 1920. The ground floor is now used as Leith Police Station.

Leith Assembly Rooms and Exchange Building

The Assembly Rooms were opened in 1783 and soon became the social centre of the port. The Exchange Building was added in 1809 the architect being Thomas Brown. The building has been converted into flats.

Burns Statue

Erected by the Leith Burns Appreciation Society in 1898 and designed by D. W. Stevenson. The red sandstone plinth is decorated with bronze reliefs depicting scenes from Burns' poetry. The statue, facing as it does Constitution Street with its back to the Docks, has been facetiously said by Leith Dockers to have been so positioned, as he could not stand the sight of hard work.

Corn Exchange

Built in 1860 by Peddie & Kinnear at a cost of £6,500 it has a frieze by John Rhind completed in 1862 depicting cherubs growing corn and milling flour. Part of the building houses the Corn Exchange Bar whose landlady for many years was the infamous Maggie Rae who kept order with the use of a cudgel and a foul tongue, indeed it was said that her language would make a passing sailor blush, and she was reputed to dry her knickers on the pie machine. When national television launched a quest to find Britain's rudest publican Maggie won hands down, a title she treasured.

Maggie died in April 2003.

Lamb's House

The home of Andrew Lamb, a prosperous merchant, it was here that Mary Queen of Scots rested after her arrival in Leith on 19 August 1561. The house was converted into flats but due to neglect fell into disrepair. In 1938 the Marquis of Bute purchased the building and had it restored at his own expense, he then gifted it to The National Trust for Scotland. In 1961 it was converted into a day centre for the elderly, the first such centre in Scotland.

Kings Wark

The Kings Wark was built by James I and extended by James II as a Royal Arsenal, citadel, palace and warehouse. Damaged by Hereford in 1544 it was rebuilt in the reign of Mary Queen of Scots. Stores for the Castle Garrison were taken ashore here and warehoused, many cannons and military materials were forged here, it being the principal arsenal of Scotland during Stuart times. A doorway still standing shows the date 1711.

James VI gave the building to Bernard Lindsay (who kept a tavern on what was called the Lang or East Sands where the sea began and now called Bernard Street after him) who rebuilt it in 1613. In 1617 he was made an honorary burgess on the occasion of a banquet given for James VI on his only visit to Scotland after becoming James I of England.

King's Landing

Hidden behind the moored ship on the shore is a plaque at the water's edge marking the spot where King George IV landed in 1822 and the Crown above it on the Quay was where the Royal Foot first touched Scottish soil. The cast iron tablet is inscribed 'Geo IV Rex O Felicem Diem (O Happy Day).

Most Royal landings took place here, including Mary Queen of Scots in 1561, Mary of Gueldres, Queen of James II in 1449, in 1469 Princess Margaret of Denmark who married James III, the French Princess Madeline first wife of James V in 1537, Mons Meg was also landed here in 1829 after having been in London.

Signal Tower

One of the oldest buildings in Leith, built in 1685 by Robert Mylne the King's Master Mason it was originally a rape seed oil windmill. In 1689 the Fraternity of Master Mariners was empowered to display warning flags to shipping showing the depth of the water and to charge 'Flag money' for the service. The monies were dispensed to the poor.

Malmaison Hotel

Originally the Sailors Home the building dates from 1883 and cost £10,000, it was built on land reclaimed from the sea.

The opening ceremony was performed by Lord Rosebery.

Statue of Sandy Irvine Robertson

He was chairman of the wine company Justerini & Brookes and was responsible for the introduction of Leith Claret. The statue was paid for by his friends and the sculptress was Lucy Poet.

Leith Links

One of the earliest homes of golf the game having been played here in the first half of the seventeenth century.

John Pattisone (Patterson) played a challenge game with the future James II and with his winnings built a house in the Canongate (Golfers Land). The Honourable Company of Edinburgh Golfers was founded in 1744 and the Town Council gave a silver club to be played for annually on the provision that the club be properly constituted and with a set of rules. This was done and the 13 rules that they laid down were adopted by St Andrews and form the basis of today's golf rulebook. Due to overcrowding on the Links the Honourable Company moved to Musselburgh and in 1891 moved to their present home at Muirfield where a copy of the original rules is on display. A cairn shows the layout of the five holes in 1744. The last professional tournament played on the links was on the 17 May 1867, among the competitors were Tom Morris and Tom Morris Jnr. Golf became a nuisance on the Links and was banned during the summer months. The Council leased land at Craigentinny and a course was laid out under the direction of Ben Sayers in 1907 and this marked the end of golf on the Links.

During July 2002 four holes were opened up and players were invited to play the holes using hickory shafted clubs. The event was such a success that in 2003 the 'Leith Rules Golf Society' was inaugurated with the intention of increasing recognition of Leith as one of the founding locations of golf.

Part of the links included Leith Sands where horse racing was a popular sport and two silver cups were given as prizes in 1665. The course stretched from the foot of Constitution Street to Seafield and a circuit measured two miles, two circuits made a heat and three heats made a race so the eventual winner would have to run twelve miles.

In the eighteenth century the races were held over a week and degenerated into a week of drunkenness, vandalism and fighting, and in 1816 much to the relief of Leithers the races were moved to Musselburgh where they are still held.

An attempt was made to re–establish the races but there was a public outcry and the last race meeting took place on 22 September 1859.

The two earthen mounds are known as Giant's Brae and Lady Fyfe's Brae and were constructed to give elevation to the English Artillery during the siege of Leith in 1560.

Mother Aitken's Bar

Built as Seafield Baths in 1813 and designed by John Patterson it had seventeen hot, cold and tepid baths as well as a plunge pool. Hotel accommodation was also provided.

Portobello

Known affectionately to the citizens as 'Porty' it was for many years Edinburgh's seaside resort. Founded by a retired sailor named George Hamilton who fought at the Battle of Puerto Bello in 1739 he built his house on a desolate spot and called it Puerto Bello.

In 1765 valuable deposits of clay were found at what today is Electra Place and William Jameson opened up the pottery industry manufacturing bricks, bottles and pottery. The Thistle Potteries moved to Crieff in 1972 and at the foot of Pipe Street are two bottle ovens dated 1906 and 1909.

Portobello was made a burgh in 1833 and amalgamated with Edinburgh in 1896.

Some notable residents in Portobello include 'Ned' Barnie who was the first Scot to swim the English Channel and in 1951 the first person to swim it in both directions. A science teacher at Portobello High School he swam in the Forth every day and to celebrate his 70th birthday swam the two miles from Musselburgh to Portobello. He died aged 87 on Christmas Day 1983.

The artist Sir William Russell Flint (1880–1970) was born in Lutton Place, he was a sickly child and on medical advice the family moved to Rosefield Place when he was three years old. He was educated at Melville College before moving to London in 1900. During the 1930s he was the leading master of water colour nudes, he was knighted in 1947.

Television presenter Gail Porter was born in 1971 and educated at

Portobello High School. Famously and unknown to her a nude photograph of her was projected onto the Houses of Parliament by a male magazine.

Andrew Marr, political journalist with the BBC, lived on the Esplanade while working as a journalist with the *Scotsman* newspaper.

J. G. Lockart, author, was Sir Walter Scott's son-in-law and biographer. He lived in what is now Bellfield Street and when he died he was buried at Scott's feet in Melrose Abbey.

At the junction of King's Road and Portobello High Street stood the Portobello Power Station with a 300 ft high chimney. It opened in 1923, closed in 1977 and was demolished in 1983. On the site next to it was Portobello open-air pool, designed by the City Engineers dept. and opened on 30 May 1936. The pool measured 300ftx130ft (90x39 metres) making it twice the size of the Commonwealth Pool. At the deep end there was a wave making machine which it is reported soaked the official party at the opening. Due to declining numbers the pool closed in 1979 and was demolished in 1987. The site is now occupied by five-a-side football pitches.

Bridge Street

No. 3 was where Harry Lauder (1870–1950) was born. A music hall singer who portrayed the Scots as being ultra careful with money, he himself could command a salary of £1,000 per week. He toured America twenty two times and entertained five American Presidents. He was the first British singer to sell a million records. Portobello by-pass is named after him.

Tower Street

In 1856 the celebrated geologist, stonemason, writer and founder of the 'Colonies' housing development, Hugh Miller, committed suicide at his home.

Joppa, ancient name for Jaffa or Tel Aviv in Israel, and the reasons for naming it thus are obscure. At one time there would have been salt pans on the shore used for making salt.

Queens Bay Lodge

Built by Charles Jenner in 1890 and now an eventide home. In front of the lodge Jenner had erected an exact copy of the 'Scalinger Railings' of Verona of 1380. The originals are on the tomb of the Scalingers of Verona.

The feature is the delicate ladders constantly repeated in the centres of the quatrefoils. This ladder (scala) is the family device. In the original the fabric is so flexible that the network may be shaken at a touch and is one of the finest examples of hammered ironwork in the world. This copy was made at Portobello in 1890 by James Ross blacksmith and David Grieg his assistant in the work.

Jewel and Esk Valley College

This was formerly the home of Leith Nautical College which moved here from Commercial Street in 1977 and explains why the building has a ship's superstructure.

Richard Corsie Leisure

Owned by what is probably Scotland's finest bowler. He has been World Champion both indoor and outdoor and is a Commonwealth Champion.

Duddingston Crescent

The twelve villas are known as 'The Twelve Apostles'.

Duddingston House

The Duddingston Estate was sold by the Duke of Argyll in 1745 to the Earl of Abercorn, who in 1763 had the house built to the design of William Chambers. The grounds were laid out by Capability Brown and are now Duddingston Golf Course. Edward VII considered buying it as a Royal residence but chose Sandringham instead.

Duddingston Golf Course

It opened in December 1894 as the Insurance and Banking Golf Course, but changed its name after the First World War. It was the home course of Ronnie Shade, Scotland's finest amateur golfer.

Who is Who of Edinburgh Residents

Adam, Robert (1728–92)
Noted for his work in New Town and also London, examples of his work include Register House, the north side of Charlotte Square and Hopetoun House, regarded as Scotland's finest stately home. He is buried in Westminster Abbey.

Anderson, Sir Robert Rowland (1834–1921)
Scotland's leading architect at the turn of century, his work includes Scottish Portrait Gallery, McEwan Hall and Medical School.

Armour, Tommy, (1895–1968)
Golfer known as 'The Silver Scot'. Won US Open 1927, USPGA1930, The Open 1931 at Carnoustie.

Barrie, James (1860–1937)
Author of *Peter Pan* whose copyright he signed over to Great Ormond Street Hospital.

Barnie, W. E. 'Ned'(1896–1983)
First Scot to swim the Channel and the first person to swim both ways.

Beaton, Cardinal David. (1494–1548)
Last Archbishop at St Andrew's, opposed John Knox, was murdered by Protestant Reformers.

Black, Joseph (1728–99)
Chemist, Professor of Medicine at Edinburgh University, discovered carbon monoxide.

Boswell, James (1740–95)
Lawyer by profession, biographer of Dr Samuel Johnston on his journey to the Highlands.

Bremner, Rory, (1961-)
Impressionist, famous for his portrayal of political figures.

Brewster, Sir David (1781–1868)
Physicist, worked on light refraction, principal of Edinburgh University 1859, invented the Kaleidoscope.

Brown, George (1818–80)
Politician, founding father of Canada, spoke against French Canadians, developing the divisions that persist today.

Brougham, Henry (1778–1868)
Lawyer, politician and inventor. Educated at the Royal High School he went on to become Lord Chancellor between 1830–34. Designed the closed four wheeled carriage that bears his name.

Bruce, William Spiers (1867–1921)
Polar explorer, advised Scott that his supply dumps were too far apart to succeed.

Buchanan, Ken (1945-)
Boxer. Turned professional in 1965 and became British Lightweight Champion. In 1970 in Puerto Rico he defeated Ismael Laguna to become World Champion. He defended the title twice more, was controversially beaten by Roberto Duran in 1972 who would not fight him again. Regained the British Title by beating Jim Watt and in 1973 won the Lonsdale Belt outright. Retired in 1983 with 62 wins and 8 defeats.

Burns, Robert (1759–96)
Poet, writer and National Bard, wrote 'Auld Lang Syne', his birthday 25 January, is celebrated all over the world.

Burke, William (1792–1829)
Labourer, mistakenly called a 'Body Snatcher' he was in fact a murderer who with his accomplice William Hare murdered 16 people, and sold the bodies to the medical school. Hare turned King's evidence and was pardoned, Burke was publicly hanged.

Burnet, James (Lord Monboddo) (1714–19)
High Court Judge, eccentric personality in pre Darwin times believed that Man was descended from Monkey.

Bryce, David (1803–76)
Architect, proponent of Scottish Baronial style, his works include Fettes College and the former Royal Infirmary at Lauriston

Carlyle, Thomas (1795–1881)
Writer and literary critic, Rector Edinburgh University 1886. Known as 'The Sage of Chelsea'

Charleston, Ian (1949–90)
Film actor best known for portrayal of Eric Liddle in film 'Chariots of Fire', educated at the Royal High School and Edinburgh University, died of Aids related disorder.

Corsie, Richard (1966-)
Bowler. Has won every title, gold, silver and bronze in the Commonwealth Games World titles both indoor and outdoors in singles, doubles and team events.

Connoly, James (1868–1916)
Trade unionist, leader of the Easter uprising in Dublin. Served in British Army 1882–89, married 1890, became involved in Independent Labour Party, moved to Dublin 1896, founded Irish Socialist Republican Party. Was wounded in the fight for the General Post Office, was captured and tried by the authorities, found guilty and condemned to death by firing squad. As he could not stand to be executed he was tied to a chair and shot. One of his many famous quotes was 'We don't want much, only the world'.

Connery, Sean (1930-)
Actor, educated Boroughmuir High School, film star best known as the character James Bond. Won Oscar for Best Supporting Actor in 'The Untouchables'

Corbett, Ronnie (1930-)
Comedy actor best known for television series 'The Two Ronnies' with Ronnie Barker.

Doyle, Sir Arthur Conan (1859–1930)
Studied medicine at University, became a writer inventing the character Sherlock Holmes, based upon his tutor Dr Joseph Bell.

Dunnett, Dorothy (1923-)
Writer and painter, attended Edinburgh College of Art and became a professional portrait painter before finding fame as an author of historical romances.

Farmer, Sir Tom (1940-)
Entrepreneur and philanthropist. Started a tyre business in 1964 and sold out in 1968. In 1971 Started Kwik Fit which went on to become Britain's biggest tyre and accessory company. Became Chairman and biggest investor, (with £6 million) in Hibernian football club. He was knighted in 1997.

Fettes, Sir William (1750–1836)
Merchant and philanthropist, left a fortune made on tea and wine to found Fettes College in 1870.

Flint, Sir William Russell (1880–1970)
Watercolour artist famous for his painting of nude women.

Geddes, Sir Patrick (1854–1932)
Regarded as father of Town Planning.

Gordon, Hannah (1941-)
Film actress most known for television sit coms.

Graham, Kenneth (1859–1932)
Author, most notably *The Wind in the Willows*

Gresley, Sir Nigel (1876–1941)
Engineer and locomotive designer, his most famous design was the A4 Pacific *Mallard* which attained a speed of 126 m.p.h. on 3 July 1938, a record that still stands today for a steam engine.

Haig, Earl Douglas (1861–1928)
Commander of Allied troops in First World War. Founder of Earl Haig Fund for Disabled Servicemen.

Hastings, Gavin (1962-)
Rugby player was capped 61 times for Scotland 20 as Captain and played in three World Cups between1987–95.

Haston, Dougal (1940–77)
Mountaineer, first Briton to climb North Face of the Eiger, in 1966 and the first to climb Changabang in India in1974. Was killed in an avalanche while skiing in the Alps.

Heatly, Sir Peter (1924-)
High Diver, won gold in three successive Empire Games (presently Commonwealth) 1950–54–58, Chairman Sports Council 1975–87 Chairman Commonwealth Games Federation 1982–90. Knighted in 1990.

Hendry, Stephen (1969-)
Snooker player. Turned professional aged sixteen, and became the youngest World Champion in 1990, a title he won five years in succession 1992–96, he holds the record for the most title wins in a season, 9 in 91–92. Has won 72 titles world wide including a record world championship 7 times.

Heriot George (1563–1624)
Known as 'Jinglin Geordie' was goldsmith to King James VI, left his fortune to found Heriots School.

Hill, David Octavius (1802–70)
Pioneer in photography. Landscape and portrait painter.

Hume David (1711–76)
Philosopher, agnostic and leading figure in the Scottish Enlightenment.

Hunter, Russell (1925–)
Film actor best known as 'Lonely' in Television series 'Callan'. Married actress Una MacLean in 1991.

Hutton, James (1726–97)
Father of modern Geology, published *Theory of the Earth* in 1785.

Johnston, Reginald Fleming (1874–1938)
Diplomat, tutor to the last Emperor of China. Portrayed in the film by Peter O'Toole.

Inglis, Elsie (1864–1917)
Leading surgeon, set up maternity hospital staffed by women. In First World War, set up hospitals for troops in Serbia and Russia.

Irvine, Andy (1951-)
Rugby Player capped 51 times for Scotland 15 as captain, made 9 appearances for British Lions on tours in 1974 '78 '80. Was the first player to amass over 300 points in International career. Retired in 1982.

James VI, (1566–1625)
Son of Mary Queen of Scots, on death of Elizabeth I in 1603 acceded to the English Throne as James I, this resulted in Union of Crowns.

Knox, John (1505–72)
Father of Protestant Reformation, preached at St Giles.

Knox, Dr Robert (1791–1862)
Anatomist at Medical School, he bought corpses from Burke and Hare.

Kennedy, Ludovic (1919-)
Writer, broadcaster, radio and television presenter, married actress Moira Shearer.

Lawson, Charles (1794–1873)
Botanist, introduced Cypress trees that bear his name *'Cupressus Lawsonii'*.

Lauder, Sir Harry (1870–1950)
Music Hall entertainer, dressed in kilt with twisted walking stick, portrayed the Scots as tight-fisted.

Liddle, Eric (1902–45)
Educated at Edinburgh University, played rugby for Scotland. At the Paris Olympics in 1924 won a Gold Medal at 400 metres and bronze in 200. Refused to run on Sunday. Worked as missionary in China

1925–45 died in Japanese internment camp. Was the subject of the film 'Chariots of Fire'.

Lister, Joseph (1827–1912)
Pioneer of antiseptics, reducing post-operative deaths due to infection.

Littlejohn, Sir Henry Duncan (1826–1914)
Medical and health pioneer, improved sanitation, instituted legal requirement to inform authorities of infectious diseases.

Magnusson, Magnus (1929-)
Author but better known as host of TV's Mastermind.

Mary, Queen of Scots (1542–87)
Last Catholic Monarch in Scotland; was forced to abdicate in favour of her son James VI. Executed for Treason by Elizabeth I.

Marshall, Alex (Tattie) (1967-)
Bowler. Won Gold outdoor and indoor in Team, Pairs and Fours and Gold in Commonwealth Games in Manchester in 2002.

Maxwell, James Clerk (1831–79)
Mathematician and Physicist, prepared the way for quantum physics. Ranks alongside Newton and Einstein.

McEwan, Dr William (1827–1913)
Brewer and philanthropist, he set up a brewery in Fountainbridge in 1856, became MP and gave money to build McEwan Hall.

MacDairmaid, Hugh (1892–1978)
Author poet, this was his pen name, his real name was Christopher Murray Grieve, founder of SNP. His best known work was, 'A drunk man looks at the Thistle'

McGonagall, William Topaz (1830–1902)
Regarded as the world's worst poet, composed such rhymes as 'The Tay Bridge Disaster'

McKenzie, Sir Compton (1883–1972)
Author of *Rockets Galore* and *Whisky Galore* based on the sinking of the ship S. S. *Politician*.

Monro, Alexander (Primus) (1697–1767)
Anatomist, Chair of Anatomy and Professor of Anatomy at University, Founder of Royal Infirmary, was succeeded by his son and grandson who shared the same name, a lineage which lasted for 126 years. It was his grandson who dissected the corpse of William Burke.

Millar, Hugh (1802–56)
Stonemason and Geologist, was one of the leaders in the Disruption of 1843.

Murray, 'Chick' (1919–85)
Comedian, with his wife Maidie was known as 'The Tall Droll with the Small Doll'.

Murray, David (1951–)
Entrepreneur, Founder of Murray International Metals, lost both his legs in car crash. Bought Glasgow Rangers Football Club for £6 million in 1989.

Murray, Yvonne (1964–)
Athlete, won Bronze in 3000 metres in 1986 Commonwealth Games and Silver in the European Championships. Bronze in 1988 Olympics, Silver at 1990 Commonwealth Games, Gold in the 1990 European Championships, Gold in 1994 and at 10,000 metres Gold in 1994 Commonwealth Games.

Napier, John (1550–1617)
Mathematician, invented Napier's bones which permitted easy multiplication by addition, defined the concept of Logarithms also the decimal point.

Nasmyth, Alexander (1758–1840)
Acclaimed portrait painter, painted many society people including Robert Burns.

Nasmyth, James (1808–90)
Son of Alexander. Owned a foundry business, invented steam hammer, planing machine and pile driver, inventions he regretted in later life.

Noble, Richard (1946–)
Fastest man on earth, in 1983 in the Nevada desert reached a speed

of 633 m.p.h. and in 1997 broke the speed of sound reaching 763 m.p.h.

Paolozzi, Sir Eduardo (1924-)
Sculptor, born in Leith and educated at Holy Cross and Edinburgh Art College, he was admitted to the Royal Academy in 1979. Three of his works are on display outside St Mary's Cathedral Broughton Street. They were commissioned by the City and Sir Tom Farmer. He was knighted in 1988.

Playfair, W. H. (1789–1857)
Architect. His classical designs earned Edinburgh the name 'The Athens of the North'. He designed Regent, Carlton and Royal Terraces, Royal Scottish Academy, National Gallery. New College and Assembly Halls and also as he described it 'That damn Donaldson's School.

Pillans, James (1778–1864)
Head of the High School between 1820–1863, Professor of Humanity at Edinburgh University. Invented the blackboard and coloured chalks and used them to teach Geography.

Porter, Gail (1971-)
Television presenter, educated Portobello High School. A nude photo of her was projected onto Houses of Parliament.

Raeburn, Sir Henry (1756–1823)
Portrait painter, painted many well-known figures of the time including Sir Walter Scott. His memory commemorated in Raeburn Place.

Rankin, Ian (1960-)
Author. Creator of the fictional Edinburgh detective Inspector Rebus.

Ramsay, Allan (1686–1758)
Poet and bookseller, founded the first travelling library in United Kingdom. His house in Ramsay Gardens was nicknamed 'Goose pie' because of its shape.

Ramsay, Allan (1713–84)
Artist. Son of the poet and bookseller.

Richardson, Ian, (1934-)
Educated Tynecastle School, Glasgow University where he studied medicine, began acting 1958, star of stage screen and television.

Rowling, J. K. (1965-)
Author of 'Harry Potter' books.

Scott, Sir Walter (1771–1832)
Lawyer, poet and writer of the 'Waverley' novels, great patriot. Commemorated by monument in Princes Street.

Shade, R. D. B. M. (Ronnie) (1938–1986)
Golfer. Winner Boys Championship in 1956, Scottish Amateur 1963–67, English Open 1961–63–67. In 1966 was the leading Amateur in the Open at Muirfield. Turning professional he won Scottish Strokeplay, Scottish Professional and the Irish Open. Because of his accuracy it was said his initials stood for 'Right down the bloody middle'.

Sharp, Cameron (1960-)
Sprinter won gold in Commonwealth Games 4x100 relay in 1978, 3 bronze in 82 Games, Bronze in 86 Games and Silver in 82 European Championships. Involved in car crash in 1991 and due to medical negligence was left physically disabled.

Sholto, Sir John, 8th Marquis of Queensberry (1844–1900)
Laid down rules for boxing in 1867. Tried for libelling Oscar Wilde which led to Wilde's downfall over affair with his son Lord Alfred.

Sibbald, Sir Robert (1641–1722)
Established first Botanical garden in City and was founder of Royal College of Physicians.

Sinclair, Catherine (1800–64)
Author and benefactor, ran a school to train girls for domestic service, first to introduce food kitchens and introduced drinking fountains to the city. Was regarded as patron saint of cab drivers. A monument to her is at the corner of North Charlotte Street and St Colme Street.

Simpson, Sir James Y. (1811–70)
Obstetrician, pioneer of anaesthetics particularly chloroform.

Sim, Alistair(1900–76)
Comedy actor best known as Headmistress in 'The Belles of St Trinians'. First actor to be Rector of Edinburgh University (1948).

Smellie, William (1740–95)
Printer, published 1st Edition of *Encyclopaedia Britannica*.

Smith, Sidney (1771–1845)
Clergyman, writer and wit. Established the Edinburgh Review in 1802.

Smith, Adam (1723–90)
Economist, wrote *Inquiry into the Nature and Causes of the Wealth of Nations*.

Smith, Alexander McCall (1948–)
Author, who introduced the world to Mma Ramotswe and the No1 Ladies Detective Agency in Botswana.

Smith, John (1938–94)
MP Leader of Labour Party widely expected to be next Prime Minister but died while his party was in Opposition.

Smyth, Charles Piazza (1819–1900)
Astronomer Royal for Scotland, instigated the One O'Clock gun.

Souness, Graeme (1953–)
Footballer with Liverpool won 3 European Cups and 5 League titles. Went on to be Manager of Rangers, Liverpool, Galatasaray, Torino, Benfica, Southampton and Blackburn, known as a hothead, abrasive and arrogant.

Spark Muriel (1918–)
Author, best known work *The Prime of Miss Jean Brodie*.

Steele, Sir John (1804–91)
Sculptor, created many of city's statues including Wellington and Sir Walter Scott.

Stevenson, Robert Louis (1850–94)
Author of many classic books including *Kidnapped* and *Treasure Island*.

Stewart, Dugald (1753–1828)

Philosopher, published *Outlines of Moral Philosophy*

Swan, Annie Shepherd (1859–1943)
Novelist is credited with writing over one hundred and fifty books.

Thomson, Robert William (1822–73)
Conceived the idea of pneumatic tyres in 1840s, John Boyd Dunlop developed and patented the idea. Invented fountain pen.

Tranter, Nigel (1909–2000)
Historical novelist. Educated at George Heriots. Published over 110 books He also wrote about the American West under the pseudonym of Nye Tredgold.

Usher, Andrew (1826–98)
Distiller and brewer, lived in Pear Tree House. Donated £100,000 to build Usher Hall.

Watson, George (1654–1723)
Accountant. In 1672 went to Rotterdam to learn bookkeeping. Returned to Edinburgh in 1676 and became the first professional accountant in Scotland. In 1695 when the Bank of Scotland was founded he was appointed the Chief Cashier. He is buried in Greyfriars churchyard. He left £12,000 to found the school that bears his name.

Welsh, Irvine (1958–)
Author. Foul mouthed, hard drinking ex heroin addict, his novel *Trainspotting* was made into a film starring Ewan MacGregor and Robert Carlisle.

Wells, Alan (1952–)
Sprinter, won gold in 100 metres and silver in 200 metres in 1978 Commonwealth Games in Canada. He repeated the feat in the 1980 Moscow Olympics becoming the oldest winner of the 100 metres. Won both golds at 1982 Commonwealth Games in Brisbane.

Williamson, Roy (193–90)
Folk singer and with Ronnie Browne performed as the 'Corries' folk singing duo, wrote many songs his most famous being 'Flower of Scotland' now regarded as our National Anthem.

Williamson, Peter (1730–99)
Known as 'Indian Peter' he was sold into slavery, captured by Cherokee Indians, escaped, joined the Army, captured by the French, returned to Edinburgh and started a postal service and published the first street directory.

Wilkie, David (1954–)
Swimmer, (Breast-stroke) won silver medal in 1972 Olympics, gold in 200 metres breast-stroke in 1976 Olympics in Montreal in world record time and silver in 100 metres in Commonwealth Games in 1970 and silver and two gold in 1974 Commonwealth Games. He was the first to wear head cap and goggles, now commonplace.

Wilson Professor John(1785–1854)
Advocate, through political connections was elected to Chair of Moral Philosophy 1820 at the University, a position he knew nothing about. Better known by his pen name Christopher North.

Calton Hill 328ft High

1718	Old Calton burial ground opened on south-western slope.
1724	City Council bought lands of Calton from Lord Balmerino.
1776	City Observatory founded. It was planned by James Craig with advice from Robert Adam.
1777	David Hume monument erected, architect Robert Adam.
1792	Building of Observatory completed.
1796	Bridewell (House of Correction) erected, architect was Robert Adam.
1808	Calton Jail begun, designed by Archibald Elliott to replace the old Tolbooth which was due for demolition, It was described as 'A piece of undoubted bad taste to give so glorious an eminence to a prison'.
1812	Astronomical Institution founded.
1814	Act for Calton Road and Regent Bridge erection.
1815	Waterloo Place cut through burial ground.
1815–19	Regent Bridge built, architect was Archibald Elliott.
1811–15	Governor's house for Calton Jail built, architect was Archibald Elliott.
1816	Nelson Monument, designed by Robert Burn was built in the shape of an inverted telescope 102ft high, a circular stair of 145 stairs leads to an observation platform with an extensive view of the city. The basement was occupied by a confectioner's shop until 1849.
1816	National Monument first mooted.
1817	Calton Jail was opened.
1817	New Calton Burial ground opened further east.
1818	New Observatory built, designed by William Playfair.
1819–60	Building of Regent Terrace Carlton Terrace and Royal Terrace to the design of William Playfair.
1822	National Monument begun, designed as a church on

the lines of the Parthenon in Athens but never completed due to lack of funds, work stopped in 1829.

1826   Playfair's monument to his uncle, Professor John Playfair, Mathematician and Natural Philosopher.

1829   Royal High School built, architect was Thomas Hamilton.

1830   Burns Monument on Regent Road was erected to the design of Thomas Hamilton.

1832   Monument to Dugald Stewart, Philosopher, designed by William Playfair.

1845   Obelisk, designed by Thomas Hamilton, to the Scottish political martyrs of 1793–4 erected in the Old Burial Ground.

1845   Tunnel completed through south flank for the North British Railway Company.

1852   Time ball on Nelson Monument, the ball 1ft 6ins. in diameter and made of zinc is raised daily by machinery and descends at 1pm. In 1861 it was linked by an electrical device to the time gun in the Castle.

1893   Monument to the Scottish soldiers killed in the American Civil War erected in the Old Burial Ground, surmounted by a statue of Abraham Lincoln. The sculptor was George Bissell and was the first statue of an American President to be erected outside America.

1925   Calton Jail closed.

1937   Calton Jail and Bridewell demolished for the building of St Andrew's House. The Governor's house remains.

1969   New co-educational Royal High School was opened at Barnton. The Calton Hill building was used as a civic arts centre, but in 1977 work started to convert it for the proposed Scottish Assembly. After the 1979 referendum the building was only used a few times by politicians. It was deemed to be unsuitable for use as a home for the Scottish Parliament and it was decided to build at Holyrood.

Holyrood Abbey and the Palace of Holyrood House

1128	Founding of Abbey by David I.
1141	Augustinian canons brought from St Andrew's.
1143	Charter of David I made Abbey very wealthy.
1161	Fergus Lord of Galloway, became a canon and his vast estates reverted to Holyrood Abbey.
1296	Edward I stayed in Abbey during siege of Edinburgh.
1322	Abbey sacked by Edward II.
1326	Robert Bruce held a parliament in Abbey.
1371	David II buried in Abbey.
1381	John of Gaunt, third son of Edward IV, lodged in Abbey,
1385	Edinburgh, including St Giles, burned by Richard II but Abbey saved by the intervention of the Englishman John of Gaunt.
1400	Now Stewart Kings used the Abbey regularly as guest house.
1430	James II born in guest house.
1437	James II crowned in Abbey aged 6
1449	James II married Mary of Gueldres in Abbey aged 19
1460	James II buried in Abbey, aged 29
1464	Rebuilt by Abbot Crawford and side buttresses introduced.
1469	James III married Margaret of Denmark in Abbey.
1486	Abbot Bellenden beautified Abbey, covered roof with lead and built outer wall with postern tower at each corner (Queen Mary's Bathhouse still standing).
1501	James IV built North Tower of Holyrood Palace.
1502	Vaulted gateway erected – The Foir Yett.
1503	James IV married Margaret Tudor in Abbey.
1524	James V crowned in Abbey.
C 1530	James V continued building of Palace front.
1536	James V's first Queen Magdalene buried in Abbey.
1538	James V married Mary of Guise and Lorraine in Abbey.
1542	James V buried in Abbey.

1544	Abbey and Palace sacked by Hereford on orders of Henry VIII. Treasures including Font and Eagle Lectern removed (now in St Albans). Thus Abbey destroyed before reformation.
1547	Second sacking by Somerset (Hereford). Took away lead roof.
1559	Became Parish church of Canongate.
1561	Palace repaired for Mary Queen of Scots, French influence changed 'Stewart' to 'Stuart'.
1565	Marriage of Mary to Lord Darnley in Abbey.
1566	Murder of David Rizzio in Palace.
1567	Darnley buried in Abbey.
1567	Mary married Bothwell in Palace.
1570	Church shortened to Nave only, eastern end destroyed by reformers.
1590	Anne, Queen of James VI crowned in Abbey.
1603	James VI advised by Sir Robert Carey of death of Elizabeth I and his accession to the throne of England. James departed to London.
1633	Coronation of Charles I in Abbey.
1650	Cromwell in Palace, troops accidentally set Palace on fire.
1660	Sundial installed in garden by Charles II.
1671–80	Palace rebuilt on orders of Charles II and South Tower added.
1679–82	Duke of York (later James VII) resided in Palace.
1684–85	Canongate Kirk founded for Parish of Canongate. Jacob DeWitte painted portraits of one hundred and eleven Scottish Kings for picture gallery in Palace.
1686	James VII converted Abbey back to Roman Catholic Chapel and took it over for the Knights of the Thistle.
1688	James VII abdicated. Mob destroyed the Chapel and desecrated Royal vaults. Neither George I, George II or George III ever came to Holyrood. Prince Charles Edward Stuart held reception in Palace.
1755	Abbey gate (Foir Yett) demolished.
1758	Abbey roof repaired with flagstones.

1768	Roof collapsed due to weight.
1789	Jewelled dagger found in Queen Mary's Bath House thought to be connected with murder of David Rizzio.
1796–1802	Comte D'Artois, younger brother of Louis XVI, took sanctuary in Abbey.
1822	Visit of George IV. Levees held in Palace but he never slept there.
1830	Second visit of D'Artois, now Charles X of France.
1848	Remains of Mary of Gueldres reburied after exhumation from Trinity College Church.
C 1850	Visits of Queen Victoria.
1851	Statue of Queen Victoria in courtyard.
1861	Statue removed, replaced with present fountain.
1898	Queen Victoria had Royal vault contents reburied.
1922	Memorial gates and Statue of Edward VII.

New Town Buildings in Georgian/Victorian Edinburgh

1767	Thistle Court Foundation Stone, Thistle Street. James Craig.
1768	No. 35 St Andrew Square. Robert Adam.
1770	No. 6 Queen Street. Robert Adam.
1772	Dundas House, St Andrew Square. Sir William Chambers.
1776	Old Observatory, Calton Hill. James Craig.
1777	David Hume Memorial, Calton Graveyard. Robert Adam.
1784	St Andrews Church, George Street. Major Frazer (Spire 1787).
1784	Belford Bridge.
1787	Assembly Rooms, George Street. John Henderson. Portico added 1818, Wm. Burn: Music Hall added 1843, Wm. Burn.
1788	Registrar House occupied.
1789	St Bernard's Well. Alex Nasmyth.
1791	Bridewell, Calton Hill. Robert Adam.
1793	St George's Episcopal Chapel, York Place. James Adam.
1795	Sir Henry Raeburn studio York Place.
1806	Nelson Monument, Calton Hill. Robt. Burn (Finished 1816 by Thomas Bonnar).
1813	St Mary's Roman Catholic Cathedral, Broughton Street. Gillespie Graham.
1814	St George's Church, Charlotte Square. Robert Reid.
1815	Calton Jail, Regent Road. Archibald Elliott.
1816	St John's Episcopalian Church, Princes Street. Wm. Burn.
1818	City Observatory, Calton Hill. Wm. Playfair.
1818	St Paul's Church, York Place. Archibald Elliott.
1821	Broughton Place Church. Archibald Elliott.
1822	National Monument, Calton Hill. Wm. Playfair and Thom. Cockerell, (abandoned 1830).
1822	Royal Scottish Academy, Princes Street. Wm. Playfair.

1823	Edinburgh Academy, Henderson Row. Wm. Burn.
1823	Deaf Institute, Henderson Row. Gillespie Graham (sold to Edinburgh Academy 1977).
1823	St Bernard's Church, Saxe Coburg Place. James Mylne.
1824	St Mary's Church, Bellevue. Thos. Bonnar.
1825	Royal High School, Regent Road. Thomas Hamilton.
1825	Prof. John Playfair Monument, Calton Hill. Wm. Playfair.
1825	Stockbridge Market, St Stephen Place. Archibald Scott.
1825	Gates and railings added to Royal Bank, St Andrew's Square.
1827	St Stephen's Church, St Vincent Street. Wm. Playfair.
1828	John Watson School (Gallery Modern Art), Belford Road. Wm. Burn.
1830	Burns Monument, Regent Road. Thomas Hamilton.
1832	Dugald Stewart Monument, Calton Hill. Wm. Playfair.
1832	Surgeons Hall, Nicholson Street. Wm. Playfair.
1832	Greenside Church, Greenside. Gillespie Graham.
1833	Dean Education Centre (Dean Gallery), Belford Road. Thomas Hamilton.
1838	Holy Trinity Church, Dean Bridge. John Henderson.
1840	Broughton Market.
1840	Canonmills Bridge (earlier bridge 1768).
1840	George Hotel, George Street. David Bryce.
1841	Clydesdale Bank (All Bar One), George Street. David Bryce.
1842	Haymarket Station. John Miller.
1843	Royal Society Building, George Street. David Bryce.
1844	Martyr's Memorial, Calton Graveyard. Thomas Hamilton.
1844	Highland Tolbooth, St John's Church. (The Hub) Castlehill Gillespie Graham.
1844	Scott Monument, Princes Street. George Meikle Kemp.
1845	Physicians Hall, No. 10 Queen Street. Thomas Hamilton.
1846	New College Assembly Halls, Mound. Wm. Playfair.
1847	Royal Bank (The Dome), George Street. David Rhind.

1850	Daniel Stewarts College, Queensferry Road. David Rhind.
1851	Donaldson School for the Deaf, West Coates. Wm. Playfair.
	British Linen Bank (HBOS) St Andrew's Square. David Bryce (Figures by A Handyside).
1854	National Gallery, Mound. Wm. Playfair.
1859	New Register House, West Register Street. Robt. Mathieson.
1860	Free Church Offices, Mound. David Cousins.
1861	Stockbridge Colonies, Glenogle Road. Edinburgh Co-op Building Society.
1862	The Café Royal, West Register Street. Robert Patterson.
1865	Merchant Company Hall, Hanover Street. David Bryce Jnr.
1866	General Post Office, Princes Street. Robert Mathieson
1869	St George's West Church, Shandwick Place. David Bryce.
1869	Ross Fountain, Princes Street Gardens.
1870	Fettes College, East Fettes Avenue. David Bryce.
1870	Bank of Scotland, Mound. David Bryce (1806 by Robt. Reid).
1873	Palmerston Place Church, Palmerston Place. Peddie & Kinnear.
1873	Waverley Bridge.
1876	Catholic Apostolic Church, East London Street. Sir Robt. Rowland Anderson. Now Mansfield Traquair Centre, Murals by Pheobe Traquair.
1879	St Mary's Episcopal Cathedral, Palmerston Place. Sir George Gilbert Scott.
1876	Medical School, Teviot Place. Sir Robt. Rowland Anderson.
1889	Belford Church, (Youth Hostel), Belford Road. Sydney Mitchell.
1890	National Museum of Antiquities, Queen Street. Sir Robt. Rowland Anderson.

1895	Jenners rebuilt, (earlier 1838). Sir William Hamilton Beattie.
1895	Royal Observatory, Blackford Hill Observatory Road. W. W. Robertson (Office of H. M. Works).
1895	Prudential Insurance Co. Building, St Andrew's Square. Sir Alfred Waterhouse.
1896	St Cuthbert's Church, Kings Stables Road. Hippolyte. J Blane.
1897	McEwan Hall, Teviot Place. Sir Robt. Rowland Anderson.
1901	North British Hotel, Princes Street. Sir William Hamilton Beattie.
1902	Caledonian Hotel, Lothian Road. Sir George Washington Browne.
1907	R. W. Forsyth's (now Burtons Top Shop), Princes Street. Sir John J Burnett.
1911	Church of Scotland Offices, 121 George Street. Sydney Mitchell.
1912	Freemasons Hall, George Street. A. Hunter Crawford.
1927	Playhouse Theatre, Greenside Place. John Fairweather.
1935	Ross Bandstand, Princes Street Gardens (old Bandstand to Meadows).
1939	St Andrew's House, Regent Road. Thomas Tait.
1972	St James' Centre, Leith Street. Hugh Martin & Partners.

Building Costs

1628	George Heriots School, Lauriston Place, £27,000
1640	Parliament House, Parliament Square, £11,600
1754	The Royal Exchange, (City Chambers) High Street, £31,000
1771	Royal Bank of Scotland (Dundas Mansion), St Andrew's Square, £33,000
1784	St Andrew's Church, George Street, £7,000
1785	South Bridge, £6,500
1786	Register House, Princes Street, £31,000
1811	St George's Church (West Register House. Charlotte Square, £33,000
1813	St Mary's R. C. Cathedral, Broughton Street, £8,000
1816	County Buildings, George IV Bridge, £15,000.
1816	St John's Episcopal Church, Princes Street, £18,000
1818	St Paul's Church, York Place, £12,000
1821	Melville Monument, St Andrew's Square, £3,500
1822	National Monument, Calton Hill, £12,000
1823	Edinburgh Academy, Hamilton Place, £12,000
1825	Royal High School, Regent Road, £34,000
1826	St Stephen's Church. St Vincent Street, £21,000
1844	Scott Monument, Princes Street, £16,000
1854	National Gallery, Mound, £40,000.
1866	General Post Office, Princes Street, £120,000
1870	Bank of Scotland H. Q. Bank Street £75,000
1874	St Mary's Episcopal Cathedral, Palmerston Place, £128,200

Buildings in Old Town

854	St Giles' Church.
1128	Holyrood Abbey.
1450	Edinburgh Tolbooth. (Demolished 1815).
1462	Holy Trinity Church.
1490	Queen Mary Bath House.
1490	John Knox House. 15th cent. Netherbow Port. (Demolished 1764).
1501	Holyrood Palace.
1544	Magdalene Chapel.
1562	Greyfriars Burial Ground.
1570	Adam Bothwell's house.
1570	Huntly House.
1572	Tweeddale House.
1587	Bailie MacMorran's house.
1590	Advocates Close.
1591	Canongate Tolbooth.
1617	Gladstone's Land.
1620	Greyfriars Church.
1621	Tailors Hall, Cowgate (Three Sisters pub).
1622	Lady Stairs House.
1623	White Horse Close.
1624	Nisbet of Dirleton's house.
1626	Moray House.
1630	Canonball House.
1633	Acheson House.
1637	Parliament House.
1638	Sempill's Close.
1646	Brodies Close.
1647	Tron Church opened.
1674	Castlehill Reservoir.
1677	Shoemakers Land.
1680	Queensberry House.
1688	Canongate Church.
1690	Mylnes Court.
1690	Reid's Close (Canongate Manse).

1696	Panmure Close.
1723	Old Assembly Close.
1726	Riddles Court.
1727	James Court.
1734	Anchor Close.
1736	Lodge Canongate Kilwinning.
1740	Ramsey Lodge (Goosepie House).
1745	Chessels Court.
1746	Old Playhouse Close.
1753	City Chambers (Royal Exchange).
1763	North Bridge.
1763	St Cecilia's Hall.
1766	New Assembly Close.
1769	Whitefoord House.
1788	South Bridge.
1806	Bank of Scotland, Mound (reconstructed1870).
1816	Regional Chambers (reconstructed1904).
1820	Parliament Square and Law Courts.
1834	George IV Bridge.
1834	Victoria Street.
1834	Johnston Terrace.
1844	Highland Tolbooth Church (The Hub).
1846	Outlook Tower.
1859	Cockburn Street.
1872	Married Quarters, Johnston Terrace.
1890	Solicitors Library.
1894	Ramsey Gardens, Castle Esplanade.
1911	Thistle Chapel.
1937	Sheriff Court.

Important Buildings

1143	Duddingston Church.
1429	Corstorphine Church.
	Fifteenth century Craigmillar Castle.
	Fifteenth century Merchiston Tower.
	Fifteenth century Liberton Tower.
	Fifteenth century Cramond Tower.
	Sixteenth century Craigentinny House.
	Sixteenth century Craigcrook Castle.
1565	Craighouse. (Napier University).
1593	Lauriston Castle.
1605	Bruntsfield House.
1617	Inch House.
1617	Pinkie House, Musselburgh.
1623	Stenhouse Mansion.
1628	Heriots Hospital. Wm. Wallace.
1636	Peffermill House.
1638	Pilrig House.
1650	Dalry House.
1656	Cramond Kirk.
1670	The White House, Whithouse Loan.
1670	Sheep Heid Inn, Duddingston Village.
1680	Cramond House.
1685	Caroline Park, Granton.
1687	Prestonfield House (rebuilt) Sir Wm. Bruce.
1696	Old Surgeons Hall, High School Yards, James Smith.
1722	Candlemakers Hall.
1741	Sciennes Hill House.
1743	Hermits and Termits, St Leonards Street. (restored 1982).
1746	Duncans Land, Stockbridge.
1756	Pear Tree House. West Nicholson Street.
1763	Gayfield House, East London Street. Chas. & Wm Buttar.
1768	Duddingston House. Sir William Chambers.

1771	St Patrick's Church, Cowgate. (Originally Episcopalian now R. C.)
1771	Colinton Church (rebuilt 1908).
1774	Warriston House, Inverleith Row/ Eildon Street.
1774	Inverleith House, Botanic Gardens.
1776	Archers Hall, Buccleuch Street.
1776	Golf Tavern Wrichthouses (not 1476).
1777	Old High School, Infirmary Street. Alex. Lang.
1780	Beechwood House, Corstorphine Road.
1785	Hermitage of Braid. Braid Road.
1788	Heriot Hill House, Rodney Street.
1791	Ravelston House, (converted in 1946 to Mary Erskine School) Alex Keith.
1795	Easter Warriston, (replaced Easter Warriston House c. 1600) now Crematorium.
1803	Lady Yester's Church, High School Wynd.
1823	Queens Hall, South Clerk Street.
1823	Botanic Gardens, Inverleith Row.
1825	Liberton Church.
1827	Loretto School, Musselburgh.
1827	Kings Bridge, Kings Stables Road. Thomas Hamilton.
1828	Belmont, Ellersley Road. Wm. Playfair.
1836	Bonaly Tower. Wm. Playfair & J. M. & W. H. Hay.
1857	Augustine Bristo Congregational Church, George IV Bridge.
1857	St Peter's Episcopalian. Church Lutton Place. Wm. Slater.
1857	Buccleuch & Greyfriars Church, Buccleuch Street. Hay of Liverpool.
1858	Palm House Botanic Gardens. Robert Mathieson.
1861	Royal Scottish Museum. Capt. Fowke.
1861	Chalmer's Hospital. Peddie & Kinnear.
1864	Barclay Church, Barclay Place. F. T. Pilkington.
1868	Castle Terrace. Sir James Gowans.
1870	Royal Infirmary. David Bryce.
1871	Clermiston Tower, Wm. MacFie.

1873	Heriot Watt University, Chambers Street (Crown Office). John Chesser.
1878	Convent of the Sacred Heart, Colinton Road. Peddie & Kinnear.
1882	Royal Victoria Hospital, Craigleith Road.
1883	Lyceum Theatre. C. J Phips.
1884	Well Court, Dean Village. Sydney Mitchell.
1887	Central Library, George IV Bridge. Sir George Washington Browne.
1895	Royal Observatory, Blackford Hill, W. W. Robertson.
1887	MacEwan Hall. R. Rowland Anderson.
1898	Fire Station (L B F B HQ.). Robert Morhum.
1905	Kings Theatre. J. D. Swanston.
1910	Usher Hall. Stockdale Harrison.
1913	Zoological Gardens. Patrick Geddes.
1935	Maybury Roadhouse. Patterson & Broome.
1956	National Library of Scotland, George IV Bridge. Reginald Fairlie.
1963	David Hume Tower. Robert Matthew.
1965	Glasshouses, Botanic Gardens. George Pearch.
1966	Hillend Ski Centre,
1966	Appleton Tower. Alan Reiach.
1966	Princes Margaret Rose Hospital (closed 2003). Morris & Steedman.
1967	Mortonhall Crematorium, Sir Basil Spence.
1967	Royal Commonwealth Pool. Johnson & Marshall.
1967	University Library, George Square. Sir Basil Spence.
1970	Meadowbank Stadium. City Architect.
1973	St James Centre. Hugh Martin & Partners.
1975	Edinburgh Airport Building. Johnson & Marshall.
1975	Scottish Widows Assurance, Dalkeith Road. Sir Basil Spence.
1976	Students Centre, Bristo Square. Morris & Steedman.
1977	Extension to Art College, Lauriston Place. Wheeler & Spooner.
1981	Bristo Square.

St Giles, High Kirk of Edinburgh

854	First church on the site named St Giles, probably because of the Auld Alliance.
1120	Alexander I founded Norman Church connected with Lindisfarne. Monks farmed Grange of St Cues.
1243	Bishop of St Andrew's dedicated St Giles.
1320	Church burned by English invasion.
1385	Burned again this time by Richard II. All that were left were the four central pillars.
1390	Church restored and now received benefactions.
1409	Albany Aisle.
1454	Wm. Preston of Gorton (Craigmillar) bequeathed the arm bone of St Giles in gold with a diamond ring on finger. Preston Aisle built.
1460	Church extended from original cruciform, to the west as a memorial to James II. Roof of choir raised. Kings Pillar and vaulting.
1466	Becomes Collegiate church with Deans, Canons etc.
1477	No further burials in church, graveyard now in Manse garden outside. Fifteenth century, Church wealthy from Guild monies, ship dues and fines. Different Guilds endowed Chapels. Lantern Tower built. Hammermen in Chapel of St Eloi (in which is now a memorial to Argyll).
1508	Gavin Douglas appointed Provost of St Giles.
1513	Walter Chepman brought printing to Scotland. Endowed a priest in St John's Chapel (now Chepman aisle).
C. 1520	After Flodden, Chapels increased to about fifty, each with images, candles and a priest. Greed now possessed the Clergy. Image of St Giles with gorgeous velvet robes, jewels etc.
1534	Now the lower orders of the clergy began to rebel; were the first martyrs in Scotland which encouraged the Reformation.

1557	St Giles' Day 1 September. During the annual procession, mob burned image of St Giles after ducking it in Nor Loch.
1559	John Knox first preached in St Giles.
1560	Mary Queen of Scots landed at Leith, never attended service at St Giles but opened Parliament in the west end of St Giles.
1560	Last Mass said in St Giles. Church cleared of all images and altars. Whitewashed inside and had long tables with white linen.
1566	Mary Queen of Scots abdicated.
1570	Assassination of Regent Moray, buried in the Moray Aisle, John Knox preached at funeral.
1572	John Knox died. Kirkaldy of Grange now holding the Castle on behalf of Queen, placed cannons in steeple of St Giles.
1578	Church partioned into four separate churches.
1585	Clock installed in Tower.
1596	James VI believing in Divine Right of Kings, wanted Episcopacy. Argued with minister from Royal Pew.
1635	Charles I elevated St Giles into Episcopalian Cathedral.
1637	Lauds Liturgy introduced, Jenny Geddes threw her stool at Dean Hannay.
1638	National Covenant signed; to maintain Presbyterianism, led to execution of Charles 1.
1639	First Lord High Commissioner at General Assembly.
1644	Sir John Haddo, Royalist, imprisoned in Tower.
1648	Crown Steeple restored and rebuilt.
1650	Cromwell's officers used to preach in St Giles.
1657	Cromwell removed the Royal Pew and expelled General Assembly.
1660	Restoration of Monarchy, Remains of Viscount Montrose collected and reburied in Chepman Aisle, his heart believed to be in America.
1666	Covenanters from Rullion Green imprisoned in Haddo's Hole. Marquis of Argyll beheaded.

1690–1707 William and Mary brought back Wm. Carstairs who secured the independence of the Scottish Church.

1707   Union of Parliaments.

1727   Daniel Defoe visited St Giles.

1736   Porteous Riots.

1745   Message from Bonnie Prince Charlie read in church.

1798   Norman doorway destroyed.

1817   Krames cleared from outside.

1822   George IV occupied the Royal Pew.

1827–1833 Disastrous reconstruction by Wm. Burn completely altered the outside of the church.

1872–1883 Magnificent restoration of the interior by Lord Provost Wm. Chambers, who died four days before the re-opening.

1878   Organ placed in church.

1883   Flags of Scottish Regiments placed in church.

1911   Thistle Chapel designed by Sir Robert Lorimer from a bequest by Earl of Leven.
             Opened by King George V.

1912   Clock removed from steeple. (Bell remains often confused with Tron church).

1940   Window behind organ bricked up in Parliament Square to prevent bomb damage.

1965   Statue of John Knox moved to outside church.

1981   Plastering on outside brickwork at Parliament Square dangerous and had to be removed.

1983   Statue of John Knox brought inside church.

1985   Robt. Burns Memorial window installed,

Statues in Edinburgh

Albert, Prince Consort	Charlotte Square	Sir John Steele	
Bruce, King Robert	Castle	T. J. Clapperton	1929
Buccleuch, Duke of	County Square	Boehm	1888
Burns, Robert	Scot. Nat. Portrait Gallery	John Flaxman	1826
Burns, Robert	Constitution Street	W. Stevenson	1898
Chalmers, Dr Thomas	George Street	Sir John Steele	1878
Chambers, William	Chambers Street	John Rhind	1891
Charles II	Parliament Square	Unknown	1685
Dickson, Dr David	St Cuthberts Churchyard	Handyside Ritchie	1844
Edward VII	Forecourt Holyrood Palace	H. S. Gamley	1922
Edward VII	Victoria Park	John Rhind	1914
'Fama'	Top H. B. O. S. Mound		1870
Forbes, Duncan	Parliament Hall	Roubillac	1752
Standing Group	Princes Street Gardens	Wm. Brodie	1862
'Golden Boy'	University dome South Bridge	John Hutchison	1888
George II	Forecourt Royal Infirmary	James Hill	1755
George III	Inside Register House	Mrs A. S. Damer	Unknown.
George IV	George Street	Sir Francis Chantry	1831
Gladstone, Wm. Ewart	Coates Crescent	Pittendrich McGillivray	1917
Greyfriars Bobby	George IV Bridge	Wm. Brodie	1873
Guthrie, Rev. Thomas	West Princes Street	Pomeroy	1910
Haig, Douglas	Castle Esplanade	Wade	1923
Heriot, George	Heriot's School	Robt. Mylne	1693
Hopetoun, John 4th Earl	St Andrew's Square	Thomas Cambell	1834
Hume, David	High Street	Alexander Stoddart	1977
James V (as Gudeman of Ballengiech)	S. S. P. C. A. Queensferry Road.	Robert Forrest	1836
Jeffrey, Francis Lord	Parliament Hall	Sir John Steele	1855
Knox, John	New College	John Hutchison	1896

Knox, John	St Giles	Pittendrich McGillivary	1906
K. O. S. B.	North Bridge	Birnie Rhind	1906
Lincoln, Abraham	Calton Graveyard	George F. Bissell	1893
Livingston, David	East Princes Street Gardens	Mrs D. O. Hill	1876
Mary Queen of Scots	Scot. Nat. Portrait Gallery	W. Birnie Rhind	1890
Melville, Henry Dundas(1st Lord)	St Andrew's Square	Robert Forrest	1827 statue on top designed by Chantry.
Melville, Robert Dundas (2nd Lord)	Melville Crescent	Sir John Steele	1857
Pitt, William (younger)	George Street	Sir Francis Chantry	1833
'Prudence'	Royal Society George Street	Percy Portsmouth	1908
Ramsey, Allan	Princes Street	Sir John Steele	1865
Ramsey, Dean	Princes Street		1879
Royal Scots Memorial	Princes Street Gardens	Sir Frank Mears	1952
Scots Greys	Princes Street	W. Birnie Rhind	1906
Scott, Sir Walter	Princes Street	Sir John Steele	1846
Scottish American War	Princes Street Gardens	Dr R. Tait MacKenzie	1927
Simpson, James Young	Princes Street	Wm. Brodie	1877
Victoria, Queen	R. S. A. Princes Street	Sir John Steele	1844
Victoria, Queen	Leith Walk	John S. Rhind	1907
Walker, John	Waverley Station	Birnie Rhind	1907
Wallace, Sir William	Castle	Alex Carrick	1929
Watt, James	Heriot Watt University	Peter Slater	1854
Wellington, Duke of	Princes Street	Sir John Steele	1852
Wilson, Prof. John	Princes Street	Sir John Steele	1865
York, Duke of	Castle Esplanade	Thomas Campbell	1839

Georgian Edinburgh

1752	The 'Proposals published.
1753	Royal Exchange started (later City Chambers) by John Adam.
1760	George Square built outside the Royalty.
1763	Foundation Stone of South Bridge (Wm. Mylne).
1767	Act of Parliament for Extension of the Royalty (a further act of extension 1805).
	Craig's plan accepted. First building in Thistle Court, St Andrew's Square started.
1769	North Bridge collapsed at South End. First house on Princes Street free of rates until 1923. (former Woolworths site now a burger bar).
1771	Earliest building on south Princes Street, West of North Bridge.
1772	North Bridge opened for traffic.
1774	Foundation Stone of Register House laid (Architect Robert Adam).
1783	Mound started.
1786	Princes Street, George Street, Queen Street built up to Hanover Street.
1788	South Bridge opened. Register House in use (enlarged 1827).
1789	University begun at Old College, South Bridge (Robert Adam).
1790	New Town built up to Frederick Street.
1791	Gayfield Place built (John Begg).
1792	New Town built up to Castle Street; Charlotte Square started (Robert Adam).
	Death of Robert Adam.
1798	York Place, Picardy Place (1800),Albany Street (1805) Forth Street and Broughton Place (1809).
1802	Start of the second New Town by Wm. Sibbald and Robt. Reid. First house in Heriot Row(1803) Abercromby Place (1804) Great King Street (1817) completed 1823

1805	Princes Street completed. Police Act, start of proper Police Force.
1814	Charlotte Square finished by Robert Reid.
1817	Regent Bridge and Waterloo Place (Archibald Elliot) Ann Street, St Bernard Crescent area (Henry Raeburn).
1818	Calton development (Playfair).
1819	Edinburgh Water Company formed.
1820	Melville Street (Robert Brown). Blacket Place by Gillespie Graham for British Linen Co.
1822	Moray Place development (Gillespie Graham).
1823	Queen Street Gardens, Bellevue Terrace (Thomas Bonnar), Royal Circus (Playfair).
1825	Shandwick Place, Atholl Crescent, Coates Crescent, Walker Street.
1826	Gardners Crescent.
1829	Manor Place (by 1860 still Western boundary of Edinburgh).
1830	Mound completed, Rutland Square (John Tait designed by Arch. Elliot 1819). Edinburgh declared bankrupt.
1832	Dean Bridge (Thomas Telford).
1833	Burgh Reform Act.
1855	Melville Crescent (John Lessels).
1860	Learmonth Estate started Buckingham Terrace.
1870	North Bridge widened by footpath.
1874	Belgrave Crescent, Learmonth Terrace/ North Bridge completely rebuilt.

Leith

1128	David I Charter gives Inverleith Harbour and fishery to Holyrood Abbey.
1134	First recorded settlement at Leith.
	Bruce's Charter confirms superiority of Edinburgh over North and South Leith.
1329	Trinity House founded by Master Mariners.
1382	Logans become Barons of Restalrig.
	Edinburgh purchased Shore from Logans.
1417	Sir Robert Logan founds Precinct of St Anthony.
1424	Jane Beaufort landed at Leith with James I.
1434	James I builds Kings Wharf.
1449	Mary of Gueldres landed at Leith. (married James II).
1469	Margaret of Denmark landed at Leith (married James III).
1483	Merchants trading from Leith must be Burgesses of Edinburgh.
1486	St Mary's Church founded, South Leith.
1489	Abbot Ballantyne builds bridge at Coalfield.
1493	Sir Andrew Wood defeats the English of Dunbar.
1493	St Ninian's Church built, North Leith. (closed 1816).
1504	James IV founds Newhaven.
1507	Sir Robert Barton, knighted.
1510	Edinburgh purchased Newhaven from James IV.
1511	Great Michael launched at Newhaven.
1537	Madeline De Valois with James V.
1544	Hereford sacks Leith.
1547	Battle of Pinkie and sacking of Leith by Somerset.
1549	French fortify Leith.
1550	Andrew Lamb's house built (rebuilt early 17th cent.)
1555	Original Trinity House founded.
1556	Mary of Guise bought Leith from the Logans.
1559	Siege of Leith, Giants Brae and Lady Fyfes Brae erected on the Links.
1560	Treaty of Edinburgh, French leave Leith.
1561	Arrival of Mary Queen of Scots.

1565	Leith Tolbooth built, demolished 1818.
1566	Edinburgh acquires superiority of Leith.
1590	Anne of Denmark arrives with James VI.
1593	St Ninian's (North Leith Parish) Church founded.
1600	Craigentinny house built by Nesbits.
1603	James VI's. Golden Charter confirms Edinburgh's superiority.
1606	St Ninian's becomes parish church of North Leith.
1609	South Leith Church becomes parish church in place of Restalrig Church.
1638	National Covenant signed in St Mary's Church South Leith and St Ninian's.
1639	Edinburgh purchased superiority of North Leith from the Earl of Roxburgh, which now came into the Burgh of the Canongate.
1645	The Great Plague.
1650	Leslie's defence of Leith against Cromwell.
1656	Citadel built.
1698	Darien Expedition sails from Leith.
1707	Treaty of Union damages Leith Trade.
1713	Turnpike Roads Act assists travel.
1720	First dry dock in Scotland opened in Leith.
1724	Edinburgh purchased Calton from Lord Balmerino.
1751	Bonnington Toll erected under Turnpike Act.
1754	Water Supply from Lochend.
1767	Peacock Hotel, Newhaven opened.
1775	Leith Street made main road.
1779	Leith Fort built after John Paul Jones scare.
1783	Assembly Rooms built, Constitution Street.
1788	Abbot Ballantyne's bridge demolished, new bridge built at Tolbooth Wynd.
1792	Leith Banking Company formed. (failed 1842).
1800	John Rankine planned Leith Docks.
1806	Old Dock, First wet Dock built in Leith. Queens Dock.
1809	Exchange Buildings built, Constitution Street.

1809	Martello Tower built, (Napoleonic Wars).
1812	Customs House built by Robert Reid.
1813	Seafield Baths.
1816	North Leith Church transferred to Madeira Street.
1816	Leith Races (held since James VI time) transferred to Musselburgh.
1816	Trinity House rebuilt.
1821	Chain Pier built, blown down in 1898.
1822	George IV landed at Leith.
1826	Dock Commission formed.
1827	Town Hall built in Charlotte Street. (Altered to Queen Charlotte Street 1 February 1968).
1833	Leith becomes Parliamentary Burgh.
1834	Tolls abolished on Leith Walk.
1835	Granton Harbour built.
1836	Edinburgh, Leith and Granton railway opened.
1838	*Sirius* built by Robt. Menzies. (First steamship to cross Atlantic).
1842	Scotland Street tunnel opened, (closed in 1861).
1848	Railway extended to Granton.
1849	Leith Hospital opened.
1852	Victoria Dock.
1862	Corn Exchange opened at the corner of Baltic Street and Constitution Street.
1869	Albert Dock.
1876	Leith Post Office opened in Constitution Street.
1880	Improvement schemes, many old houses demolished.
1881	Edinburgh Dock.
1898	Burns Statue by D. W. Stevenson unveiled.
1903	Leith Central Station opened.
1904	Imperial Dock.
1905	First electric trams in Leith.
1906	Queen Victoria Statue by John Rhind.
1920	Leith amalgamated with Edinburgh.
1937	Last crossing from Burntisland to Granton by the 'Willie Muir'.
1960	Demolition of Kirkgate.

1961	Bernard Street Bridge rebuilt (stationary).
1967	Forth Ports Authority replaced Leith Dock Commission.
1969	Western Dock Gates, port no longer tidal.
1977	Henry Robb Shipbuilder, became Robb Caledon.
1984	*St Helen* launched by Robb Caledon, yard closes.
1998	Former Royal Yacht *Britannia* opened as tourist attraction.

Miscellaneous Dates

1128	Burgh of Canongate founded by King David I.
1296	William Wallace mustered two hundred patriots on Figgate Whins.
1374	Simon Preston bought Craigmillar.
1457	Statute by James I that 'Fute-ball and the Golfe to be utterly cryed doon and not to be used'.
1505	Work started on the *Great Michael* and was launched in 1511
1507	Walter Chepman introduced printing to the town.
1540	Magdalen Chapel built.
1565	First execution using the Maiden.
1579	Golf was being played on Bruntsfield Links.
1581	Sunday bowling declared illegal.
1593	Golf being played on Leith Links.
1610	Comiston House built, rebuilt in 1815 by Sir James Forrest, Lord Provost.
1621	Tailors Hall in Cowgate built.
1623	Death of George Heriot.
1676	Company of Archers formed,
1637	Charles I attempts to anglicise the Church in Scotland.
1638	National Covenant, a lowland movement forms, Charles I regards protest against prayer book treason forcing Scots to choose between King and Church. Covenant signed in Greyfriars Churchyard.
1650	Earl of Montrose executed.
1651	First newspaper published (*Mercurius Scoticus*).
1660	Restoration of Monarchy, Charles II restored to throne.
1661	Marquis of Argyle executed.
1661	Dalry House built by Walter Chieslie.
1661	First sedan chair in City.
1681	Tea drunk in town for first time.
1685	Earl of Argyle executed.
1685	Caroline Park House built.
1685	Duckings ceased in the 'Nor Loch'.
1695	Bank of Scotland chartered.

1696	Window Tax imposed.
1704	Royal Company of Archers incorporated by Queen Anne. Became the Sovereign's bodyguard in Scotland in 1822
1707	Last meeting of the Scottish Parliament.
1725	Allan Ramsey opened circulating library, the first in Britain.
1727	Royal Bank of Scotland founded.
1730	'Gardy Loo' abolished by Town Council.
1736	Grand Lodge of Scotland formed.
1736	Lodge Room of Canongate Kilwinning opened. The oldest Masonic Lodge still in use.
1739	Black Watch raised, the regiment was formed to watch over the Highlands not to help the Highlanders.
1740	Duddingston Curling Club formed.
1744	Honorable Company of Edinburgh Golfers founded.
1762	St Cecilia's Hall in Cowgate built by Robt. Mylne for Musical Society of Edinburgh.
1763	Foundation stone of the North Bridge laid by Lord Provost George Drummond.
1769	First house on Princes Street Built by John Neale and to be free of burgh tax for all time.
1771	*Encyclopaedia Britannica* first published.
1771	Walter Scott born in College Wynd.
1774	Penny Post introduced by Peter Williamson ('Indian Peter') from Luckenbooths.
1776	Archers Hall built.
1780	Surgeon Alexander Wood introduced the umbrella to Edinburgh.
1783	Royal Society of Edinburgh founded.
1784	First ascent by a man in a balloon from British soil made by James Tytler.
1785	First balloon flight over the city (by Lunardi).
1786	Robert Burns made his first visit to City.
1789	St Bernard's Well built. Designed by Alexander Nasmyth.
1808	Work started on Calton Jail.

1812	'Deid Chack' abolished. This was the meal eaten by Magistrates after attending an execution.
1816	Horse racing moved from Leith to Musselburgh.
1817	*The Scotsman* newspaper first published.
1817	Hackney carriages first registered.
1822	Union Canal opened.
1828	Work started on Surgeons Hall, Nicholson Street, designed by Wm. Playfair.
1831	Dean Orphanage built, (now Dean Gallery) designed by Thomas Hamilton.
1834	New Club opened.
1845	Pneumatic tyre invented by Robert Thomson.
1848	Greenwich Mean Time adopted, clocks adjusted by 12½ minutes.
1851	Window Tax abolished.
1855	George Hotel opened.
1860	Meadows opened as park.
1861	First colour photograph taken by James Clerk Maxwell.
1861	General Post Office foundation stone laid by Prince Albert.
1864	Last public hanging, at junction of High Street and George IV Bridge.
1865	General Post Office opened.
1870	Powderhall professional sprint begun on New Year's Day, now run at Meadowbank.
1871	Clermiston Tower built by Wm. MacFie to mark centenary of the birth of Sir Walter Scott.
1873	Statue of 'Greyfriars Bobby' by Wm. Brodie unveiled.
1873	The *Edinburgh Evening News* first published.
1874	Heart of Midlothian football club formed.
1875	Hibernian football club formed.
1879	First telephone exchange opened, the location St Andrew's Square.
1889	Braid Hills acquired by City Council for golf course.
1895	Royal Observatory built.
1903	First private car registered in the city.
1903	Floral Clock electrically worked.

1907	First motor taxi cab registered.
1913	Usher Hall built, gifted by the Brewer Thomas Usher.
1925	Calton Jail closed, prisoners transferred to Saughton Prison.
1934	Peirshill Barracks demolished to make way for housing namely Peirshill Square East and West.
1936	Portobello open air pool opened. Closed in 1979
1947	Edinburgh International Festival of Music and Drama inaugurated.
1948	First performance of Military Tattoo on Esplanade.
1962	Traverse Theatre opened in West Bow.
1964	Princes Street Station closed.
1977	Last of the 'Steamies' (public washhouses) closed.
1977	New terminal building opened at Airport.
1978	Haymarket Ice Rink closed.
2003	Royal Infirmary moved to Little France.